# INTERPRETING THE
# PAULINE LETTERS

# INTERPRETING THE PAULINE LETTERS

## An Exegetical Handbook

John D. Harvey

AUTHOR AND SERIES EDITOR

*Interpreting the Pauline Letters: An Exegetical Handbook*
© 2012 by John D. Harvey

Published by Kregel Publications, a division of Kregel, Inc., P.O. Box 2607, Grand Rapids, MI 49501.

The Greek font GraecaU and the Hebrew font New JerusalemU are both available from www.linguistsoftware.com/lgku.htm, +1-425-775-1130.

Unless otherwise noted, all Scripture quotations are from the NEW AMERICAN STANDARD BIBLE". Copyright © 1960, 1962, 1963, 1968, 1971, 1972, 1973, 1975, 1977, 1995 by The Lockman Foundation. Used by permission. (www.Lockman.org)

ISBN 978-0-8254-2767-1

Printed in the United States of America
12 13 14 15 16 / 5 4 3 2 1

*To Paul W. Fowler,*
*William J. Larkin, Jr.,*
*and Paul O. Wright,*
*who taught me to love Greek*
*and to handle the New Testament text with care*

# CONTENTS IN BRIEF

# CONTENTS

# SERIES PREFACE

THE AUTHORS OF THE NEW TESTAMENT communicated their witness to the good news of Jesus Christ using a variety of types of literature (literary genres). Those different types of literature require different principles and methods of interpretation and communication. Those principles and methods are best understood in the context of a series of handbooks that focus on the individual types of literature to which they apply. There are three basic literary genres in the New Testament: narrative, letter, and apocalypse. Other subgenres are present within those basic types of literature (e.g., parable), but narrative, letter, and apocalypse provide the framework for those subgenres.

The four volumes in this series will offer the student of Scripture the basic skills for interpreting and communicating the message of the New Testament in the context of the various literary genres. The four volumes will be

- *Interpreting the Gospels and Acts (Matthew–Acts)*
- *Interpreting the Pauline Letters (Romans–Philemon)*
- *Interpreting the General Letters (Hebrews–Jude)*
- *Interpreting the Apocalypse (Revelation and other prophetic-apocalyptic passages)*

Each volume is designed to provide an understanding of the different types of literature in the New Testament, and to provide strategies for interpreting and preaching/teaching them. The series is intended primarily to serve as textbooks and resources for seminary and graduate-level students who have completed at least a year of introductory Greek.

However, because an English translation is always provided whenever Greek is used, the series is also accessible to readers who lack a working knowledge of Greek. For that reason, upper-level college students, seminary-trained pastors, and well-motivated lay people should also benefit from the series.

The four volumes will cover the twenty-seven books of the New Testament. Each volume will (a) include a summary of the major themes present in the New Testament books covered by it; (b) set methods of interpretation in the context of the New Testament books to which those methods apply; (c) go beyond exegesis to exposition, by providing strategies for communicating each type of New Testament literature; (d) provide step-by-step examples which put into practice the methods and strategies set out in each volume, in the context of an overall exegetical-homiletical framework.

In order to enhance the usefulness of the series, the length, style, and organization of each volume will be consistent. Each volume will include the following elements:

- *The nature of the literary genre (including important subgenres)*
- *The background of the books (historical setting)*
- *The major themes of the books*
- *Preparing to interpret the books (textual criticism, translation)*
- *Interpreting passages in the context of their genre*
- *Communicating passages in the context of their genre*
- *From exegesis to exposition (two step-by-step examples)*
- *A list of selected resources and a glossary of technical terms*

Authors are given freedom in how they title each chapter and in how best to approach the material in it. Using the same basic organization for each book in the series, however, will make it possible for readers to move easily from volume to volume and to locate specific information within each volume.

The authors in this series represent a variety of theological backgrounds and educational institutions, but each is committed to handling God's Word accurately. That commitment reflects a key element in living the Christian life: the functional authority of Scripture. Whatever theological position we might hold, we submit ourselves to the authority of the Bible and align our understanding of life and doctrine to its teaching. It is the prayer of the authors and the publisher that these handbooks will enable those who read them to study the Bible, practice its teachings, and share its truth with others for the advance of Christ's kingdom purposes.

—JOHN D. HARVEY
Series Editor

# PRELUDE

AMONG THE BOOKS OF THE NEW TESTAMENT, Paul's letters are second only to the Gospels in interest and popularity. From the magisterial presentation of the gospel he preached (Romans) to his personal appeal on behalf of Onesimus (Philemon), Paul's letters have fascinated lay people and scholars alike. The message in Galatians, of salvation by grace alone through faith alone in Christ alone, captured Luther's heart and sparked the Protestant Reformation. Five centuries after Luther, the "new perspective on Paul" continues to stir discussion of Paul's letters.

Written by the first great missionary church planter to the churches he planted and the co-workers with whom he labored, Paul's letters breathe the spirit of the age in which he wrote. Yet the challenges his readers faced are eerily similar to the challenges the twenty-first-century church faces. It is necessary only to read 2 Timothy 4:3–4 to note the parallels (NASB): "For the time will come when they will not endure sound doctrine, but wanting to have their ears tickled, they will accumulate for themselves teachers in accordance to their own desires; and will turn away their ears from the truth, and will turn aside to myths." The advice and instruction Paul offered his readers continue to guide churches and individuals today. It is only natural that we turn to his letters to understand the significance of what Christ has done for us and how we can follow him more closely.

Yet the historical, cultural, and linguistic distance between Paul's time and ours poses challenges for understanding and applying the teaching of his letters. It is those challenges that prompt this handbook on *Interpreting the Pauline Letters*. The first three chapters seek to place Paul's letters within the genre of first-century letter writing, to set

Paul's ministry within its historical context, and to provide an overview of Paul's theology. Then the focus shifts to the tasks of interpreting, appropriating, and communicating the message of passages from Paul's letters. The objective is to set out a method for taking a passage from text to sermon, and two passages (Col. 3:1–4; Phil. 3:12–16) serve as examples of applying that method.

Abbreviations are kept to a minimum and appear in the list that follows this prelude. Technical terms appear in bold font at their first use and are listed in the glossary at the end of the book. Resources noted throughout the book appear together in the eighth chapter along with a selected list of commentaries.

I am grateful to all the teachers and authors who have taught me about Paul and his letters over the past twenty-five years. My colleagues at Columbia International University Seminary & School of Ministry have helped refine both the exegetical and homiletical methods that form the basis for much of chapters four through six. I would like to thank Jim Weaver who opened the door for this volume as well as for the New Testament series. Finally, my wife, Anita, has been my most patient and persistent encourager all along the way.

# ABBREVIATIONS

| | |
|---|---|
| *Ant.* | Josephus, *Jewish Antiquities* |
| BAGD | W. Bauer, W. F. Arndt, F. W. Gingrich, and F. W. Danker, *A Greek-English Lexicon of the New Testament and Other Early Christian Literature,* third edition (Chicago: University of Chicago Press, 2000) |
| BDF | F. Blass, A. Debrunner, and R. W. Funk, *A Greek Grammar of the New Testament and Other Early Christian Literature* (Chicago: University of Chicago Press, 1961) |
| ESV | English Standard Version |
| HNTE | Handbooks for New Testament Exegesis |
| JETS | *Journal of the Evangelical Theological Society* |
| JSOT | *Journal for the Study of the Old Testament* |
| NASB | New American Standard Bible |
| NIV | New International Version |
| NKJV | New King James Version |
| UBS4 | United Bible Societies Greek New Testament, 4th edition |
| Virt. | Philo, *On Virtue* |

# 1

# THE GENRE OF PAUL'S LETTERS

## The Chapter at a Glance

- Paul wrote his letters in a complex environment that combined orality, literacy, and rhetoric.

- Paul's letters are both similar to and different from other first-century Greek letters.

- Paul's letters exhibit three levels of structure: the overall structure of the letter, structure within the letter body, and structure at the sentence level.

- Paul's use of the letter genre allowed him to tailor his message to his readers and their circumstances.

PAUL'S LETTERS ARE CLEARLY DISTINCT from both the narrative **genre** of the Gospels and Acts and the prophetic-apocalyptic genre of Revelation. They share their epistolary genre with the General Letters, but they were written by a single author and have more in common with each other than with the letters written by James, Peter, John, Jude, and the unknown author of Hebrews. The number of extant letters ascribed to Paul provides a significant database that has attracted numerous scholars, including those who have sought to analyze their literary genre. Before considering the genre of Paul's letters, however, it is essential to set them against the backgrounds of communication in the first century and of other ancient letters.

## COMMUNICATION IN THE FIRST CENTURY

Paul wrote his letters within a complex culture characterized by the interaction of oral, rhetorical, and literary environments. It will be helpful to understand each of these environments and the interaction among them.

### The Oral Environment

Scholars who study oral cultures have identified certain characteristics within them. Such cultures tend to be more concrete than abstract because they are organized around the events of life. They tend to use words as more than mere functional tools because that which is spoken is intended to educate and entertain. Oral cultures tend to promote thematic memory skills rather than verbatim recall because themes of the overall story are more important than the exact words used. The stories produced by oral cultures tend to be redundant rather than concise, additive rather than subordinate, aggregative rather than synthetic, and conservative rather than creative.[1] Finally, expression in oral cultures is acoustically oriented rather than visually oriented. Storytellers in such cultures compose for the listeners' ears rather than for the readers' eyes.[2]

Because they compose for the ear, speakers in oral cultures adopt certain habits of composition. Their speech tends to be formulaic in that it leans heavily on stock phraseology to enhance recognition, understanding, and acceptance. It also tends to be repetitive because repetition facilitates comprehension, reflection, and memory. These habits of oral composition persist long after a culture begins to make the transition away from **orality** toward **literacy**, and their residual impact may still be found in later, written works. For example, as this chapter notes, Greek letter writers tend to use common formulaic language to introduce various portions of their letters.

The persistence of oral speech habits means it is possible to speak of various degrees of orality. Walter Ong has suggested the categories of radically oral, largely oral, and residually oral.[3] Using those categories, it is probably most accurate to speak of first-century Mediterranean culture as "largely oral." That is, reading and writing were done aloud; sound shaped thought and expression; and there was a premium placed on the spoken word. That premium on the spoken word is reflected in the rhetorical environment in which Paul's letters were composed.

---

1. A. B. Lord, "Characteristics of Orality," *Oral Tradition* 2 (1987): 54–62.

2. Although it is not story, Jesus' Sermon on the Mount in Matthew 5-7 demonstrates many of the characteristics of oral composition.

3. W. Ong, *The Presence of the Word* (New Haven, CT: Yale University Press, 1967), 22.

## The Rhetorical Environment

**Rhetoric** was important in the first century. When students reached the ages of fifteen to seventeen, their secondary education included "first exercises" in rhetoric. Above the age of eighteen, schools of rhetoric prepared students for such professions as teacher, lawyer, public official, and civic leader. In addition to the formal rhetoric taught in schools, what might be considered "practical" rhetoric was widely used in public arenas such as the marketplace and city chambers.

As Ong has suggested categories of orality, George Kennedy has suggested three broad categories of rhetoric: traditional rhetoric, conceptual rhetoric, and classical rhetoric.[4] Traditional rhetoric consists, basically, of a formalization of the ways in which speech is used in oral cultures. Conceptual rhetoric refers to the organization of traditional rhetorical processes and techniques into a system that could be formally studied and taught. Out of the system of conceptual rhetoric grew the classical rhetoric practiced by the orators of Greece and Rome after the fifth century b.c.

The rhetoric of everyday first-century Mediterranean culture might best be described as "practical," a combination of traditional and classical: "Rhetorical categories and figures were part of the culture of the day. They were 'in the air,' and everyone, whether formally or informally educated, was influenced by rhetoric."[5]

## The Literary Environment

In addition to oral and rhetorical aspects of first-century culture, the **literary** aspect must also be noted. Evidence for systems of writing can be found as early as 3000 B.C. The Greek alphabet was in use by the middle of the eighth century B.C., and it has been suggested that the average Athenian could read script around 400 B.C.

Here too, Eric Havelock has suggested various degrees of literacy, including craft-literate, recitation-literate, and script-literate.[6] In a craft-literate culture, reading and writing are restricted to specialists (e.g., scribes). In a recitation-literate culture, more individuals possess the ability to decipher written texts, but that ability is largely secondary to memorization and recitation of the important works of the culture. In a script-literate culture, the average member of the culture is able to read written texts.

---

4.  G. A. Kennedy, *Classical Rhetoric in Its Christian and Secular Tradition from Ancient to Modern Times* (Chapel Hill, NC: University of North Carolina Press, 1984), 6.

5.  J. D. Harvey, *Listening to the Text: Oral Patterning in Paul's Letters* (Grand Rapids. MI: Baker, 1998), 49.

6.  E. A. Havelock, "The Preliteracy of the Greeks," *New Literary History* 8 (1977): 372.

Using these categories, first-century culture is best described as script-literate. Within that culture, a spectrum of writing activities existed, including reproduction, transcription, and composition. **Papyrus** was the most commonly used writing material, and because writing materials were expensive, economy took precedence over beauty. Dictation to a secretary or scribe was the normal method of composition, and texts were read aloud. Systems of shorthand existed so that secretaries and scribes could record an author's dictation before producing a finished copy of the manuscript.

| First-Century Culture | | |
|---|---|---|
| **Largely oral** | **Script-literacy** | **Practical rhetoric** |
| • Spoken word central<br>• Acoustically oriented<br>• Formulaic | • Reading done aloud<br>• Dictation common<br>• Secretaries and shorthand | • Traditionally based<br>• Classically influenced<br>• Aimed at persuasion |

## Summary

So, the culture in which Paul ministered and wrote involved a complex interaction of the oral, rhetorical, and literary environments. Because the culture was still largely oral, there was a premium placed on the spoken word, and communication was shaped for the ear more than it was for the eye. Because of the strong emphasis on practical rhetoric within the culture, the techniques of classical rhetoric were adopted and adapted for persuasive purposes. Because the culture was script-literate, writing and reading were done aloud, systems of shorthand and note taking existed, and secretaries were commonly used. Each of these aspects of the culture has implications for understanding Paul's letters. Before looking at Paul's letters, though, it will be helpful to consider them against the background of ancient letters in general.

## ANCIENT LETTERS

The Old Testament attests to the existence and use of letters well before the first century A.D. (2 Sam. 11:15; 1 Kings 21:9–10; 2 Kings 5:6; 10:6; 19:9–14; 2 Chron. 2:11–15; 21:12–15; Ezra 1:1–4; 7:11–26; Neh. 6:5–7; Est. 8:9–14; Jer. 29:3–23). This evidence is embedded in narrative passages and often supplies a summary of a letter's content. As such, they lack the formulaic character of later letters. Hans-Josef Klauck also provides an extensive list of references to letters and writing in Second Temple Judaism, including evidence from 1–2 Maccabees, the Letter of Aristeas, 2 Baruch, and multiple passages from the works of Josephus.[7] It is clear, therefore, that Judaism was familiar with the practice of letter writing and, in fact, used letters to communicate.

## Hebrew Letters

The documents noted above preserve evidence of official letters produced as literary documents. Outside those literary documents, few common letters exist. Those that are extant are generally late (early second century A.D.), fragmentary, and preserved on **ostraca**. They tend to be brief with few formal features; address, greeting, and closing are more common only in later letters, Two examples from the Wadi Murabba'at papyri, written about the time of the second Jewish revolt in A.D. 132–135 are typical.

> *papMur 43*
>
> From Shimon ben Koshiba to Yeshua ben Galgula
> and to the men of your company: Greetings [Shalom].
> I swear by the heavens: should harm come to any one
> of the Galileans who are with you, I will put your feet
> in fetters as I did to ben Aful.

> *papMur 44*
>
> From Shimon to Yeshua son of Galgula: Greetings
> [Shalom]. You are to send five kor-measures of wheat
> by men of my house who are known to you. Prepare
> for them an empty place. They will be with you this
> sabbath, if they desire to come. Keep up your courage
> and strengthen that place. Best wishes. I have designated
> the person who is to give you his wheat. They
> may take it after the Sabbath.

## Greek Letters

In contrast to the scarcity of extant Hebrew letters, entire collections of Greek letters of different types exist. This wealth of documents has resulted in various ways of classifying them. Perhaps the best approach

---

7. H. J. Klauck, *Ancient Letters and the New Testament* (Waco, TX: Baylor University Press, 2006), 229–97.

uses the three broad categories noted by Jeffrey Weima: literary letters, official letters, and private letters.[8]

Literary letters are documents in letter form that were written with the intent that they be copied and distributed to a wider audience. The letters of Epicurus, Cicero and Seneca and the Cynic Epistles fit in this category. Subcategories include letter-essays, philosophical letters, and novelistic letters. Although some scholars have suggested that Paul's letters correspond to literary letter-essays, that conclusion has not gained widespread acceptance.

Official letters include correspondence written to conduct state business. This category includes royal and imperial letters that carry some political weight. The following imperial letter of thanks from the emperor Hadrian is a representative example.

> To good fortune.
>
> The Emperor and Caesar, of the god Trajan Parthicus
> a son, of the god Nerva a grandson, Trajan Hadrian
> Augustus, of tribunician power, to the association of
> young men in Pergamum, greetings ([*chairein*]).
>
> Since I have learned – by your letter and the fact that
> you have sent Claudius Kyros – the amount of joy that
> you, as you declared, have shared with me, I decided
> that this demonstrates your character as excellent men.
>
> Be well.
> On the 3$^{rd}$, before the Ides of November, from
> Juliopolis.

The primary parallel between official letters and Paul's letters is the authority involved in a superior writing to subordinates—in Paul's case, his authority as an apostle.

Private letters include all correspondence in the personal domain and not intended for publication. They include family letters, letters of petition, letters of introduction, and business letters. Of those four types, the family letter is probably the closest to Paul's.

---

8.  J. A. D. Weima, "Greco-Roman Letters" in *Dictionary of New Testament Background*, eds. C. A. Evans and S. E. Porter (Downers Grove, IL: InterVarsity Press, 2000), 640–4.

| Types of Greek Letters | | |
| --- | --- | --- |
| **Literary Letters** | **Official Letters** | **Private Letters** |
| • Essays in letter form<br>• Copied and distributed<br>• Instruct and/or entertain | • Formal edicts<br>• Preserved in archives<br>• Conduct state business | • Occasional documents<br>• Not for publication<br>• Conduct personal business |

Generally speaking, all Greek letters have certain elements in common. William Doty, following Koskenniemi, notes that Greek letters tend to exhibit the characteristic features of relationship, presence, and dialogue.[9] John White suggests that every Greek letter seeks to accomplish at least one of three common purposes: to convey information, to make requests or give commands, and to enhance or maintain personal contact.[10] Doty also notes the general form used in Greek letters:[11]

> Introduction (sender, addressees, greetings, health wish)
> Body
> Conclusion (greetings, wishes, final greeting or prayer sentence)

In addition, Greek letter writers tend to use common formulaic language to introduce various portions of their letters. The following letter from the Zenon archive (104b) demonstrates each of these elements.

> Apollinarios to his mother and lady, Taesis, many greetings. Before all else I pray that you are well; I myself am well and make obeisance on your behalf to the gods here.
>
> I want you to know, mother, that I arrived in Rome safely on the twenty-fifth of the month Pachon and was assigned to Misenum. But I do not know my century yet, for I had not gone to Misenum when I wrote this letter to you. I request you, therefore, mother, attend to yourself; do not worry about me, for I came to a fine place. Please write me a letter about your welfare and that of my brothers and of all your people. And, for my part, if I ever find someone [to carry the letter], I will write to you; I certainly will not hesitate to write to you.

---

9. W. G. Doty, *Letters in Primitive Christianity* (Philadelphia: Fortress, 1973), 11–12.

10. J. L. White, *Light from Ancient Letters* (Philadelphia: Fortress, 1986), 197.

11. Doty, *Letters*, 14.

> I greet my brothers much, and Apollinarios and
> his children, and Karalas and his children. I greet
> Ptolemy, and Ptolemais and her children. I greet all
> your friends, each by name. I pray that you are well.

It is worth making several observations about this family letter. Relationship and dialogue are, naturally enough, present since Apollinarios is writing to his mother and is seeking to continue their relationship. His purpose is to convey information about his situation and to maintain contact with his family. The characteristic Greek letter form is readily evident, consisting of (a) an introduction with sender, addressee, greeting, and a health wish, (b) a two-part body including both information and a request, and (c) a closing with greetings and a prayer sentence. Formulaic language is particularly evident in the use of an information/disclosure formula ("I want you to know . . .") and a request/appeal formula ("I request you . . ."). It is also interesting to note the use of the so-called "epistolary aorist" in which the letter is viewed from the perspective of the reader when she receives it rather than from the perspective of the writer when he composes it (". . . for I had not gone to Misenum when I wrote this letter to you"). Instances of Paul's use of the epistolary aorist occur in Galatians 6:11; Philippians 2:28; Philemon v.12.

The structure of this somewhat longer letter parallels the model Klauck proposes:[12]

- Letter Opening
  - » Prescript (sender, addressee, greeting)
  - » Proem (prayer wish, thanksgiving, remembrance before gods, joy expression)[13]

- Letter Body
  - » Body opening (disclosure, request, recommendation of self or others)
  - » Body middle (information, appeal, instructions, exhortation, request)
  - » Body closing (possible request or exhortation, travel and visitation plans)

- Letter Closing
  - » Epilogue (concluding exhortation, act of writing, possible visit)
  - » Postscript (greetings, wishes/farewell, autograph)

---

12. Klauck, *Ancient Letters*, 42.

13. Klauck uses "proem" as a general term for a letter's introductory section.

The prescript and **proem** are clearly delineated, as are the epilogue and postscript. A **disclosure formula** ("I want you to know . . .") introduces the body opening, and a **request formula** ("I request you . . .") introduces the body middle. The body closing consists of the request and promise related to writing ("Please write me a letter . . . I will write to you . . .").

## PAUL'S LETTERS

Paul's letters are both similar to and different from other first-century letters. Similarities include (a) the overall form of introduction, body, and closing; (b) the features of relationship, dialogue, and presence; (c) the purposes of informing, requesting, exhorting, and commanding; and (d) the use of formulaic language. Differences include length, complexity, and flexibility.

Paul's letters are considerably longer than the average extant papyrus letter. Randolph Richards provides the following comparisons:[14]

| Length of Greco-Roman Letters | | |
| --- | --- | --- |
| Extant Papyri | 18–209 words | 87 words on average |
| Cicero's Letters | 22–2,530 words | 295 words on average |
| Seneca's Letters | 149–4,134 words | 995 words on average |
| Paul's Letters | 335–7,114 words | 2,495 words on average |

Given their greater length, it is not surprising that Paul's letters are also more complex. Whereas most papyrus letters deal with a single topic, Paul's letters usually address more than one. That complexity is particularly clear in 1 Corinthians, for example, where Paul introduces multiple topics with the formula περὶ δὲ ("now concerning . . ."). Paul also uses the letter form flexibly, adapting it to the needs of the moment. Although the general structure of opening-body-closing is always present, the bodies of Paul's letters follow a variety of patterns. For that reason, it is difficult to establish a "typical" structure for Paul's letters, and it is especially tenuous to draw definitive conclusions based on variations from that supposedly "typical" structure. In fact, it is possible to speak of three "levels" of structure in Paul's letters.

---

14. R. E. Richards, *Paul and First-Century Letter Writing: Secretaries, Composition, and Collection* (Downers Grove, IL: InterVarsity Press, 2004), 163.

## Macro-Level: The Overall Structure of the Letter

In light of the flexibility with which Paul uses the letter genre, the best approach to establishing the overall structure of individual letters is to identify clusters of **epistolary conventions** and formulaic language within each letter and let those clusters suggest the structure. For example, a close reading of Romans in its canonical from yields the following clusters of items:

| | |
|---|---|
| **1:1–13** | • Sender (1:1)<br>• Recipients (1:7)<br>• Greeting (1:7)<br>• Thanksgiving (1:8)<br>• Attestation (1:9)<br>• Visit wish (1:10–11)<br>• Disclosure formula (1:13) |
| **11:25–12:3** | • Disclosure formula (11:25)<br>• Doxology (11:33–36)<br>• Request formula (12:1)<br>• Verb of saying (12:3) |
| **15:13–16:27** | • Peace wish (15:13)<br>• Confidence formula (15:14)<br>• Writing statement (15:15)<br>• Visit wish (15:22–23)<br>• Intention to visit (15:28–29)<br>• Request formula (15:30)<br>• Peace wish (15:33)<br>• Greetings (16:3–16)<br>• Request formula (16:17)<br>• Peace wish (16:20a)<br>• Grace benediction (16:20b)<br>• Greetings (16:21–23)<br>• Doxology (16:25–27) |

These clusters suggest the following overall structure for the letter:

- Salutation (1:1–7)

- Thanksgiving (1:8–12)

- Body (1:13–15:33)

> » Section A (1:13–11:36)
> » Section B (12:1–15:33)

- Closing (16:1–27)

This overall structure for Romans corresponds well to both Klauck's proposed model and the family letter included above, although with significant Pauline modifications. The salutation (1:1–7), for example, is considerably longer than usual. Klauck notes it as the longest salutation found in Greek antiquity.[15] It expands considerably the author's self-identification and highlights Paul's status as an apostle. The characteristic Pauline greeting of "Grace . . . and peace" (χάρις . . . καὶ εἰρήνη) combines the Greek greeting, χαίρειν, with the Hebrew greeting (shalom).

The thanksgiving (1:8–12) corresponds to Klauck's "proem" and is also longer than usual. It follows the most common form in Paul's letters of a thanksgiving statement followed by a prayer report (cf. 1 Cor. 1:4–9; Eph. 1:15–23; Phil. 1:3–11; Col. 1:3–23; 1 Thess. 1:2–10; 2 Thess. 1:3–13; Philem. vv.4–7; 2 Tim. 1:3–5). In other letters, Paul includes a blessing (2 Cor. 1:3–7; Eph. 1:3–14) and/or a rebuke (Gal. 1:6–10).

The body of Romans is obviously longer than most extant papyrus letters. Yet it opens with a disclosure formula (1:13) similar to that used in the family letter from Apollinarios to his mother. Paul commonly uses such a disclosure formula to introduce new information (cf. 1 Cor. 11:3; 15:1; Phil. 1:12; Gal. 1:11). Elsewhere, he also uses request formulas to exhort his readers to undertake an action (cf. 1 Cor. 1:10; Eph. 4:1; Rom. 12:1), **joy formulas** to provide data for a subsequent request (cf. Phil. 4:10; Philem. v.7), and **compliance formulas** to remind of previous instructions (cf. 1 Tim. 1:3–4; 2 Tim. 1:6; Titus 1:5).

The two main sections of the letter body are readily identified by the doxology that closes the first (11:33–36) and the request formula that introduces the second (12:1). A peace wish in 15:13 suggests the end of the body middle, and the so-called **apostolic parousia** that follows (15:14–33) confirms that impression.[16] This latter section functions as the body closing in which Paul weaves together his plans to visit Rome and his reflections on his apostolic ministry. It closes with another peace wish (15:33).

---

15. Klauck, *Ancient Letters,* 20, 302.

16. R. W. Funk first proposed the term "apostolic parousia" for those sections of Paul's letters where he seeks to make his "presence" (παρουσία) felt in at least one of three ways: (1) mention of writing, (2) mention of an emissary, or (3) mention of a visit ("The 'Apostolic Parousia': Form and Significance," in *Christian History and Interpretation: Studies Presented to John Knox,* eds. W. R. Farmer, C. F. D. Moule, and R. R. Niebuhr [Cambridge: Cambridge University Press, 1967], 249–68).

The closing of Romans (16:1–27) is the longest in Paul's letters. Numerous analyses have been suggested, but Weima's is perhaps the most helpful:[17]

- *Letter of commendation (16:1–2)*
- *First greeting list (16:3–16)*
- *Hortatory section (16:17–20a)*
- *Grace benediction (16:20b)*
- *Second greeting list (16:21–23)*
- *Doxology (16:25–27)*

The fact that Tertius inserts his own greetings as the one who wrote the letter (16:22) lends credence to the idea that Paul used secretaries when he wrote, as do references elsewhere to writing "in [his] own hand" (cf. 1 Cor. 16:21; Gal. 6:11; Col. 4:18; 2 Thess. 3:17; Philem. v.19). The latter references also have led some scholars to identify possible autograph sections in Paul's letters. Harry Gamble, for example, has proposed that Romans 16:1–20 comprises such a section,[18] while Weima argues for 16:16–20.[19]

The following table sets out the overall structures of the remaining twelve letters ascribed to Paul.

| 1 Corinthians | 2 Corinthians | Galatians |
|---|---|---|
| • Salutation (1:1–3)<br>• Thanksgiving (1:4–9)<br>• Body (1:10–16:14)<br>» Section A (1:10–4:21)<br>» request formula (1:10)<br>» apostolic parousia (4:14–21)<br>» Section B (5:1–16:14)<br>• Closing (16:15–24) | • Salutation (1:1–2)<br>• Blessing (1:3–7)<br>• Body (1:8–13:10)<br>» Section A (1:8–9:15)<br>» disclosure formula (1:8)<br>» Section B (10:1–13:10)<br>» request formula (10:1)<br>» apostolic parousia (13:1–10)<br>• Closing (13:11–13) | • Salutation (1:1–5)<br>• Rebuke (1:6–10)<br>• Body (1:11–6:10)<br>» Section A (1:11–2:21)<br>» disclosure formula (1:11)<br>» Section B (3:1–4:11)<br>» rebuke formula (3:1)<br>» Section C (4:12–6:10)<br>» request formula (4:12)<br>• Closing (6:11–18) |

17.  J. A. D. Weima, *Neglected Endings: The Significance of the Pauline Letter Closings* (Sheffield: JSOT Press, 1994), 222.

18.  H. Gamble, *The Textual History of the Letter to the Romans* (Grand Rapids: Eerdmans, 1977), 93–4.

19.  Weima, *Neglected Endings*, 123.

| Ephesians | Philippians | Colossians |
|---|---|---|
| • Salutation (1:1–2)<br>• Blessing (1:3–14)<br>• Thanksgiving (1:15–23)<br>• Body (2:1–6:22)<br>  » Section A (2:1–3:21)<br>    » doxology (3:20–21)<br>  » Section B (4:1–6:22)<br>    » request formula (4:1)<br>    » apostolic parousia<br>      (6:21–22)<br>• Closing (6:23–24) | • Salutation (1:1–2)<br>• Thanksgiving (1:3–11)<br>• Body (1:12–4:20)<br>  » Section A (1:12–2:30)<br>    » disclosure formula<br>      (1:12)<br>    » apostolic parousia<br>      (2:19–30)<br>  » Section B (3:1–4:20)<br>    » doxology (4:20)<br>• Closing (4:21–23) | • Salutation (1:1–2)<br>• Expanded Thanksgiving<br>  (1:3–23)<br>• Body (1:24–4:9)<br>  » joy formula (1:24)<br>  » apostolic parousia<br>    (4:7–9)<br>• Closing (4:10–18) |

| 1 Thessalonians | 2 Thessalonians | Philemon |
|---|---|---|
| • Salutation (1:1)<br>• Thanksgiving (1:2–10)<br>• Body (2:1–5:22)<br>  » Section A (2:1–3:13)<br>    » disclosure formula<br>      (2:1)<br>    » apostolic parousia<br>      (2:17–3:13)<br>  » Section B (4:1–5:22)<br>    » request formula (4:1)<br>• Closing (5:23–28) | • Salutation (:1–2)<br>• Thanksgiving (1:3–12)<br>• Body (2:1–3:16)<br>  » Section A (2:1–17)<br>    » request formula<br>      (2:1–2)<br>    » benediction<br>      (2:16–17)<br>  » Section B (3:1–15)<br>• Closing (3:16–18) | • Salutation (v.1–3)<br>• Thanksgiving (v.4–7)<br>• Body (v.8–22)<br>  » request formula<br>    (v.8, 10)<br>  » apostolic parousia<br>    (v.21–22)<br>• Closing (v.23–25) |

| 1 Timothy | 2 Timothy | Titus |
|---|---|---|
| • Salutation (1:1–2)<br>• Body (1:3–6:19)<br>  » compliance<br>    formula (1:3–4)<br>  » apostolic parousia<br>    (3:14–16)<br>• Closing (6:20–21) | • Salutation (1:1–2)<br>• Thanksgiving (1:3–5)<br>• Body (1:6–4:18)<br>  » compliance<br>    formula (1:6)<br>  » apostolic parousia<br>    (4:9–18)<br>• Closing (4:19–21) | • Salutation (1:1–4)<br>• Body (1:5–3:14)<br>  » compliance<br>    formula (1:5)<br>  » apostolic parousia<br>    (3:12–14)<br>• Closing (3:15) |

A review of Paul's other letters reveals many of the same features found in Romans. Yet only a salutation, a body, and a closing are common to all of them. Sometimes a blessing section (2 Corinthians) or a rebuke section (Galatians) replaces the thanksgiving section.

Ephesians has both a blessing section (1:3–14) and a thanksgiving section (1:15–23), while 1 Timothy and Titus have neither. Within the letter body, the apostolic parousia moves around from early in the letter (1 Corinthians) to the middle of the letter (Philippians), to the end of the letter (2 Corinthians). Most of Paul's letters have a two-part body (e.g., 1 Thessalonians), but some of the shorter letter bodies have only a single part (e.g., Philemon), while Galatians appears to have a three-part body.

Given these variations in macro-level structure, it is probably less important to draw conclusions about the arrangement of the subunits of individual letters and more important to be aware of the functions of the subunits and to take into account those functions when investigating their content. The study of each subunit has generated a significant amount of research, but it will be worthwhile to touch on each of them briefly.

### Greeting

The three-part framework of Paul's salutations is well known: sender, recipient, and greeting.[20] Familiarity with that framework could easily result in a tendency to skip over the salutation in order to get to the "good stuff." There are, however, any number of questions to ask of each part of a letter's salutation. As the sender, for example, how does Paul describe himself? As an apostle (ἀπόστολος, nine times) highlighting his authority? As a bond-servant (δοῦλος, three times) highlighting his commitment to service? As a prisoner (δέσμιος, Philem. v.1) highlighting his suffering for the gospel? Particularly when he identifies himself as an apostle, how does Paul clarify that role (e.g., "by the will of God" in 1 Cor. 1:1; "according to the commandment of God our Savior and of Jesus Christ who is our hope" in 1 Tim. 1:1), or does he expand the self-designation in some way (e.g., Rom. 1:1–6; Gal. 1:1–2; Titus 1:1–3)? Does Paul include any of his coworkers as senders? If so, whom does he include, and how does he describe them (e.g., "Sosthenes our brother" in 1 Cor. 1:1; "all the brethren who are with me" in Gal. 1:2)? How does each detail relate to the context and the content of the letter in which it appears?

When he identifies the recipient(s), who are they, and what descriptors does Paul use when he names them? Do those descriptors affirm the recipients' relationship with Christ (e.g., "to all who are beloved of God in Rome, called as saints" in Rom. 1:7)? Or do they point out the

---

20. The passages in question are Rom. 1:1–7; 1 Cor. 1:1–3; 2 Cor. 1:1–3; Gal. 1:1–5; Eph. 1:1–2; Phil. 1:1–2; Col. 1:1–2; 1 Thess. 1:1; 2 Thess. 1:1–2; 1 Tim. 1:1–2; 2 Tim. 1:1–2; Titus 1:1–4; Philem. vv.1–3.

need for the recipients to align themselves with the attitudes and practices of the other churches Paul has planted (e.g., "to the church of God
which is at Corinth with all the saints who are throughout Achaia" in
2 Cor. 1:1)?

Paul uses the same basic greeting in each of his letters: "Grace to
you and peace from God our Father and the Lord Jesus Christ" (e.g.,
2 Cor. 1:2). Ann Jervis suggests that such a greeting functions "to affirm the faith Paul shares in common with his readers, to (re)establish
the common bond they have in Christ, and to remind them of his apostolic hopes for them."[21] What, then, is significant about the extended
addition Paul includes in the salutation of Galatians (1:4–5)? How does
it relate to the situation he is addressing in the letter? Asking these and
other questions of Paul's salutations contributes to a more informed
interpretation of his letters.

## Thanksgiving

Paul includes thanksgiving subunits in nine of his letters.[22] Those
thanksgivings potentially serve one or more of four purposes.[23] They
can serve an epistolary purpose in introducing main themes present in
the letter. In Romans, for example, the thanksgiving introduces both
the major theme of faith and the subordinate theme of Paul's anticipated visit to Rome. The thanksgiving sections can serve a pastoral
purpose in expressing concern for the readers. Again in Romans, Paul
introduces the ideas of establishing the readers in their faith while, at
the same time, being encouraged by them in return. The thanksgiving
sections of Paul's letters can also serve a didactic purpose in reminding
the readers of previous teaching (e.g., Gal. 1:9) and/or a **paraenetic**
purpose in indicating areas for growth (e.g., Eph. 1:18–19a).

As noted above, Paul sometimes replaces the thanksgiving with a different subunit (e.g., a rebuke section), adds a second subunit to it (e.g.,
a blessing section), or in the case of Colossians, expands it considerably
by including a Christological hymn. The best-known example is the
absence of a thanksgiving in the letter to the Galatians. In its place, Paul
includes a strong rebuke subunit (1:6–10) in which he sets the tone for
the letter and raises his primary concern: the Galatians are following
false teachers who teach a "different gospel" that is diametrically opposed to the true gospel Paul preaches and, therefore, is no gospel at all.

---

21. L. A. Jervis, *The Purpose of Romans: A Comparative Letter Structure Investigation* (Sheffield: JSOT
    Press, 1991), 34.

22. The passages in question are Rom. 1:8–12; 1 Cor. 1:4–9; Eph. 1:15–23; Phil. 1:3–11; Col.
    1:3–23; 1 Thess. 1:2–10; 2 Thess. 1:3–12; 2 Tim. 1:3–5; Philem. vv.4–7.

23. P. T. O'Brien, *Introductory Thanksgivings in the Letters of Paul* (Leiden: Brill, 1977), 262.

The function of the Galatians rebuke subunit, then, is comparable to that of the thanksgivings found in Paul's other letters, but the circumstances are so dire that he can find nothing worthy of commendation and moves directly to the attack.

Perhaps less discussed but equally significant is the blessing subunit in 2 Corinthians that replaces the more common thanksgiving (1:3–7). Peter O'Brien notes that Paul's introductory blessing subunits focus on God's blessings in which he himself participates rather on than God's work in the lives of others as is true in the thanksgivings.[24] In 2 Corinthians, Paul uses the blessing subunit to introduce the twin themes of affliction and comfort that run throughout the letter, and to express his pastoral concern for the readers while identifying closely with them. The circumstances surrounding this letter, however, make it particularly appropriate to bless God for the way in which he has restored the relationship between Paul and the Corinthian church. In Ephesians, Paul adds a blessing subunit (1:3–14) before the thanksgiving (1:15–23), and in Colossians Paul expands the thanksgiving (1:3–14) by including a Christological hymn (1:15–20) and comment (1:21–23).

### Apostolic Parousia

At least eleven of Paul's letters include a subunit in which he seeks to make his presence felt.[25] Each of these "apostolic parousia" sections includes at least one of three themes: (1) Paul's act of writing the letter, (2) Paul's sending an emissary to the church or individual addressed, or (3) Paul's plans to visit the recipient(s).[26] Paul uses the writing theme to state his authority to write and/or to ask his readers to fall into line with the content of the letter. He uses the emissary theme to set out the credentials of the emissary and to explain what he expects the emissary to do. The visit theme expresses either Paul's intent or desire to visit. Only 1 Corinthians includes all three themes (4:19–21), while 2 Thessalonians includes none of them. The presence of an apostolic parousia in Galatians is debated, with the discussion usually focused on Galatians 4:12–20. In 2 Timothy and Titus, the corresponding sections focus as much on the recipient coming to Paul as the other way around (cf. 2 Tim. 4:9–15; Titus 3:12–14).

---

24. P. T. O'Brien, "Benediction, Blessing, Doxology, Thanksgiving" in *Dictionary of Paul and His Letters*, eds. G. F. Hawthorne, R. P. Martin, and D. G. Reid (Downers Grove: InterVarsity Press, 1993), 68.

25. The passages in question are Rom. 15:14–33; 1 Cor. 4:19–21; 2 Cor. 13:1–10; Eph. 6:20–22; Phil. 2:19–30; Col. 4:7–9; 1 Thess. 2:17–3:13; 1 Tim. 3:14–16; 2 Tim. 4:9–15; Titus 3:12–14; Philem. vv.21–22.

26. Jervis, *Purpose of Romans*, 113.

Identifying which theme(s) Paul includes in a given apostolic parousia can provide insight into the way in which he views his relationship with the recipients. In Romans, for example, Paul uses the writing theme to introduce himself and his ministry (15:14–21) and the visit theme to signal both his desire and his intent to come to Rome (15:22–33). In Philippians and 1 Thessalonians, the letter itself is less important than the emissaries he is sending (Phil. 2:24; 1 Thess. 3:1–10) and his own desire to visit (Phil. 2:19–23, 25–30; 1 Thess. 2:17–20; 3:11–13). In Ephesians and Colossians, Tychicus's role as Paul's emissary is clearly most important (Eph. 6:20–22; Col. 4:7–9).

### Apostolic Apologia

Related to the apostolic parousia is the **apostolic apologia**.[27] In eight of the nine letters he writes to churches, Paul includes a subunit related to his ministry as an apostle.[28] In those sections, he deals with the gospel, defends his ministry, and/or presents his credentials. These sections are particularly useful sources of information in seeking to develop an understanding of Pauline biography and chronology from his letters. They also provide insight into what the recipients know about Paul and his ministry and/or what aspects of his activities support the argument of the letters in which they occur. For example, the apostolic apologia of Ephesians directly supports one of Paul's primary concerns in that letter: the bringing together of Jews and Gentiles into a single body, the Church (3:1–13; cf. 2:11–22).

### Closing

The closings of Paul's letters are as varied as the churches and individuals to whom he wrote.[29] Based on a study of eight letters, Weima suggests that a typical Pauline closing includes four elements: peace wish, hortatory section, greetings, and grace benediction.[30]

---

27. I am indebted to Grand LeMarquand for the phrase "apostolic apologia," which he used in a class presentation when we were doctoral students at Wycliffe College in Toronto. Although I have not seen the idea developed elsewhere in the intervening years, I have found it a helpful concept in thinking about the structure of Paul's letters and, therefore, include it here.

28. The passages in question are Rom. 15:14–21; 1 Cor. 1:10–4:21; 2 Cor. 1:12–6:10; Gal. 1:11–2:21; Eph. 3:1–13; Phil. 1:12–26; 3:13–16; Col. 1:24–2:5; 1 Thess. 2:1–10.

29. The passages in question are Rom. 16:1–27; 1 Cor. 16:13–24; 2 Cor. 13:11-13; Gal. 6:11–18; Eph. 6:23-24; Phil. 4:21–23; Col. 4:10–18; 1 Thess. 5:23–28; 2 Thess. 3:16–18; 1 Tim. 6:20–21; 2 Tim.. 4:19–21; Titus 3:15; Philem. vv. 23–25.

30. Weima, *Neglected Endings*, 154. Weima studied Romans, 1 Corinthians, 2 Corinthians, Galatians, Philippians, 1 Thessalonians, 2 Thessalonians, and Philemon.

Of those four elements, though, only the grace benediction appears in all thirteen letters ascribed to Paul. Eight letters include a greeting element, and seven letters include a hortatory section. Paul uses the greetings to maintain and develop his relationship with the recipients and to promote unity among congregations. Interestingly, the longest greeting lists appear in letters to churches Paul had not planted (Rom. 16:3–16, 21–23; Col. 4:10–17), suggesting that one function of the greetings in those letters was to associate Paul with individuals who were well known to the congregations. In at least some instances, Paul uses the hortatory section to reinforce instruction that appears earlier in the letter (e.g., Rom. 16:17–20; 2 Cor. 13:11).

## Middle-Level: Structural Features within the Letter Body

Three categories of middle-level structure that occur within the bodies of Paul's letters are worth noting. They are subgenres, **oral patterns,** and epistolary conventions. Although each category deserves a volume in its own right, a brief introduction to each will provide an overview for the purposes of this handbook.

### Subgenres

Scholars have long identified and discussed subgenres in Paul's letters. The Christological hymns or confessions of Philippians 2:5–11, Colossians 1:15–20, 1 Timothy 3:16, and 2 Timothy 2:11–13, for example, each have generated extensive literature in its own right, as have other proposed instances. Even the casual reader readily recognizes doxologies such as those in Romans 11:33–36 and Ephesians 3:20–21. **Vice and virtue lists** offer concrete examples of acceptable and unacceptable ethical behavior (e.g., Gal. 5:19–23; Col. 3:5–15).

Some subgenres have distinctive forms. For example, three elements comprise the sections of a **household code:** (1) the person addressed, (2) one or more commands, and (3) a motive for the behavior commanded (e.g., Eph. 5:21–6:9; Col. 3:18–4:1; Titus 2:1–10). A **topos** is a self-contained unit that treats a topic of proper thought or action. It also consists of three elements: (1) an injunction, (2) a reason, and (3) an analysis of the topic. Paul's use of topos is easy to see in his discussion of the believer's relationship to governmental authorities in Romans 13:1–7:

> Injunction:  "Let . . ." (13:1a)
> Reason:      "For . . ." (13:1b)
> Analysis:    "Therefore . . ." (13:2–7)

Elsewhere in Romans Paul uses **diatribe** to address possible incon-
sistencies or answer possible objections. Diatribe includes the tech-
nique of addressing an imaginary questioner (e.g., 2:1–5; 2:17–24;
9:19–21; 11:17–24), interaction with objections and/or false conclusions (e.g., 3:1–9; 6:1–2, 15–16; 7:7, 13; 9:14–15), and dialogical ex-
change (e.g., 3:27–30).

### Oral Patterns

Given the largely oral culture of the first century and the strong emphasis on practical rhetoric within that culture, it should come as no
surprise that the spoken word and the listener's ear shaped thought and
expression. "Oral patterns" is one label that has been given to seven
middle-level compositional techniques that help Paul's listeners find
their way through the complex argumentation of his letters.[31]

*Inversion* is the reversal of the order in which two or more topics are
introduced and subsequently discussed; one example of this pattern occurs in 1 Corinthians 1:13–4:13.

*Alternation* is the interplay between two alternate choices or ideas,
such as the extended discussion of flesh and Spirit in Galatians 5:16–25.
Alternation is closely related to *word-chain,* which is the frequent repetition of a given word and its cognates within a clearly delimited context;
Paul's repetition of law and faith in Galatians 3:1–14 is a good example.

*Inclusion* uses cognate words to begin and end a discussion (e.g., Phil.
2:25, 30), while *ring-composition* uses a correspondence in wording between sentences to frame a section. The latter pattern may use the sentences to begin and end the section to which they belong ("inclusive,"
e.g., Phil 1:12–14, 25–26), or the sentences may stand outside the section and resume a discussion interrupted by that section ("anaphoric,"
e.g., Phil. 3:1; 4:4).

*Concentric symmetry* and the *ABA' pattern* describe structures that extend beyond the sentence level and are sometimes labeled as "chiastic."
Concentric symmetry consists of multiple, inverse correspondences
that extend over a considerable expanse of material and have a single element at the center (e.g., 1 Cor. 12:1–14:40). In the ABA' pattern, Paul
returns to an initial theme after a digression (e.g., 2 Cor. 8:1–9:15).

### Epistolary Conventions

As noted above, disclosure, request, joy, and compliance formulas
are common epistolary conventions. Others include the confidence
formula, the περὶ δὲ formula, and the use of "finally." The *confidence*

---

31. Harvey, *Listening to the Text.*

*formula* strengthens a request or admonition by creating a sense of obligation through praise. Examples are present in Romans 15:14; 2 Corinthians 2:3; Galatians 5:10; Philippians 2:24; 2 Thessalonians 3:4; and Philemon v.21.

The περὶ δὲ formula most commonly addresses an issue raised in a previous letter Paul had received. The best-known examples are in 1 Corinthians (7:1, 25; 8:1; 12:1; 16:1, 12), but Paul also uses it in 2 Corinthians (9:1, περὶ μὲν) and in 1 Thessalonians (4:9; 5:1). Because Paul uses "finally" λοιπὸν / τοῦ λοιποῦ / τὸ λοιπόν in places that seem premature to twenty-first-century readers (e.g., Phil. 3:1; 1 Thess. 4:1), it is easy to overlook the other times when he consistently uses it to introduce the last major item he will discuss in a letter (2 Cor. 13:11; Gal. 6:17; Eph. 6:10; Phil. 4:8; 2 Thess. 3:1; 2 Tim. 4:8). Each of these epistolary conventions, along with the oral patterns and the subgenres that occur at the middle level, helped the original readers/listeners make sense of the longer-than-usual body sections of Paul's letters.

## Micro-Level Structure: Structural Features at the Sentence Level

Structural features at the sentence level include aspects of figurative language and aspects of word arrangement. Instances of proverb (e.g., 1 Cor. 15:33; Gal. 5:9) and metaphor (e.g., 1 Cor. 3:4–9; 9:24–27; 12:12–17; Eph. 6:10–17) occur with some frequency in Paul's letters. Allegory might well fit here also, although the best-known example in Paul's letters (Gal. 4:21–31) extends well beyond the sentence level.

Two repeated sentence-level structures found in Paul's letters are parallelism and chiasm. *Parallelism* reflects Paul's Hebrew background and uses similarities or contrasts in thought between successive sentences. The parallelism may be either synonymous (similarity):

| | |
|---|---|
| Romans 10:11 | [F]or with the heart a person believes, resulting in righteousness, and with the mouth he confesses, resulting in salvation. |

or antithetic (contrast):

| | |
|---|---|
| 1 Corinthians 1:25 | Because the foolishness of God is wiser than men, and the weakness of God is stronger than men. |

Although "*chiasm*" has been used to describe structures of any length—including the structures of entire books—it is best used to describe the transposition of corresponding words or phrases within a sentence. Galatians provides several examples, including a double chiasm involving flesh and Spirit in 6:8:

Galatians 6:8                        For the one who sows
                                     to his own flesh
                                     will from the flesh
                                     reap corruption,

                                     but the one who sows
                                     to the Spirit
                                     from the Spirit
                                     reap eternal life.

In classical rhetoric, these micro-level structures would fit under the task of "style." As such, they offer a point of transition to a brief consideration of the role of rhetoric in interpreting Paul's letters.

## The Role of Rhetoric

Beginning in the 1970s, scholarly interest in the relationship between Paul's letters and classical Greek rhetoric increased rapidly. Ancient handbooks on rhetoric divided the discipline into five tasks: invention, arrangement, style, memory, and delivery.[32] Hans-Deiter Betz's commentary on Galatians was the first major work to adopt a consistently "rhetorical" approach to one of Paul's letters.[33] In it, Betz focused on the task of arrangement and argued that the body of Galatians (1:6–6:10) corresponds to a judicial speech with five major sections, each with a specific function:

| 1:6–11 | Introduction | (exordium) | gives the reason for the speech |
| 1:12–2:14 | Statement of fact | (narratio) | gives the background for the speech |
| 2:15–21 | Proposition | (propositio) | gives the main thesis of the speech |

---

32. Harvey, *Listening to the Text*, 28.

33. H. D. Betz, *Galatians: A Commentary on Paul's Letter to the Churches in Galatia* (Philadelphia: Fortress, 1979).

| 3:1–4:31 | Proofs | (probatio) | gives evidence in support of the thesis |
| 5:1–6:10 | Exhortation | (exhoratio) | encourages the listeners to embrace and apply the thesis |

Betz's commentary fueled a burst of monographs and articles seeking to apply all five tasks of classical rhetoric to Paul's letters, although the major focus tended to be on arrangement. There is a spectrum of views regarding the value of rhetorical analysis for interpreting letters, but it is probably best used at the "middle level" to analyze individual passages within the letter body. For example, James Bailey and Lyle Vander Broek provide the following rhetorical analysis of 1 Corinthians 15:1-58:[34]

| 15:1–2 | *Exordium* |
| 15:3–11 | *Narratio* |
| 15:12–20 | *Propositio* |
| 15:21–50 | *Proofs* |
| | Contrast between Adam and Christ (15:21–28) |
| | Baptizing on behalf of the dead (15:29) |
| | Dying daily (15:30–31) |
| | Enduring persecution (15:32–33) |
| | Nature of the resurrection body (15:34–44) |
| | Old Testament citation (15:45–50) |
| 15:51–58 | *Exhortatio* |

Klauck's comment on the application of rhetorical analysis to letters rings true:[35]

> A . . . mechanical application of the classical . . . speech model to letters and letter components is more likely to discredit rhetorical analysis than to promote it. Rhetorical analysis must not be pursued at the expense of the unique features of the letter genre that episto-lography has helped us understand. Inflated use of the

---

34. J. L. Bailey and L. D. Vander Broek, *Literary Forms in the New Testament: A Handbook,* (Louisville, KY: Westminster/John Knox, 1992), 33.

35. Klauck, *Ancient Letters*, 225.

term "rhetoric" should be avoided and the scope of
its applicability precisely determined and stated. . . . If
these boundaries are respected, then obviously rhetoric can be of great value in illuminating the argumen-
tative structure of letters—for example, by working
through enthymemes and examples or by relating the
letter elements to the classical means of persuasion by
ethos, pathos, and logos.

## PAUL AND THE LETTER GENRE

Letters were a common means of communication in first-century
Mediterranean culture. Writers used them to convey information, to
give instructions, to conduct both personal and state business, and to
maintain contact with friends and family members. Superiors used letters to give instructions to subordinates, and subordinates used letters
to make requests of those in positions above them. It was common for
individuals to arrange for friends to deliver letters for them, and the fact
that the culture was largely oral meant that those friends often read the
letters aloud to the recipients. Although the general letter form (introduction—body—conclusion) was fixed, there was considerable flexibility within the letter body itself.

Paul wrote letters because they were the most personal means available for communicating over a distance. Letters made it possible for him
"to stay in near-oral touch with his addressees."[36] They made it possible
for him to instruct, encourage, rebuke, and correct the congregations
he planted during his missionary travels. They made it possible for him
to exercise his apostolic authority even while he was absent from those
congregations. By sending coworkers to carry his letters, Paul could insure that his message was communicated correctly and could enhance
his apostolic "presence" with the recipients.

The flexibility of letters allowed Paul to address a variety of topics in
the manner and style most appropriate to the readers' circumstances.
To the Galatians, he could write an impassioned defense of the gospel;
to the Romans, he could write a comprehensive explanation of that
gospel. For the Ephesians, he could address the nature of the universal
church; for the Corinthians, he could address a series of issues facing a
particular local church. To Timothy and Titus, he could give instructions on church leadership; to Philemon, he could make an appeal to
receive a run-away slave. In each letter, Paul was able to shape his communication to the needs of the audience.

---

36. W. G. Kelber, *The Oral and Written Gospel: The Hermeneutics of Speaking and Writing in the
Synoptic Tradition, Mark, Paul and Q* (Philadelphia: Fortress, 1983), 168.

Because Paul wrote to specific congregations and individuals in specific circumstances, his letters cannot be treated as connected chapters in a systematic theology textbook (although Romans comes closest in that respect). Proper consideration must be given to their occasional nature, including the historical context of Paul's ministry activities and the religious and cultural context of the city in which the recipients were located. Proper consideration must also be given to the fact that the letters are literary documents, for any given verse or teaching exists within the context of a specific letter. At the same time, it is possible to identify themes that run throughout Paul's letters because they were written by a single author. Taken together, these factors highlight both the benefits to Paul of using the letter genre and the challenges facing those who would interpret his letters.

The first step in interpreting Paul's letters is to establish the authenticity and integrity of the letters ascribed to him. Then, it is important to synthesize the historical contexts in which Paul wrote his those letters. Those steps are the focus of Chapter 2.

## The Chapter in Review

In the oral-rhetorical-literary environment of first-century Mediterranean culture, letters were a common means of conveying information, giving instructions, and maintaining personal contact. Paul adopted and creatively adapted the letter genre to facilitate the growth of the congregations he had planted.

In addition to the overall structure of Paul's letters, subgenres, oral patterns, and epistolary conventions within the letter body are worth analyzing, as are structural features at the sentence level. Rhetorical analysis can also be helpful when considering individual passages within letters.

The flexibility of letters allowed Paul to address multiple topics and shape his communication to his readers and their circumstances. Because each of his letters is an occasional document related to the specific congregation to which he was writing, it is important to consider the historical context against which each was written.

# 2

# THE HISTORICAL BACKGROUND OF PAUL'S LETTERS

## The Chapter at a Glance

- External and internal evidence support the authenticity and integrity of the thirteen canonical Pauline letters.

- A chronology based on the evidence from Paul's letters aligns well with the account in Acts.

- Six of Paul's letters date from his time of active missionary work (A.D. 49–57); four letters date from an imprisonment period (A.D. 57–63); and the Pastoral Letters most likely date from a release-and-second-imprisonment period (A.D. 63–67).

PAUL'S LETTERS ARE OCCASIONAL documents that communicate timeless truth. Because they are occasional documents, understanding the historical contexts in which their timeless truth was communicated is an important part of interpreting them. Scholars have debated those historical contexts. Central to that discussion have been the questions of **authenticity**, **integrity**, and **chronology**. This chapter will address each of those issues in turn and, then, will seek to provide a synthesis of the historical background as a basis for interpretation.

## AUTHENTICITY: HOW MANY LETTERS?

Although the New Testament ascribes thirteen letters to Paul, scholars have raised questions about the authorship of several of them. In 1845, F. C. Baur and the so-called **Tübingen School** first suggested that only four of Paul's letters were genuine: Romans, 1–2 Corinthians, and Galatians. By labeling these letters the **Hauptbriefe**, the Tübingen School cemented their primacy within the Pauline corpus. In 1886, Carl Weizsäcker "corrected" Tübingen and argued that Philippians, 1 Thessalonians, and Philemon were also genuine. By bringing the number of "genuine" letters to seven, Weizsäcker set the direction much of critical Pauline scholarship still follows. Ephesians, Colossians, and 2 Thessalonians are sometimes viewed as "deutero-Pauline," while 1–2 Timothy and Titus are sometimes viewed as "pseudo-Pauline." Since the number of genuine letters affects multiple areas (e.g., the tracing of major Pauline themes), it is essential to establish the database to use in understanding Paul and his teaching.

| Seldom Disputed | Sometimes Disputed | Strongly Disputed |
|---|---|---|
| • Romans<br>• 1 Corinthians<br>• 2 Corinthians<br>• Galatians<br>• Philippians<br>• 1 Thessalonians<br>• Philemon | • Ephesians<br>• Colossians<br>• 2 Thessalonians | • 1 Timothy<br>• 2 Timothy<br>• Titus |

The authenticity of Romans, 1–2 Corinthians, and Galatians is seldom disputed. There is, however, some discussion of whether the original form of Romans was the same as the canonical form. That discussion centers on the floating doxology that appears variously at 14:23, 15:33, and 16:23 and on the presence or absence of the grace benediction in 16:24. Similarly, considerable discussion revolves around the integrity of 2 Corinthians. The Pauline origin of both letters, however, is widely accepted. In the same way, few commentators dispute the authenticity of Philippians, 1 Thessalonians, or Philemon, although some question the integrity of Philippians. Since opinion on 2 Thessalonians, Colossians, and Ephesians is divided, it will be helpful to consider each letter separately. The "pastoral" letters of 1–2 Timothy and Titus will be considered together.

## 2 Thessalonians

Scholars raise two concerns in connection with the authenticity of 2 Thessalonians: its less personal tone and its similarities to 1 Thessalonians. In particular, they argue that similarities in structure, language, and subject matter suggest dependence on 1 Thessalonians. In response, three counterarguments may be offered. First, George Barr has suggested that **literary dependence** is best evaluated in terms of themes occurring in clusters using the same words (rather than synonyms) that occur in more or less the same order.[1] The actual points of contact 2 Thessalonians has with 1 Thessalonians constitute less than one-third of the letter, and those points of contact are often in different contexts. Second, the structure, language, and style of 2 Thessalonians are not un-Pauline, and the letter has strong external support from the time of Ignatius, Polycarp, and Justin. Third, the differences in tone between the two letters may be explained by different circumstances and/or different subject matter. 1 Thessalonians reflects the encouraging news Paul had received about the church (1 Thess. 3:1–8), while 2 Thessalonians reflects reports that the problems addressed in his first letter had deepened.

## Colossians

The primary issues raised in connection with the authenticity of Colossian are stylistic and theological. Scholars note that the style of the letter is more complex and uses many words and phrases not present in other Pauline letters. They also argue that the theology of the letter reflects the fully developed **Gnosticism** of the second century. Again, several counterarguments may be offered in response to these concerns. First, the more complex style is most evident in sections dealing with the false teaching that threatened the church and in preformed material such as the Christological hymn in 1:15–20.[2] Further, Paul has probably borrowed many of the new words from the false teaching he is addressing in order to refute it. Second, the vocabulary of the expanded section on slaves and masters (3:22–4:1) and the individuals mentioned in the letter's closing (4:7–17) support a close connection between Colossians and the uncontested letter to Philemon. Third, the **syncretistic** heresy addressed combines the ritual practices of **legalism** (2:16–17), the worship of supernatural powers present in **mysticism** (2:18–19), and

---

1. G. K. Barr, "Literary Dependence in the New Testament Epistles," *Irish Biblical Studies* (1997): 148–60.

2. Note the criteria Richards proposes for preformed material in *First-Century Letter Writing*, 97–9.

the teachings of asceticism that the body is evil (2:20–23). As such, it is better understood as an earlier precursor to the Gnosticism of the second century. Finally, the letter has solid external support as Pauline from the time of Justin and Marcion.

## Ephesians

Four areas of concern contribute to the question of the authenticity of Ephesians: stylistic/linguistic, literary, historical, and doctrinal. The complex style and unusual vocabulary of the letter raise questions similar to those raised in connection with Colossians. Similarities in themes suggest that Ephesians is dependent on Colossians. The letter does not appear to be addressed to a concrete historical situation, and Paul's relationship to the readers seems more remote than in his authentic letters. The letter's portrayal of Christ as cosmic reconciler and its emphasis on the universal (rather than the local) church differ from Paul's teaching in his authentic letters.

In response to these concerns, it is possible to suggest that the style and vocabulary of Ephesians are appropriate to the themes discussed and are not far removed from the style and vocabulary of Colossians. The literary similarities to Colossians may be explained by Ephesians being written after, but close in time to, Colossians and by the possibility that Paul used notes.[3] Barr concludes "It should be noted that there is no evidence of direct literary dependence [between Ephesians and Colossians], although the two epistles have points of contact. . . . It is more likely that the author wrote two works in succession with different aims, developing different ideas and in different moods."[4] The possibility that Paul wrote Ephesians as a general letter to be circulated among the churches planted in the province of Asia as the result of his ministry in Ephesus explains the less specific historical references in the letter (cf. Acts 19:10).[5] It is also true, however, that both the interest in spiritual warfare (6:10–20) and the concern for reconciliation between Jews and Gentiles (2:11–22) found in the letter echo the circumstances of Paul's ministry in Ephesus as seen in Acts (19:11–20, 23–41). The Christology and ecclesiology of Ephesians are not incompatible with the theology of Paul's undisputed letters and most likely represent somewhat later reflection on the themes involved. As was true with 2 Thessalonians and Colossians, Ephesians also has solid external support from as early as the second century.

---

3.  See Richards' discussion of "recycled" material in *First-Century Letter Writing,* 160.

4.  G. K. Barr, *Scalometry and the Pauline Epistles* (London: T & T Clark, 2004), 73.

5.  A similar practice most likely lies behind the list of addressees in 1 Peter and the churches included in the book of Revelation.

## 1–2 Timothy and Titus

Less conservative scholars often consider 1–2 Timothy and Titus to be non-Pauline. It is common to designate these three letters the Pastoral Letters and treat them together because of their content, style, vocabulary, and frequent use of preformed material. The empirical evidence in support of authenticity includes the clear statements of Paul's authorship in each letter and the fact that none of the thirteen letters—other than Romans and 1 Corinthians—are better attested as Pauline.

Nevertheless, four considerations seem to argue against authenticity. Historically, the allusions in the letters to Paul's ministry do not appear to fit into the framework of Acts. Ecclesiastically, the concept of church leadership found in the letters seems to be more developed than might have been true during Paul's lifetime. Doctrinally, references in the letters to such concepts as "the faith," "the deposit," and "sound doctrine" appear to reflect a more fixed understanding of doctrine than is present in Paul's other letters. Linguistically, the vocabulary of 1–2 Timothy and Titus seems to differ from that of the other letters ascribed to Paul. Each of these arguments will be addressed in turn.

| | Issue | Response |
|---|---|---|
| Historical | Historical allusions do not fit account of Acts. | Letters were written subsequent to Acts. |
| Ecclesiological | Concept of church leadership is later than Paul. | Elders and deacons were appointed early. |
| Doctrinal | Understanding of doctrine is later than Paul. | Preformed material occurs in other letters. |
| Literary | Vocabulary differs from Paul's other letters. | Written style differs from oral style. |

The suggestion that the allusions to Paul's ministry do not fit into the record of Acts is an argument from silence. The most common explanation is a "release-and-second-imprisonment" chronology based on evidence provided by Clement of Rome (1 Clem. 5.6–7) and Eusebius (*Hist. Eccl.* 2.22.1–8; 2.25.5–8). The usual understanding is as follows:

| A.D. 61–63 | Imprisoned |
| A.D. 63 | Acquitted and freed |
| A.D. 63-66 | Further missionary work |
| A.D. 66–67 | Rearrested and imprisoned |
| A.D. 67 | Martyred |

In such a chronology, 1 Timothy and Titus date from the period of further missionary work of A.D. 63–66, while 2 Timothy dates from Paul's second imprisonment period of A.D. 66–67.[6]

The concern about a later concept of church leadership is overstated. Paul appointed elders early in his missionary work (Acts 14:23; 20:17), and the early church recognized the need for qualified leaders early in its development (Acts 1:21–22; 6:3). The uncontested letter to the Philippians includes "overseers and deacons" among its addressees. Similarly, the idea of a fixed body of truth (e.g., Phil. 1:27; Col. 2:7; Eph. 4:5) and the use of **preformed traditions** (e.g., Rom. 1:2–4; Phil. 2:5–11; Col. 1:15-19; Eph. 5:14) are both present in other Pauline letters.

The usual argument from vocabulary is that the language used in 1–2 Timothy and Titus also appears in the writings of the second century church fathers. For that reason, the argument runs, those later writings must be the source of the language in the Pastorals.[7] This conclusion, however, has been contested from several perspectives. On the basis of his study of the style of Paul's letters, Anthony Kenny concludes that 2 Timothy is as close to the "center" of Pauline style as Romans and Philippians.[8] In his study of vocabulary, Armin Baum notes that "The vocabulary of the Pastorals can easily be made to conform to the (semantically) poorer vocabulary of the Paulines by substituting the distinctive words of the Pastoral Epistles with synonyms from the other Paulines. . . . The style of the Pastoral Epistles is both semantically and syntactically closer to written language and style than the other Paulines, which show more characteristics of (conceptual) orality."[9] Barr believes that the vocabulary of the Pastorals is actually a reflection of language Paul used in his preaching: "The

---

6. There are also other ways of relating the Pastorals to Paul's life and ministry. They will be included in the discussion of chronology that follows.

7. Perhaps the most influential study on the vocabulary of the Pastorals is P. N. Harrison, *The Problem of the Pastoral Epistles*, (London: Oxford University Press, 1921). Barr, however, is not persuaded and concludes, "All that can be usefully taken from Harrison's diagrams is that there are generally more unusual words in the Pastorals than in the other Paulines, and these occur in second-century writings" (*Scalometry*, 99).

8. A. Kenny, *A Stylometric Study of the New Testament* (Oxford: Clarendon Press, 1986), 94–100.

9. A. D. Baum, "Semantic Variation within the Corpus Paulinum: Linguistic Considerations Concerning the Richer Vocabulary of the Pastoral Epistles," *Tyndale Bulletin* (2008): 291–2.

Pastorals were not written as literary works to be preserved. They were very personal letters and preserve colloquial habits not found in Paul's formal letters addressed to congregations."[10] Each of these approaches suggests it is as likely that the Pastorals were the source of the language used by second-century writers as vice versa. Finally, Earle Ellis argues that "The role of the secretary and the use of preformed traditions in the composition of the Pastorals cut the ground from under the pseudepigraphical hypothesis with its mistaken nineteenth-century assumptions about the nature of authorship. They require the critical student to give primary weight to the opening ascriptions in the letters and to the external historical evidence, both of which support Pauline authorship."[11] Taken together, the preceding arguments suggest there are no insurmountable obstacles to the authenticity of 1–2 Timothy and Titus.

## INTEGRITY: ONE LETTER OR MORE?

Commentators have offered partition theories for several of Paul's letters, but the question of integrity has tended to focus on two of them: 2 Corinthians and Philippians. It should be noted that there is no manuscript evidence either letter ever existed in any form other than what is present in the canon. Nevertheless, it will be helpful to summarize the discussions related to each letter.

### 2 Corinthians

Paul's relationship with the Corinthians is the most complex of all the churches he planted. The two canonical letters provide evidence of three visits. In addition to a founding visit (1 Cor. 1:16; 3:6–10; 4:15; 9:1–2; 16:15) and the so-called "painful" visit (2 Cor. 2:1; 13:2), Paul mentions a planned third visit (2 Cor. 12:14; 13:1; cf. 1 Cor. 16:6). There is also evidence of additional correspondence between Paul and the church. The so-called **previous letter** preceded canonical 1 Corinthians (1 Cor. 5:9–11) as did a letter from the church to Paul (1 Cor. 7:1), and 2 Corinthians mentions a **sorrowful letter** (2 Cor. 2:1–4). In particular, the mention of the painful visit and the sorrowful letter fuel the discussion of the integrity of 2 Corinthians.

---

10. Barr, *Scalometry*, 117.
11. E. E. Ellis, "Pastoral Letters" in *Dictionary of Paul and His Letters,* eds. G. F. Hawthorne, R. P. Martin, and D. G. Reid (Downers Grove: InterVarsity Press, 1993), 661.

| Paul and the Corinthians | | |
|---|---|---|
| Founding visit in Corinth | 1 Cor. 1:14–16 | A.D. 50–52 |
| Previous letter to Corinth | 1 Cor. 5:9–11 | |
| Letter from Corinth | 1 Cor. 7:1 | |
| 1 Corinthians from Ephesus | 1 Cor. 16:5–9 | Spring, A.D. 55 |
| Painful (second) visit | 2 Cor. 2:1; 13:2 | Summer/Fall, A.D. 55 |
| Sorrowful letter | 2 Cor. 2:1–4 | Spring, A.D. 56 |
| Report from Titus | 2 Cor. 7:5–7 | Summer, A.D. 56 |
| 2 Corinthians from Macedonia | 2 Cor. 8:1; 9:2–4 | Fall, A.D. 56 |
| Planned third visit to Corinth | 2 Cor. 12:14; 13:1 | Spring, A.D. 57 |

Although both 2 Corinthians 2:14–7:4 and 8:1–9:15 have been proposed as separate letters, the discussion most frequently centers on 10:1–13:14. That discussion commonly notes four contrasts between chapters 1–9 and chapters 10–13. First, the tone of chapters 1–9 is one of relief, while the tone of chapters 10–13 is one of self-defense. Second, the content of the first nine chapters focuses on the congregation's fidelity, while the content of the last four chapters focuses on false apostles. Third, the style of chapters 1–9 is said to be expository, while the style of chapters 10–13 is said to be apologetic. Fourth, the first nine chapters are written in the first person plural, while the last four chapters are written in the first person singular.

These contrasts lead some scholars to suggest two possible relationships between chapters 1–9 and chapters 10–13: either 2 Corinthians 10:1–13:14 is the sorrowful letter written between 1 Corinthians and 2 Corinthians 1–9,[12] or 2 Corinthians 10:1–13:14 comprise a fifth letter written after 2 Corinthians 1–9.[13] In addition to the fact that no manuscript evidence exists for multiple sources, however, several questions may be raised regarding partition theories. If chapters 10–13 were written first, why is the order of compilation reversed in the canonical

---

12. J. Moffat, *Introduction to the Literature of the New Testament*, third edition (Edinburgh: T & T Clark, 1918), 119–23.

13. V. P. Furnish, *II Corinthians* (Garden City, NY: Doubleday, 1984), 35–41.

version? Since 2 Corinthians 12:18 refers to the visit that carried the sorrowful letter, how can chapters 10–13 be the sorrowful letter? Were both the ending of 1:1–9:15 and the beginning of 10:1–13:14 lost, or were they deliberately discarded?

Scholars who accept the integrity of 2 Corinthians have offered several explanations for the differences present in the letter. For the sake of space, these suggestions will be noted without detailed discussion. It might be that the differences in subject matter of the three sections of the letter (chapters 1–7, 8–9, 10–13) account for the differences in tone and style. It might be that a period of time intervened between the writing of chapters 1–9 and the writing of chapters 10–13. It might be that 1:1–9:15 was written by a secretary, while 10:1–13:14 was written by Paul. It might be that Paul saved the most controversial topic for last, in keeping with the rhetorical practice of including a special emotional appeal toward the end of a speech. It might be that Paul followed the common practice seen in other speakers and writers (e.g., Pliny) of varying style and tone within the same speech or document. Although none of these explanations is conclusive, they offer alternatives that suggest there are no insurmountable obstacles to the integrity of 2 Corinthians.

## Philippians

The integrity of Philippians is discussed less than that of 2 Corinthians, but the abrupt change of tone at 3:2 and what is often perceived as a delayed thank-you note in 4:10–20 have led a few commentators to suggest that the canonical form is a **composite letter**. Some suggest that Philippians was originally two shorter letters; others suggest that it was three. Under the two-letter theory, an earlier letter (Letter A) consisted of 1:1–3:1 + 4:2–7 + 4:10–23. A later letter (Letter B) consisting of 3:2–4:1 + 4:8–9 was woven into the first to arrive at the canonical form. The three-letter theory is similar, but it identifies 4:10–20 as the first letter (Letter A) with the second letter (Letter B) shortened accordingly (1:1–3:1 + 4:2–7 + 4:21–23), and the third letter (Letter C) remaining the same (3:2–4:1 + 4:8–9).

Again, it should be noted that there is no manuscript evidence to support a composite letter theory. The only extant manuscripts of Philippians preserve the letter in its canonical form. Further, the letter has a thematic unity that weighs against partition theories, and 4:10–23 might well be a Pauline autograph. If 4:10–23 is an autograph, it explains why the thank-you note is "delayed": Paul wanted to express his gratitude in his own hand and did so when he took the pen to close the letter. In any event, the composite letter theories do not remove the supposed difficulty of the abrupt change in tone from rejoicing in

3:1 to a sharp attack on false teachers in 3:2–4:3 followed by a renewed exhortation to rejoice in 4:4. Rather than resorting to a composite letter theory, however, the more likely answer lies in the oral pattern of anaphoric ring-composition in which sentences standing outside a section (3:1 and 4:4) serve to resume a discussion interrupted by that section (3:2–4:3).[14] As was true with 2 Corinthians, the reasons to accept the integrity of Philippians are at least as strong as the arguments to question it.

## CHRONOLOGY: THE LETTERS, ACTS, OR BOTH?

With the extent and integrity of the Pauline corpus established, the next step is to develop a chronology of Paul's ministry and to understand where his letters fit within that chronology. During the second half of the twentieth century, a number of scholars raised questions about the value of Acts for developing such a chronology. For that reason, it is important to address the method used in the discussion that follows.

### A Question of Method

John Knox first suggested that basic considerations of method argue against the conventional approach of beginning with Acts in order to develop a chronology of Paul's life.[15] Instead, Knox argued (1) that the letters, as products of Paul's mind, are "primary" documents and, therefore, firsthand sources for information about the apostle's personality, thought, and life; (2) that Acts is a "secondary" document with regard to Paul since it is the product of Luke's compositional and editorial work and, therefore, at least one step removed from events involving Paul; (3) that the material in the letters should be analyzed thoroughly before the material in Acts is considered; and (4) that the material in Acts should be viewed as supplementary to, but not corrective of, the material in the letters. Although Knox's presuppositions regarding Acts led him to minimize that book's contribution to the process, his suggestion that developing a Pauline chronology beginning with the letters is worth adopting.

The basic method used in the following discussion is simple. First, collect from Paul's letters all the explicit statements about his life that might serve as chronological clues. Next, seek relationships between these clues that might contribute to an outline of Paul's ministry and the letters written during that ministry. Finally, compare the outline

---

14. For a fuller discussion of this approach to Philippians 3:1–4:4, see Harvey, *Listening to the Text*, 239–40.

15. J. Knox, *Chapters in a Life of Paul* (New York: Abingdon-Cokesbury, 1950).

developed from the letters against the details of Paul's ministry as recorded in Acts. Space necessarily prohibits a detailed listing of the results of the first step, but the clues collected will be documented in the discussion of the second step.

## Pauline Data

It it possible to gather ten of Paul's letters into three natural groupings. Mention of Paul, Silas, and Timothy in 1–2 Thessalonians link those letters, for no other letter includes Silas in its salutation.[16] References to the collection for the saints in Jerusalem link Romans and 1–2 Corinthians.[17] Philemon, Colossians, Ephesians, Philippians, and 2 Timothy all include references to Paul's imprisonment.[18] The coworkers mentioned in the latter five letters also link them.[19] These natural groupings will serve as the starting point for seeking relationships between the letters and clues about Paul's movements.

### Macedonia and Achaia

In 1 Thessalonians 2:1–12 Paul reviews the ministry he, Silas, and Timothy had in Thessalonica. That ministry took place after they had suffered and been mistreated in Philippi (2:2). Shortly after leaving Thessalonica, Paul wanted to return but was hindered by unspecified circumstances (1 Thess. 2:17–18). 1 Thessalonians 3:1 reveals that sometime after the ministry in Thessalonica Paul was in Athens alone. After visiting Thessalonica in order to encourage the church (3:2), Timothy joined Paul (3:6), although the exact location at which he did so is unclear from this passage.

The combination of Paul, Silas, and Timothy also occurs in 2 Corinthians 1:19, where Paul alludes to the fact that it was the three of them who had first preached Christ among the Corinthians (cf. 1 Cor. 1:14–17). It seems likely that this initial visit to Corinth followed Paul's time in Athens. Later in the same letter, Paul mentions the fact that brethren from Macedonia supplied his need in Corinth (2 Cor. 11:8–9). It seems likely that Paul's comment in Philippians 4:15–16 also reflects events of this period. In those verses, he mentions that the Philippians had sent to his need both while he was in Thessalonica and

---

16.   1 Thess. 1:1; 2 Thess. 1:1

17.   Rom. 15:25–27; 1 Cor. 16:1–4; 2 Cor. 8:1–6; 9:2–3

18.   Philem. vv.9–10, 13, 23; Col. 4:3, 10; Eph. 3:1; 4:1; 6:20; Phil. 1:7, 13–14, 17; 2 Tim. 1:8, 16; 2:9; 4:16

19.   Philem. vv.1, 12, 23–24; Col. 1:1; 4:7–14; Eph. 1:1; 6:21; Phil. 1:1; 2:19–24; 2 Tim. 4:11–13, 19–20

after he had departed from Macedonia. The contribution sent after he departed from Macedonia may well refer to the gift Paul received in Corinth. From these clues the likely itinerary of Philippi \ Thessalonica \ Athens \ Corinth emerges.

| Macedonia and Achaia | Philippi | 1 Thess. 2:2 |
| --- | --- | --- |
| | Thessalonica | 1 Thess. 2:2; Phil. 4:15–16 |
| | Athens | 1 Thess. 3:1 |
| | Corinth | 2 Cor. 1:19; 11:7–9 |

### Ephesus and Corinth

Not only do references to the collection link Paul's letters to the Romans and the Corinthians, those same references help establish the order in which the letters were written. In 1 Corinthians 16:1–4, Paul directed the saints in Achaia to begin the collection.[20] In 2 Corinthians 8:1–6, we learn that the collection had been completed in Macedonia and begun in Achaia. By the time Paul wrote Romans 15:25–27, the collection had been completed in Achaia as well. The order of the three letters is thus clear: 1 Corinthians, 2 Corinthians, and Romans.

Those letters, however, were not the only ones Paul wrote during this period. 1 Corinthians 5:9–13 refers to a "previous letter" he had written to the Corinthians, and 2 Corinthians 2:1–11, 7:8–12 refer to a "sorrowful letter" that he also sent to Corinth. A fuller summary of Paul's letter-writing activity from this period, therefore, is Previous Letter, 1 Corinthians, Sorrowful Letter, 2 Corinthians, and Romans.

The chronological clues in 1–2 Corinthians and Romans are comparatively numerous and provide a relatively full itinerary of Paul's travels. When he wrote 1 Corinthians, Paul was in Ephesus until Pentecost (16:8) and had been in contact with the churches in Galatia (16:1). Timothy was en route to Corinth (4:17) with plans to return to Ephesus (16:10–11). Once Timothy returned, Paul would travel to Corinth via Macedonia (16:5). In 2 Corinthians, we find Paul and Timothy (1:1) beyond Troas (2:12–13) and into Macedonia (7:5–6) on their way to Corinth (12:20; 13:1). Titus, however, had already been to Corinth once (7:7, 13–14; 8:6; 12:18) and was on his way back again (8:16–24; 9:3–5; 12:18)—this time accompanied by "the brother" and probably carrying 2 Corinthians. References in Romans to Phoebe (16:1–2), Gaius (16:23), and Erastus (16:23) suggest that Paul had arrived in Corinth, as does his comment that the collection in Achaia was

---

20.   1 Corinthians 7:1 suggests that 1 Corinthians was written in response to a letter Paul had received from the Corinthians.

complete (15:26).[21] From Corinth, Paul planned to travel to Jerusalem in order to deliver the collection (15:25). He then hoped to travel to Spain via Rome (15:28), although he was uncertain of his reception in Jerusalem (15:30–32). From the preceding details, the following itinerary emerges: Ephesus \ Troas \ Macedonia \ Corinth \ Jerusalem.

| Ephesus and Corinth | Ephesus | 1 Cor 16:8 |
| --- | --- | --- |
| | Troas | 2 Cor. 2:12 |
| | Macedonia | 2 Cor. 2:13; 7:5 |
| | Corinth | 1 Cor. 16:6 (planned) |
| | Jerusalem | Rom. 15:25 (planned) |

Although there is overlap with the itinerary derived from the Thessalonian correspondence, the visit to Corinth during the period centered on Ephesus and Corinth is Paul's third (2 Cor. 12:14; 13:1–2) and, so, subsequent to that in the earlier itinerary (cf. 1 Cor. 1:16–17). Some details remain tantalizingly obscure. What were the timing and occasion of Paul's second visit to Corinth?[22] What was the relation of that visit to the sorrowful letter mentioned in 2 Corinthians?[23] When and how was the gospel preached "round about as far as Illyricum" (Rom. 15:19)?[24]

## Imprisonment

Among the letters that mention Paul's imprisonment, Philemon and Colossians include the same authors (Paul and Timothy), the same messenger (Onesimus), the same coworkers present with Paul (Aristarchus, Mark, Epaphras, Luke, and Demas), and the same person present with the recipients (Archippus).[25] Colossians also mentions Tychicus as a messenger (Col. 4:7), the same coworker who would carry the letter to the Ephesians (Eph. 6:21). The similarities in subject matter between Colossians and Ephesians are well documented. Those similarities, as

---

21. Phoebe was a member of the church at Cenchrea, the port for Corinth. Gaius, Paul's host, and Erastus, the city treasurer, both had connections to Corinth (1 Cor. 1:14; 2 Tim. 4:20).

22. The most likely conjecture is that it occurred during Paul's ministry in Ephesus and consisted of a round trip to Corinth by sea.

23. The most likely conjecture is that it followed Paul's second visit.

24. Possibilities are (1) that Paul himself did so during the Macedonian/Achaian period, (2) that Paul himself did so during the Ephesian/Corinthian period, or (3) that just as "all who lived in Asia" heard the gospel as a result of Paul's ministry in Ephesus (Acts 19:10), so the impact of Paul's ministry in Macedonia extended to the neighboring province of Illyricum.

25. Compare Philem. vv.1–2, 12, 23–24; Col. 1:1; 4:7–17.

well as the fact that Tychicus was the messenger for both letters, suggest that Ephesians should be linked chronologically to Philemon and
Colossians. Ephesians differs, however, in that Paul alone is mentioned
as the author (Eph. 1:1), suggesting that Timothy might have been absent when that letter was composed.

There is general agreement that Paul's circumstances when he
wrote Philippians were different from those when he wrote Philemon,
Colossians, and Ephesians. Although Timothy was present (1:1) and would
later visit Philippi (2:19–24), the messenger who would actually carry the
letter was Epaphroditus (2:25–30), an individual mentioned in none of
Paul's other letters. Paul's comments about "the whole Praetorium"(1:13)
and "Caesar's household" (4:22) most naturally point to Rome as the
place of composition. The differences and the Roman location suggest
a separation in time (and, perhaps, in space) between the composition of
Philemon, Colossians, Ephesians and the composition of Philippians. If
so, it is possible to speak of an earlier portion of the captivity period and a
later portion. Paul's hope that he might be able to visit Philippi "shortly"
(2:24) suggests that the legal proceedings are further advanced than in the
other letters and, therefore, places Philippians in the later portion (and
Philemon, Colossians, and Ephesians in the earlier portion).

|  | **Colossians** | **Philemon** | **Ephesians** | **Philippians** |
|---|---|---|---|---|
| Author(s) | Paul and Timothy | Paul and Timothy | Paul | Paul and Timothy |
| Coworkers | Aristarchus Mark Epaphras Luke Demas Jesus Justus | Aristarchus Mark Epaphras Luke Demas | | Timothy |
| Messenger(s) | Tychicus and Onesimus | Onesimus | Tychicus | Epaphroditus |

2 Timothy is traditionally assigned to a second imprisonment following Paul's release and a time of renewed ministry. If, however, a second
imprisonment origin is not assumed *a priori*, the similarities between
2 Timothy and the other letters that mention Paul's imprisonment are
suggestive. Paul is in Rome (1:16–18; compare Philippians).[26] Tychicus

---

26.   The most natural reading of 2 Tim. 1:16–18 is that Onesiphorus is in Rome rather than that

has been dispatched to Ephesus (4:20; compare Ephesians). Although Luke is still present with Paul, Demas and Mark are elsewhere (4:10–11; compare Philemon and Colossians). Timothy is also absent (4:19; compare Ephesians)—most likely in the vicinity of Ephesus (4:19)—although Paul expects him to return soon via Troas (4:13; compare Philippians).[27]

These similarities at least open the possibility that 2 Timothy belongs to the same imprisonment period as do Philemon, Colossians, Ephesians, and Philippians. Within that general time frame, 2 Timothy seems to have stronger affinities to Philippians, given its Roman origin and Paul's perspective on his confinement. An interesting detail in this regard is that in both letters Paul speaks of being "poured out" for the sake of his readers (Phil. 2:17; 2 Tim. 4:6)—the only two uses of the verb σπένδομαι in Paul's writings.

If 2 Timothy is assigned to the later portion of Paul's imprisonment period, it is most likely chronologically prior to Philippians since Timothy is in Asia Minor at the writing of 2 Timothy but in Italy at the writing of Philippians. Paul's mention of a "first defense" (2 Tim. 4:16) makes sense under such a scenario.[28] Furthermore, the idea of Timothy using the Via Egnatia and the Via Appia to travel from Asia Minor through Troas to Rome is certainly within the realm of possibility. Such a route would have taken him through Philippi. Is it possible that Epaphroditus accompanied Timothy across Macedonia and on to Rome?

One possible reconstruction of Paul's imprisonment period, therefore, is that early in his captivity Paul, together with Timothy, wrote Philemon and Colossians. He then sent Timothy to Ephesus and shortly thereafter completed his letter to the same city. Tychicus and Onesimus carried all three letters to Asia Minor. Later in his imprisonment, Paul wrote to Timothy in Asia Minor directing him to come to Rome. Sometime after Timothy's arrival in Rome, Paul and he wrote the letter to Philippi and dispatched it with Epaphroditus.

---

he had searched for Paul in Rome but found him elsewhere.

27. The mention of Priscilla, Aquila, and the household of Onesiphorus (4:19) place Timothy in the vicinity of Ephesus. Priscilla and Aquila are associated with Ephesus in 1 Corinthians 16:19, although Acts also connects them with Corinth and Rome (Acts 18:1-2; cf. Rom. 16:3) as well as with Ephesus (Acts 18:24–26). Onesiphorus, however, is specifically mentioned as having "rendered service" to Paul in Ephesus (1:18).

28. I. H. Marshall sets out three possible referents for the phrase: (1) a trial during a previous captivity, (2) an earlier trial during the same captivity, or (3) the first hearing in a current two part trial (*The Pastoral Letters* [Edinburgh: T & T Clark, 1999], 823). Under the third, it is possible that Paul wrote 2 Timothy shortly after the first part of the trial and Philippians shortly before the second part. Such a scenario would explain why, in Philippians, Paul expected a verdict soon.

## The Evidence of Galatians

Galatians 1:11–2:14 is the most extensive passage on the apostle's activities, but it also has surprisingly little in common with the information found in the other letters. Two, or at the most three, points of contact are possible. First, the mention of time spent in Damascus (1:17–18) might well be linked to the brief description of Paul's escape from Aretus in 2 Corinthians 11:32–33. Second, Galatians relates two visits to Jerusalem (1:18–19; 2:1–10), while Paul mentions a visit to Jerusalem in Romans 15:25. Although it is unlikely that the visit mentioned in Romans is the same as either of those mentioned in Galatians, it is clear that Paul was periodically in contact with the leaders of the church in Jerusalem. Finally, it is possible—although by no means certain—that the injunction from the leaders of that church to "remember the poor" (2:10) might refer to the collection Paul intended to deliver to Jerusalem (1 Cor. 16:1–4; 2 Cor. 8:1–6; Rom. 15:25–27).

Furthermore, there are no hints in Galatians as to Paul's whereabouts when he wrote the letter. When that fact is added to the question of whether the letter was addressed to churches in North or South Galatia, the possible combinations and the corresponding scholarly suggestions increase geometrically.[29] The result is that the place assigned to Galatians in the sequence of Paul's correspondence tends to float from early in his ministry—often viewed as his first letter—to a later point (although never placed after Romans). All that can be said for certain is that the letter was written subsequent to a second visit to Jerusalem (2:1–10) and subsequent to the confrontation with Peter in Antioch (2:11–14).[30]

The basic chronological clues of Galatians 1:11–2:14, then, set out two periods early in Paul's ministry. The first centered in Damascus and Arabia (1:11–20). It opened with his conversion (1:13–15a), lasted three years (1:18), and closed with a visit to Jerusalem (1:18–20). The second centered in Syria and Cilicia (1:21–2:10). It lasted either eleven or fourteen years (2:1) and also closed with a visit to Jerusalem (2:1–10). In all probability, the Antioch incident (2:11–14) followed Paul's time in Syria and Cilicia, although how closely it did so is uncertain. A summary of the itinerary derived from Galatians, therefore,

---

29. For an even-handed discussion of the destination of the letter, see R. N. Longenecker, *Galatians* (Dallas: Word, 1990), lxii–lxxiii. John Hurd provides a helpful table that summarizes the various critical assumptions (*The Origin of 1 Corinthians*, [New York: Seabury, 1965], 18).

30. Although it is likely that the Antioch incident followed the second Jerusalem visit, the possibility that it did not must be left open, for the sequence marker "then" that appears in 1:18, 21; 2:1 is replaced by the less specific "when" in 2:11.

is Damascus (conversion) \ Arabia \ Damascus \ Jerusalem \ Syria and Cilicia \ Jerusalem \ Antioch(?).[31]

| Damascus and Arabia | Damascus | Gal. 1:17 |
| | Arabia | Gal. 1:17 |
| | Damascus | Gal. 1:17; 2 Cor. 11:32–33 |
| | Jerusalem | Gal. 1:18 |
| Syria and Cilicia | Syria and Cilicia | Gal. 1:21 |
| | Jerusalem | Gal. 2:1–10 |
| | Antioch | Gal. 2:11–14 |

## 1 Timothy and Titus

The two remaining letters, addressed to Paul's representatives Timothy and Titus, are the most problematic. Neither contains much information in connection with an itinerary of Paul's movements. In 1 Timothy, Paul has recently departed from Ephesus where he left his "true child in the faith" (1:2) and is currently in Macedonia (1:3). In Titus, Paul is in an unspecified location, and Titus is in Crete (1:5). Paul expects that Titus will later travel to Nicopolis, after being relieved in Crete by either Artemus or Tychicus (3:12). This scarcity of clues combined with an *a priori* tendency to assign both letters to a release-and-second-imprisonment scenario leads many to omit 1 Timothy and Titus from attempts to create a single integrated outline of Paul's ministry and letters. The similarities in style and subject matter are such that both letters are commonly assigned to the same time period. If, therefore, a case can be made that one of them fits into the general outline developed from the other letters, it is likely that the other fits as well.[32]

---

31. That Paul's conversion may be linked to Damascus is supported by his remark that after he departed into Arabia, he "again returned" to Damascus (1:17).

32. In answer to the argument that Titus 1:5 specifically says Paul "left behind" Titus in Crete and must, therefore, imply a visit by Paul himself to Crete (unmentioned in either Acts or the other letters), see Marshall who argues that the meaning of the verb is closer to "dispatched, deployed, assigned" (*Pastoral Letters*, 150). G. W. Knight's argument that the uses of the verb in 2 Tim. 4:13, 20 require the nuance of "behind" in Titus 1:5 fails to acknowledge the range of meaning with which the word is used (*The Pastoral Epistles* [Grand Rapids: Eerdmans, 1992], 287). B. Reicke translates the phrase "I let you stay" and concludes, "the expression . . . does not imply that Paul had been with Titus on the island, but that he had his collaborator remain there when he himself left Corinth for Macedonia" (B. Reicke, *Re-examining Paul's Letters. The History of the Pauline Correspondence*, ed. D. P. Moessner and I. Reicke [Harrisburg, PA: Trinity Press International, 2001], 69).

One reading of 1 Timothy 1:3, in light of Paul's other correspondence, is that the letter was written during the period centered in
Ephesus and Corinth subsequent to the travel plans envisioned in
1 Corinthians 16:1–11. Paul had sent Timothy to Corinth (1 Cor.
4:17) but expected him to return to Ephesus (1 Cor. 16:9–11).[33]
During this same period Titus was making multiple trips to and from
Corinth in a comparatively short time (2 Corinthians 7–9). It is not
outside the realm of possibility that Timothy could have completed a
round trip relatively quickly—especially if the return leg were made
by sea. If Paul waited for Timothy's return before leaving Ephesus,
the statement that he "urged [Timothy] to remain in Ephesus while
I was traveling in(to) Macedonia" (παρεκάλεσά σε προσμεῖναι ἐν
Ἐφέσῳ πορευόμενος εἰς Μακεδονίαν) makes perfect sense (1 Tim.
1:3). From Ephesus, Paul stopped in Troas before moving on to
Macedonia (2 Cor. 2:12; cf. 1 Cor. 16:5). That stop allowed time to
pass before Timothy joined Paul in Macedonia for the composition of
2 Corinthians (2 Cor. 1:1).[34]

Titus appears elsewhere in Paul's letters only three times. In Galatians
2:1–10, he accompanied Paul and Barnabas to Jerusalem at the end of
the Syria and Cilicia period. He was particularly active as a messenger
to and from Corinth during the Ephesus and Corinth period (2 Cor.
2:12–13; 7:13–8:24; 12:18). In the later imprisonment period, he had
gone to Dalmatia (2 Tim. 4:10). None of these clues has specific points
of correspondence to any of Paul's other letters, although Reicke correctly notes that the port city of Nicopolis (Titus 3:12) in Epirus lay just
south of Dalmatia (i.e., the coastal region of Illyricum).[35] Negatively,
there is no mention in his letter to Titus that Paul is in prison, nor
does Paul mention Titus in the greetings he sends from Corinth to the
church in Rome (Rom. 16:21–24).

As noted above, the similarities in style and subject matter between
1 Timothy and Titus incline most scholars to assign them to the same
general time period. If, therefore, 1 Timothy fits into the time Paul
spent in Ephesus and Corinth, Titus was probably composed during
the same general period. Given the lack of specific information in the

---

33.  An interesting point to consider is Paul's description of Timothy in 1 Corinthians 4:17 as his
     "beloved and faithful child in the Lord," which is not far removed from "true child in the
     faith" found in 1 Timothy 1:2.

34.  Knight argues that the Acts account does not permit such an itinerary (*Pastoral Epistles*,
     15—6). The length of time, however, that elapsed between Timothy's dispatch from
     Ephesus (Acts 19:21—22) and the representatives' departure for Syria with the collection
     (Acts 20:1—4) is indefinite. It included Paul's stay "for a while" in Asia (Acts 19:22), his
     travels through Macedonia and Achaia (Acts 20:2), and his three-month stay in Achaia
     (Acts 20:3).

35.  Reicke, *Paul's Letters*, 60, 112.

letter itself, Reicke's proposal is as good as any. He suggests that after Paul arrived in Corinth he sent Titus to Crete (thus explaining Titus's omission from Romans). Paul sent Titus the letter bearing his name while he was in route to Jerusalem (thus explaining the unspecified place of origin). When Artemus later relieved him in Crete (Tychicus had gone to Ephesus), Titus traveled to Nicopolis to meet Paul (cf. Titus 3:12). Failing to find Paul in Nicopolis, Titus moved on to Illyricum (cf. Rom. 15:19) in order to continue the work already begun there (thus explaining his presence in Dalmatia).[36]

## Synthesis

An outline of Paul's ministry based solely on his letters includes six periods. The first centered in Damascus and Arabia. It began with the apostle's conversion in the vicinity of Damascus and covered parts of three years. Included in those three years were time spent in Arabia, a return to Damascus, and a visit to Jerusalem. The second period centered in Syria and Cilicia, covered parts of eleven years, and also concluded with a visit to Jerusalem. None of the canonical letters belongs to either of these periods, although the letter to the Galatians documents them and must have been written subsequent to them.

During a time of unspecified length in Macedonia and Achaia, Paul traveled from Philippi through Thessalonica and Athens to Corinth. 1–2 Thessalonians date from this third period. Sometime subsequent to the Macedonia and Achaia period, Paul's ministry centered in Ephesus and Corinth. During that unspecified length of time Paul traveled from Ephesus through Troas and Macedonia to Corinth, with plans to travel onward to Jerusalem, Rome, and Spain. The apostle wrote 1–2 Corinthians and Romans during this fourth period as well as, possibly, 1 Timothy and Titus.

Paul wrote Philemon, Colossians, and Ephesians during an earlier imprisonment period. It is impossible to ascribe a length of time to this fifth period, but it appears to have been separated in time from a later captivity period. Rome is the venue for a later imprisonment period—also of unspecified length. The apostle wrote Philippians during this sixth period as well as, possibly, 2 Timothy.

---

36. Ibid., 68–73, 112.

| Macedonia and Achaia | 1–2 Thessalonians |
|---|---|
| Ephesus and Corinth | 1–2 Corinthians, Romans<br>1 Timothy, Titus (?) |
| Imprisonment        (earlier)<br>(later) | Colossians, Philemon, Ephesians<br>Philippians, 2 Timothy (?) |

It is important to note that it is not possible to derive absolute dating for this outline derived from the letters alone. Galatians 1:11–2:14 assigns parts of three years to the Damascus and Arabia period and parts of eleven years to the Syria and Cilicia period. No other time spans are given. It is true that Paul mentions the Nabatean King, Aretus, in connection with the Damascus and Arabia period (2 Cor. 11:32–33). Yet Aretus IV lived from 9 B.C. until A.D. 39/40, and within those years precise dating of Paul's escape is impossible from the brief comment in 2 Corinthians. Even the dating of the first two periods, therefore, must rest at least indirectly on data from Acts, for only Acts supplies a detailed context for Paul's conversion. Since any chronology of Paul's ministry depends, to a greater or lesser degree, on a consideration of Acts, the final step in developing a chronology is to compare the outline derived from the apostle's letters with the outline presented by Acts.

## Comparison with Acts

Paul's activity in Acts is generally organized under five headings: conversion and early ministry (9:1–30; 11:25–30), first missionary journey and the Jerusalem conference (12:25–15:35), second missionary journey (15:36–18:22), third missionary journey (18:23–21:16), and imprisonment (21:17–28:31). Interestingly, there are significant parallels between major portions of the Acts outline and an outline derived from the letters.[37] Those parallels may be sketched briefly.

Luke's account of Paul's conversion and first visit to Jerusalem (9:1–29) directly parallels the summary of the Damascus and Arabia period in Galatians 1:13–20. Similarly, Luke's brief summary of Paul's time in Tarsus (= Cilicia; 9:30; 11:25) and Antioch (= Syria; 11:26) along with his second visit to Jerusalem (11:27-30) directly parallels the summary

---

37. Even Gerd Lüdemann—no advocate of Luke's historical accuracy—concludes, "With the exception of the journey through southern Galatia and Cyprus, most of the stations in Acts, and even their order, are confirmed by the letters" (*Paul, Apostle to the Gentiles: Studies in Chronology* [Philadelphia: Fortress, 1984], 15).

of the Syria and Cilicia period in Galatians 1:21–2:10.[38] It is possible that the time between Paul, Barnabas, and Mark's return to Antioch and the beginning of the first missionary journey (Acts 12:25–13:3) is when the Antioch incident described in Galatians 2:11–14 occurred, but there is no way of knowing for certain.

The largest single **lacuna** in the letters involves the activities described in Acts 13:4–16:10. Those activities include Paul's missionary activity in Cyprus, Pamphylia, and Pisidia (13:4–14:26); his return visit to Antioch (14:27–28); the events surrounding the Jerusalem Conference (15:1–35); his trip through Syria, Cilicia, Phrygia, and Galatia (15:36–16:6); and the events surrounding the Macedonian vision (16:7–10). It is possible that Paul's letter to the Galatians relates to one or more of these activities in some way, but again, there is no explicit mention of them in any of his letters.

With Paul's arrival in Europe, the parallels resume. Luke's account of Paul's travels from Philippi to Corinth (16:11–18:17) parallels the itinerary of the Macedonia and Achaia period derived from 1–2 Thessalonians; 2 Corinthians 1:19, 11:8–9, Philippians 4:15–16.[39] Paul's return visit to Caesarea and Antioch (18:18–22), another trip through Galatia and Phrygia (18:23), and the events surrounding Apollos (18:24–28)—all included in Acts—have no parallels in the letters, although references to Apollos's ministry in Corinth appear in 1 Corinthians (1:12; 3:4–6,

---

38. It is at this point, of course, that the issue of the relationship between the five visits of Acts and the three visits of the letters arises. It is not necessary, however, (a) to explain the visits in Acts 11:27–30 and 18:22 as Lukan creations as Knox does (*Chapters*, 61–73), (b) to view Acts 11:27–30; 15:1–29; and 18:22 as a "tripling" of Paul's second visit to Jerusalem—which was "originally" located at Acts 18:22—as Lüdemann does (*Paul*, 149–56), or (c) to reject the historicity of Acts 14:21–15:41 as Hurd does (*1 Corinthians*, 35–41). It is obvious from the discussion above that Paul's letters do not chronicle all his movements. The fact that he mentions only three visits to Jerusalem does not necessarily rule out additional visits. In any event, the natural answer to the question of the relationship between Galatians 2:1–10 and the Acts visits is that Galatians 2 describes the so-called "famine visit" of Acts 11 rather than the "conference visit" of Acts 15. For a fuller discussion of the relationship between Galatians 1–2 and the Acts visits, see Longenecker, *Galatians*, lxxii–lxxxiii.

39. Lüdemann agrees: "The correspondence of the stops mentioned in Acts 16ff for the second missionary journey and those that may be inferred from 1 Thessalonians . . . is astonishing" (*Paul*, 14). Hurd, however, argues that 1 Thessalonians 3:1–2, 6 and Acts 17:14, 18:5 differ to such a degree that "there would seem to be more reason for separating these reports than for assuming that they concern a single series of events," and he bridles at what he sees as the "scholarly ingenuity" necessary to reconcile the accounts (*1 Corinthians*, 25–6). It is true that the most common solution—that Timothy joined Paul in Athens, then traveled to Thessalonica, and later rejoined Paul in Corinth—is complex, but a simpler reading is possible. Paul was "left behind at Athens alone" (1 Thess. 3:1) when the Berean brethren departed with instructions for Silas and Timothy (Acts 17:14). After Timothy visited Thessalonica (1 Thess. 3:2), he and Silas joined Paul (1 Thess. 3:6; cf. Acts 18:5) who had, in the meantime, moved on to Corinth (Acts 18:1; cf. 2 Cor. 11:8–9).

22 ; 16:12; cf. Titus 3:13). Luke's account of Paul's ministry in Ephesus and his subsequent travels in Macedonia and Achaia (19:1–20:12) parallels the itinerary of the Ephesus and Corinth period derived from 1–2 Corinthians and Romans.

Paul's trip to Jerusalem with the collection is anticipated in Romans 15:26 as is the potential for a hostile reception in Romans 15:30–32, but the detailed description provided by Acts (20:13–21:26) is absent. Acts records two locales for Paul's imprisonment, separated by his sea voyage to Rome. The initial imprisonment is in Jerusalem and Caesarea (21:27–26:32); the second is in Rome (28:16–31). Interestingly, the names of several of Paul's companions on his trip to Jerusalem (20:4) also appear in the letters to Philemon, to the Colossians, and to the Ephesians.[40] If the "we-passages" indicate authorial participation, Luke was also present on the trip to Jerusalem (20:5–16; 21:1–18; cf. Philem. v.20; Col. 4:14). This correlation has led Reicke and others to conclude that the earlier imprisonment period derived from Philemon, Colossians, and Ephesians coincided with the initial imprisonment in Jerusalem and Caesarea.[41] Although the letters have no parallel for Paul's voyage to Rome (27:1–28:15), the later imprisonment period in Rome derived from 2 Timothy and Philippians corresponds to the second locale described in Acts 28:16–31.

| Ministry Periods | Passages in Acts | Jerusalem Visits |
|---|---|---|
| Damascus and Arabia | Acts 9:1–29 | Acquaintance visit (9:26–30) |
| Syria and Cilicia | Acts 9:30; 11:25–30; 12:25–13:3 | Famine visit (11:27–30) |
| Cyprus and Galatia | Acts 13:4–16:10 | Council visit (15:1–12) |
| Macedonia and Achaia | Acts 16:11–18:23 | Greeting visit (18:22) |
| Ephesus and Corinth | Acts 19:1–21:16 | |
| Imprisonment | Acts 21:17–28:31 | Collection visit (21:17–19) |

---

40. Aristarchus is mentioned in Philem. v.24, Col. 4:10; Timothy is mentioned in Philem. v.1; Col. 1:1; Tychicus is mentioned in Col. 4:7–9; Eph. 6:21.

41. Peter O'Brien argues that Caesarea was too small to have been the base for missionary work requiring such a large group of Gentile coworkers (P. T. O'Brien, *Colossians, Philemon* [Waco: Word, 1982], lii). His suggestion, however, may be countered by Gene Smillie's historical survey of the Gentiles' presence in Palestine ("'Even the Dogs': Gentiles in the Gospel of Matthew," *JETS* 45 [2002]: 78–84).

## The Contribution of Acts

It is, indeed, possible to develop a tentative outline of Paul's ministry from his letters alone. Admittedly, however, doing so takes work, for—aside from Galatians 1:11–2:14—the clues are brief and scattered. A degree of inference is necessary both to piece together Paul's movements within the natural groupings of the letters and to suggest relationships between those groupings. 1 Timothy and Titus are particularly problematic. It is impossible to assign absolute dates to the outline based on information from the letters alone, although relative chronological relationships are possible within the first two periods.

On the other hand, the book of Acts provides a connected account of Paul's ministry. Although a number of scholars have questioned that account, it corresponds well to the basic periods derived from the letters. This correspondence suggests that at least some of the objections raised against the historical portrait of Paul in Acts are based on presuppositions rather than on evidence. Furthermore, it is only by using information present in Acts that it is possible to assign tentative dates to Paul's activities.

It is not necessary to use the material in Acts to "correct" material from Paul's letters, as some scholars fear. Instead, the material from Acts supplements the clues found in the letters. That material provides an overall framework for Paul's ministry that is impossible to derive from the letters alone. It provides information omitted from the letters and it gives historical context that makes suggesting dates possible. Using Acts to supplement the material from Paul's letters brings us closer to being able to trace his steps and establish a chronology for the ministry within which his letters fit. The next step, then, is to attempt to assign tentative dates to the different period of Paul's ministry.

## Deciding on Dates

The actual chronological data provided by both Paul's letters and Acts is limited. The letters provide five pieces of evidence. In Galatians 1:18 Paul writes, "Three years later I went up to Jerusalem to become acquainted with Cephus, and stayed with him fifteen days." The phrase "three years later" is usually understood to mean "three years after Paul's conversion." In Galatians 2:1 Paul writes, "Then after an interval of fourteen years I went up again to Jerusalem with Barnabas, taking Titus along also." There is considerable discussion over whether those "fourteen years" are consecutive or concurrent. In other words, should the fourteen years of 2:1 be *added to* the three years of 1:18, or do the fourteen years of 2:1 also *include* the three years of 1:18?[42] In 2 Corinthians 12:2, Paul also mentions that it was "fourteen years ago" that "a man in Christ"—most likely Paul himself—was caught up into the third heaven and heard "inexpressible words which a man is not permitted to speak" (12:4). It seems unlikely, however, that the fourteen years of 2 Corinthians 12:2 refer to the same period mentioned in Galatians 2:1.[43]

Two other pieces of evidence come from 1 Corinthians. In 1 Corinthians 16:6 Paul writes, "and perhaps I will stay with you, or even spend the winter, that you may send me on my way wherever I may go." In 1 Corinthians 16:8, Paul continues, "But I will remain in Ephesus until Pentecost." Both of these statements appear to relate to Paul's planned movements during the Ephesus and Corinth period, but neither provides a starting point for assigning tentative dates to that period. In fact, the same is true with the statements from Galatians and 2 Corinthians. Each provides information *relative* to other events, but none provides a fixed point from which to reckon the time periods mentioned.

For the most part, Acts also provides relative chronological information. From Acts 18:11, we know that Paul spent "a year and six months" in Corinth. Acts 19:10 tells the reader that Paul's teaching in the school of Tyrannus "took place for two years." Acts 20:3 notes that Paul spent "three months" in Greece, while Acts 20:6 notes that Paul sailed from Philippi "after the days of Unleavened Bread." From Acts 24:27, we know that Paul spent at least "two years" in Caesarea while Felix did little regarding his case. When Paul was shipwrecked on Malta, it was "[a]t the end of three months" that his group set sail for Italy (Acts 28:11), and when he finally arrived in Rome, "he stayed two full years in his own rented quarters" (Acts 28:30).

Acts 18, however, provides two helpful references. Acts 18:2 notes that Priscilla and Aquila had recently arrived in Corinth from Italy "because Claudius had commanded all the Jews to leave Rome," and Acts 18:12 notes that the events of that chapter happened "while Gallio was proconsul of Achaia." Together, these statements suggest a fixed point around which the other, relative information may be arranged. C. K. Barrett notes that "the ninth year of Claudius corresponds almost exactly with A.D. 49."[44] He also sets the likely start of Gallio's proconsulship as A.D.

---

42. This discussion adopts a concurrent understanding. For detailed discussions, see Longenecker, *Galatians*, lxxx-lxxxiii, and R. Y. K. Fung, *The Epistle to the Galatians* (Grand Rapids, MI: Eerdmans 1988), 18.

43. Based on a date of a.d. 56 for the writing of 2 Corinthians and using inclusive dating, M. L. Harris concludes that Paul's vision took place in a.d. 43, during the time he spent in Syria and Cilicia (*The Second Epistle to the Corinthians* [Grand Rapids, MI: Eerdmans, 2005], 835–7). Such a date is too early to correspond with the "fourteen years" of Galatians 2.1, whether a consecutive or a concurrent understanding is adopted.

44. C. K. Barrett, *The Acts of the Apostles*, 2 vols. (Edinburgh: T&T Clark, 1998), 2:862.

51 (summer).[45] Together, these statements from Acts suggest that Paul arrived in Corinth sometime in A.D. 50 and appeared before Gallio sometime in A.D. 52, setting the dates of his ministry in Corinth at A.D. 50–52.

Using Barrett's dates for Paul's time in Corinth, along with a date of A.D. 33 for Jesus' crucifixion,[46] and a concurrent understanding of the three and fourteen years in Galatians, therefore, it is possible to suggest a basic chronology:

| | |
|---|---|
| A.D. 34 | Conversion |
| A.D. 37 | First visit to Jerusalem |
| A.D. 48 | Second visit to Jerusalem |
| A.D. 50–52 | Ministry in Corinth |
| A.D. 53–55 | Ministry in Ephesus |
| A.D. 57–59 | Imprisonment in Caesarea |
| A.D. 61–63 | House arrest in Rome |

The following table seeks to set out a fuller overview that integrates the data from the letters, the letters themselves, and the data from Acts.

| Damascus and Arabia (A.D. 34–37) | | |
|---|---|---|
| Letters | | Acts |
| Damascus (Gal. 1:17) | | Damascus (Acts 9:1–22) |
| Arabia (Gal. 1:17) | | |
| Damascus (Gal. 1:17; 2 Cor. 11:32–33) | | Damascus (Acts 9:23–25) |
| Jerusalem (Gal. 1:18) | | Jerusalem (Acts 9:26–29) |
| Syria and Cilicia (A.D. 37–48) | | |
| Letters | | Acts |
| Syria and Cilicia (Gal. 1:21) | | Tarsus (Cilicia) (Acts 9:30) |
| | | Antioch (Syria) (Acts 11:26) |
| Jerusalem (Gal. 2:1–10) | | Jerusalem (Acts 11:27–30) |
| Antioch (Gal. 2:11–14) | | Antioch (Acts 12:25–13:3) |

---

45. Ibid., 2:870–1. Although Barrett is open to the possibility that the date might be a.d. 50, he prefers a.d. 51.

46. See H. W. Hoehner, "Chronology" in *Dictionary of Jesus and the Gospels*, eds, J. B. Green, S. McKnight, and I. H. Marshall (Downers Grove, IL: InterVarsity Press, 1992), 118–22.

| Cyprus and Galatia (A.D. 48–50) | | |
|---|---|---|
| | Galatians | **Acts** <br> Cyprus (Acts 13:4–12) <br> Psidia (Acts 13:13–14:25) <br> Antioch (Acts 14:26–28) <br> Jerusalem (Acts 15:1–12) <br> Antioch (Acts 15:30–35) <br> Syria and Cilicia (Acts 15:41) <br> Psidia (Acts 16:1–5) <br> Phrygia (Acts 16:6) <br> Troas (Acts 16:8) |
| **Macedonia and Achaia (A.D. 50–53)** | | |
| **Letters** <br> Philippi (1 Thess. 2:2) <br> Thessalonica (1 Thess. 2:2; Phil. 4:15–16) <br> Athens (1 Thess. 3:1) <br> Corinth (2 Cor. 1:19; 11:7–9) | 1-2 Thess. | **Acts** <br> Philippi (Acts 16:11–40) <br> Thessalonica (Acts 17:1–9) <br> Berea (Acts 17:10–14) <br> Athens (Acts 17:15–34) <br> Corinth (Acts 18:1–18) <br> Ephesus (Acts 18:19–21) <br> Jerusalem (Acts 18:22) <br> Antioch (Acts 18:22) <br> Phrygia (Acts 18:23) |
| **Ephesus and Corinth (A.D. 53–57)** | | |
| **Letters** <br> Ephesus (1 Cor. 16:8) <br> Troas (2 Cor. 2:12) <br> Macedonia (2 Cor. 2:13; 7:5) <br> Corinth (1 Cor. 16:6 planned) <br><br> Jerusalem (Rom. 15:25 planned) | 1 Cor. <br><br> 2 Cor. <br> Romans <br><br> 1 Tim. (?) <br> Titus (?) | **Acts** <br> Ephesus (Acts 19:1–41) <br><br> Macedonia (Acts 20:1) <br> Greece (Acts 20:2) <br><br><br> Jerusalem (Acts 21:17) |

| Imprisonment (A.D. 57–63) | | |
|---|---|---|
| Letters | | Acts |
| | | Caesarea (Acts 23:33–26:32) |
| | | Malta (Acts 28:1–10) |
| Rome (Rom. 15:24, 28 planned) | Colossians Philemon Ephesians Philippians 2 Tim. (?) | Rome (Acts 28:16–31) |

## SYNTHESIS OF HISTORICAL BACKGROUND

Of the thirteen letters ascribed to Paul, at least six date from his active missionary ministry, and at least four date from his imprisonment. The three "pastoral" letters are usually thought to have been written during a release-and-second-imprisonment period, although a possible case can be made to fit them into one of the other two groups. Establishing a chronology has set the stage; now it is time to sketch a suggested historical background for each letter.

### The Missionary Letters

#### Galatians

The destination and date of Paul's letter to the Galatians are interrelated issues and have generated considerable discussion. The two most common suggestions are (1) that Paul wrote the letter after his first "missionary journey" to churches planted in Southern Galatia (Psidia and Lycaonia) during his ministry there (cf. Acts 13:13–14:24), or (2) that Paul wrote the letter during or after his second journey to churches planted in Northern Galatia (Phrygia) when he passed through that region on his way to Troas (cf. Acts 15:6–8). An early date (e.g., A.D. 49–50) usually accompanies a South Galatian destination, while a later date (e.g., A.D. 53–57) is usually linked to a North Galatian destination. On balance, a Southern Galatian destination seems somewhat more likely. If that destination is accepted, the likely date is A.D. 49–50, and Galatians is the earliest of Paul's letters. The likely place of composition is Syrian Antioch, since Acts tells us that Paul spent "a long time" in that city between the end of his first journey and the Jerusalem Conference (14:26–28).

In contrast, there is no dispute regarding the occasion and purpose of the letter. Paul writes because Judaizing false teachers arrived in Galatia.

These false teachers were preaching "a different gospel" and were casting doubt on Paul's apostolic credentials (Gal. 1:6–17). Apparently, they were similar to "certain men from James" who had also appeared in Antioch and had led both Barnabas and Peter to withdraw from table fellowship with the Gentile disciples there (Gal. 2:11–21). Naturally enough, Paul's purpose in writing to the Galatians was to refute these false teachers just as he had previously opposed similar teaching in Antioch. "Defending the True Gospel" captures well the theme of the letter.

### 1–2 Thessalonians

The evidence suggests that Paul wrote 1–2 Thessalonians during the Macedonia and Achaia period, most likely while he was in Corinth between A.D. 50 and 52.[47] It is fairly clear from 1 Thessalonians itself that Paul wrote that letter after receiving Timothy's report on the church (3:6–8). His primary purpose was to assure them of his satisfaction with their progress and to help them address issues that had arisen in his absence. In particular, he was concerned about certain misunderstandings regarding the return of Christ (4:13–5:11). Apparently, those misunderstandings deepened at some point after Paul had written 1 Thessalonians, and Paul wrote a second letter to provide additional instruction for the church. He wrote 2 Thessalonians to give them comfort in the face of persecution (1:3–12), to correct information they had received in a letter purporting to be from Paul (2:1–12; cf. 3:17), and to address idleness that had taken root among some members of the congregation (3:6–15). In both letters, the topic of Christ's return is especially prominent. A possible theme for 1 Thessalonians might be "Living Expectantly until Christ Returns," while a possible theme for 2 Thessalonians might be "Standing Firmly until Christ Returns."

### 1–2 Corinthians

Paul's Corinthian correspondence dates from the latter part of the Ephesus and Corinth period (A.D. 55–57) and reflects the complexity of his relationship with the church. Initially, Paul spent at least eighteen months in Corinth planting the church (Acts 18:1–8). Sometime after that founding visit, Paul wrote the so-called "previous" letter instructing the Corinthians to dissociate from professing Christians who were

---

47. Although some scholars argue that Paul wrote 2 Thessalonians first, that position has failed to gain widespread support. For reversing the order, see C. A. Wanamaker, *Commentary on 1 & 2 Thessalonians* (Grand Rapids, MI: Eerdmans, 1990), 37–44; for the traditional order, see R. Jewett, *The Thessalonian Correspondence* (Philadelphia: Fortress, 1986), 26–30.

living immorally (1 Cor. 5:9). After receiving oral reports (1 Cor. 1:11) and a letter from the church (1 Cor. 7:1), Paul wrote 1 Corinthians from Ephesus sometime before Pentecost of A.D. 56 (1 Cor. 16:5–9). His purpose in 1 Corinthians was to rectify doctrinal errors, moral sins, and disorderly conduct in worship. A theme of "Correcting the Morals, Manners, and Meetings of the Church" reflects that purpose.

After a quick, "painful" visit (2 Cor. 2:1; 12:14, 21; 13:1–2), Paul wrote a third letter—the so-called "sorrowful" letter (2 Cor. 2:3–9; 7:8, 12)—intended to discipline his opponents and organize the collection. Concerned about the Corinthians' response to the sorrowful letter, Paul sent Titus ahead as he traveled through Troas into Macedonia. In response to Titus's report, Paul wrote from Macedonia to express his joy over their response and to prepare for his coming visit (2 Cor. 7:5; 8:1; 9:2–4). After writing 2 Corinthians with a suggested theme of "Pastoring the Problem Church," Paul spent three months in Greece, primarily in Corinth (Acts 20:2–3).

| Paul's Opponents in 2 Corinthians |
|---|
| **Identity** |
| • Jewish Christians (11:22)<br>• Carried letters of commendation (3:1) |
| **Character** |
| • Commended themselves (10:12–13)<br>• Emphasized eloquence and appearance (5:12; 10:10; 11:6)<br>• Expected monetary remuneration (11:7–11) |
| **Teaching** |
| • Preached "another Jesus . . . a different spirit . . . a different gospel" (11:4)<br>• Perhaps imposed Jewish practices upon Gentiles (3:6) |
| **Effect** |
| • Undermined Paul's apostolic authority (10:8–11)<br>• Led Corinthians astray from devotion to Christ (11:3) |

## Romans

Also written toward the end of the Ephesus and Corinth period, most likely from Corinth during A.D. 56–57, Romans is Paul's final letter from his active missionary ministry. He wrote because he anticipated traveling and ministering in the western Mediterranean area after he had delivered the collection to the church in Jerusalem (15:14–33). With those travel plans in mind, Paul wrote to introduce himself to the church in Rome and to correct the attitudes and behavior of the Jewish and Gentile believers in the church. Romans stands as Paul's most comprehensive statement "Explaining the Gospel of Justification by Grace through Faith in Christ."

## The Imprisonment Letters

### Colossians and Philemon

Because Paul mentions many of the same individuals in both Colossians and Philemon (Col. 1:1, 7; 4:10–17; Philem. vv.1–2, 23–24), the two letters are usually considered together. Paul wrote both letters while he was in prison (Col. 4:3, 10, 18; Philem. vv.1, 9, 13), and three theories exist as to the location of his imprisonment: Ephesus, Caesarea, and Rome. No record exists of an imprisonment in Ephesus, and because Paul expected to be released soon (Philem. v.22), Caesarea seems unlikely. On the other hand, Rome was a more likely place for the runaway slave Onesimus to try to hide his identity (Philem. vv.8–16). If Paul wrote the letters from Rome, the probable date is A.D. 61–62.

Although Paul had not planted the church in Colossae (2:1), it probably owed its existence to his extended ministry in Ephesus (cf. Acts 19:8–10). When Epaphras arrived in Rome (1:7–8), he brought news of heretical teaching that threatened the church. That syncretistic teaching focused on ritual observances (2:16–17), affirmed the worship of supernatural powers (2:18–19), and taught that the body was evil (2:20–23). In response, Paul wrote to express his personal interest in the congregation and to refute the heretical teaching by emphasizing both the preeminence of Christ (1:15–20) and the Christian's completeness in him (2:8–15). "Proclaiming Completeness in Christ" summarizes the theme of the letter.

| The Colossian Heresy | | |
|---|---|---|
| Legalism (2:16–17) | Mysticism (2:18–19) | Asceticism (2:20–23) |
| • Dietary laws<br>• Holy days | • Worship of angels<br>• Heavenly visions | • Do not handle, taste, touch<br>• Severe treatment of body |

Since Tychicus would carry the letter to Colossae, Paul used the opportunity to write to Philemon regarding Onesimus, who would be making the same trip (Col. 4:7–9). Onesimus had become acquainted with Paul during his imprisonment and became a follower of Christ through Paul's witness. With Onesimus's return to Colossae, Paul wrote to Philemon asking him to receive his runaway slave as a brother in Christ (vv.12–20). This brief letter highlights the importance of "Remaking Relationships in Christ."

## Ephesians

Paul most likely wrote Ephesians from Rome at about the same time he wrote Colossians and Philemon (A.D. 61–62). Because Tychicus also carried this letter (6:21–22), the occasion was probably his departure for Asia with the other two letters. The fact that the phrase "in Ephesus" is missing from some manuscripts (1:1), however, raises questions regarding the letter's original destination and leads to several suggested explanations: (1) the letter originally was known by another name (e.g., Laodicea; cf. Col. 4:16), (2) the letter was Paul's parting message to the Church as a whole, (3) the letter originally carried no place name, and (4) the letter was written to circulate among churches in the province of Asia. At least as likely as those explanations is a scenario in which the letter was originally addressed to the church in Ephesus but was cast in a form suitable for circulation among other churches in Asia; as copies circulated, the original destination was omitted. Paul's purpose in writing was to develop the doctrine of the unity of humankind in Christ (2:11–22) and to relate that doctrine to daily living in a hostile world (4:17–32). The theme of the letter is "Understanding the Believer's Wealth, Walk, and Warfare in Christ."

## Philippians

Also written from prison (1:12–18) but most likely at a slightly later date, Philippians may be dated around A.D. 62–63. Mention of the "Praetorium" (1:11) and "Caesar's household" (4:22) most naturally point to Rome as the place of origin. The church had sent a gift to Paul by the hand of Epaphroditus (4:18) who had fallen ill while in Rome (2:26–27). When Paul sent Epaphroditus back to Philippi, he carried the letter with him (2:25, 28). The letter appears to have had multiple purposes: (1) to commend Epaphroditus on his return, (2) to prepare for an impending visit by Timothy and Paul, (3) to warn against divisiveness within the church, and (4) to thank the congregation for their gift. The attitude of joy that pervades the letter despite Paul's imprisonment suggests a theme of "Standing United in Joyful Confidence."

## The Pastoral Letters

### 1 Timothy

Adopting a release-and-second-imprisonment scenario suggests that Paul wrote 1 Timothy sometime after Philippians, perhaps around A.D. 63–65. After departing for Macedonia, he wrote to Timothy who had remained in Ephesus (1:3). Timothy's task was to counter the activity of false teachers who were disrupting the life of the church (1:3–4), and Paul wrote to help counter both their teaching and their behavior. The word "godliness" (εὐσέβεια) appears eight times in the letter and is connected to Paul's explicit purpose for writing in 1 Timothy 3:14–16. For that reason, "Practicing Godliness in God's Household" is a logical theme for the letter.

### Titus

Since similarities of style and subject matter link Paul's first letter to Timothy and his letter to Titus, the likely date for the latter is also A.D. 63–65. Paul's location when he wrote is uncertain. It is possible that he was in Macedonia or Achaia, but it appears clear that he had not yet reached Nicopolis (3:12). Titus was in Crete where Paul had left (or sent) him to organize the church and appoint elders (1:5). Paul wrote to encourage and strengthen Titus in his task. His emphasis on truth as the key to the believer's life in Christ suggests a theme of "Basing Good Works on God's Salvation."

### 2 Timothy

Sometime after writing 1 Timothy and Titus, Paul wrote a second letter to Timothy during a period of imprisonment (1:8; 2:9). Mention of Onesiphorus's presence in Rome suggests that city as the place of origin (1:16–18), and Paul's comment that his "departure" was near suggests a date of A.D. 66–67 (4:6–8). The facts that Timothy had to pass through Troas to reach Paul and that Priscilla and Aquila were present with Timothy suggest Ephesus as a likely destination (4:13, 19; cf. 1 Tim. 1:3; Acts 18:24–28). Paul's purpose in writing was to prepare Timothy for his ministry of "Guarding the Gospel" after Paul's death.

## THE BIG PICTURE

Nine of Paul's letters address a church or group of churches. Each congregation lived and worshipped in a specific locale and faced specific challenges. In general, those congregations included a majority of Gentile believers; yet they faced a wide variety of problems. Judaizing false teachers sought to impose legalism on the Galatians; the false apostles in Corinth led that church into antinomianism and schismatic tendencies; the syncretistic heresy in Colossae combined legalism, mysticism, and asceticism; the church in Thessalonica adopted an extreme response to Paul's teaching on the second coming of Christ. For these reasons, it is important to interpret Paul's letters in the context of the churches to which they were written. Although the letters themselves are the starting point for that process, the book of Acts complements the letters and can contribute helpful background. Together, the letters and Acts establish the framework of Paul's ministry, both in terms of the churches he planted and his own circumstances when he wrote to those churches.

Paul wrote four letters to individuals, but they fit less readily into the framework of his ministry. The letters to Timothy and Titus pose particular challenges in this regard, whether the letters alone, Acts alone, or both sources together form the basis for that framework. It is these three letters, however, that provide particular insight into Paul's view of how the leadership of local congregations should function. Fortunately, the letters to individuals provide any number of clues to the issues Paul sought to address. Although there is no data outside Philemon, for example, that contributes to understanding it, the relational context of the letter is comparatively easy to construct. Further, each of Paul's letters to individuals includes a clearly stated purpose for writing. Those purpose statements help set the interpretive framework for the letters in which they occur.

With the authenticity, integrity, and historical background for each of Paul's letters established, it is time to turn to the major themes present in those letters. Chapter 3 will summarize those themes and will seek to sketch an outline of the theology of Paul's letters.

## The Chapter in Review

There is reasonable evidence to accept as authentic all thirteen letters ascribed to Paul, and no manuscript evidence exists to support a composite letter theory for either 2 Corinthians or Philippians. The Acts account of Paul's travels and ministry corresponds well to a basic outline derived from his letters, although Acts includes an extended account of Paul's ministry in Cyprus and Galatia that the letters do not mention (Acts 13:4–16:12).

Six letters (Galatians, 1–2 Thessalonians, 1–2 Corinthians, and Romans) date from Paul's active missionary period and address challenges present in local churches. Four letters (Colossians, Philemon, Ephesians, and Philippians) date from a somewhat later imprisonment period and are more reflective in nature, although Colossians and Philippians still address challenges in those churches. The three so-called Pastoral Letters (1–2 Timothy and Titus) differ in style and subject matter in that they focus on personal instructions for Paul's apostolic representatives. They are probably Paul's final letters and might well be the source for similar writings by the second-century church fathers.

# 3

# THE THEOLOGY OF PAUL'S LETTERS

---

## The Chapter at a Glance

- Paul recognized two spheres of human existence—"in Adam" and "in Christ"—each with distinct character, conduct, and consequences.

- Faith in Christ results in a transfer from one sphere to the other, and places a person in the Church as the context for living the Christian life.

- Common themes run throughout the five major groups of Paul's letters: 1–2 Thessalonians, 1–2 Corinthians, Romans–Galatians, the Prison Letters, and the Pastoral Letters.

- The paradigm of "coherence and contingency" provides a helpful model for understanding the theology of Paul's letters.

---

JAMES DUNN SUGGESTS FOUR models for doing Pauline theology.[1] One model is to use systematic theology categories such as man, sin,

---

1. J. D. G. Dunn, "Paul's Theology" in *The Face of New Testament Studies*, eds. S. McKnight and G. R. Osborne (Grand Rapids, MI: Baker, 2004), 326–48.

salvation, church, and last things. A second model is to move let-
ter-by-letter through the Pauline corpus; a third is to move chronologically by scholarly discussion. The fourth model—which Dunn
advocates—approaches Paul's theology in terms of levels, or stories.
Gordon Fee suggests a similar approach using four "essential elements": (1) the foundation is God as creator; (2) the framework is
present salvation as the initial fulfillment of God's promise; (3) the focus is Jesus as the Messiah who secured salvation and is exalted Lord;
and (4) the fruit is the Church as the eschatological community of
God's new covenant people.[2]

Each of these models is essentially deductive and imposes a preconceived structure on Paul and his thinking. Paul's own language, however, suggests a fifth model that is more inductive. In many ways Paul's
language is antithetic. For example, the opposing pairs of flesh and
Spirit, of law and grace, of Adam and Christ, and of old man and new
man are readily apparent to anyone who reads Paul's letters. Those opposing pairs do not exhaust Paul's thought, but they provide a starting
point for understanding the major contours of his theology.

## TWO SPHERES OF EXISTENCE

For Paul, there are only two spheres of human existence: every person is either "in Adam" or "in Christ" (e.g., 1 Cor. 15:21–22). Apart
from a faith response to the message of the gospel, every person is "in
Adam," a condition Paul also calls "the old man" (Eph. 4:22; Col. 3:9).
The contrasting sphere of existence is "in Christ," a condition Paul also
calls "the new man" (Eph. 4:23–24; Col. 3:10–11). Each of these two
spheres of existence has a distinct character, exhibits distinct conduct,
and carries with it distinct consequences.

When a person is "in Adam" (ἐν τῷ Ἀδάμ), his existence is characterized as "in the flesh" (ἐν τῇ σαρκί) and "under law" (ὑπὸ νόμον). His
conduct consists of "the works of the flesh" (τὰ ἔργα τῆς σαρκός) and
marks him as a "slave of sin" (δοῦλος τῆς ἁμαρτίας). He finds himself among other "children of wrath" (τέκνα ὀργῆς) who face the consequences of "condemnation" (κατάκριμα), "death" (θάνατος), and
"eternal destruction" (ὄλεθρος αἰώνιος).

In contrast, when a person is "in Christ" (ἐν τῷ Χριστῷ), her existence is characterized as "in the Spirit" (ἐν πνεύματι) and "under grace"
(ὑπὸ χάριν). Her conduct consists of "the fruit of the Spirit" (ὁ καρπὸς
τοῦ πνεύματός) and marks her as a "slave to righteousness" (δοῦλος τῇ
δικαιοσύνῃ). Instead of being under wrath, she has "peace with God"
(εἰρήνη πρὸς τὸν θεόν); instead of condemnation, she receives "acquit-

---

2. G. D. Fee, *Paul, the Spirit, and the People of God* (Peabody, MA: Hendrickson, 1996), 6.

tal" (δικαίωμα); instead of death, she looks forward to "life" (ζωή); instead of destruction, she looks forward to "salvation" (σωτηρία).

| | In Adam | In Christ |
|---|---|---|
| Character | In the flesh<br>Under law | In the Spirit<br>Under grace |
| Conduct | Works of the flesh<br>Slave of sin | Fruit of the Spirit<br>Slave of righteousness |
| Consequences | Child of wrath<br>Condemnation<br>Death<br>Destruction | Peace with God<br>Acquittal<br>Life<br>Salvation |

The phrase "in Christ" occurs 172 times in Paul's letters, and highlights four different aspects of that state of existence. *Redemptively*, it expresses the objective facts of the salvation God has accomplished in Christ (e.g., 1 Cor. 1:2; 2 Cor. 3:14; 5:19; Gal. 2:17; Eph. 1:3–14). *Corporately*, it expresses the result of becoming part of the people God has gathered together in Christ (e.g., Rom. 12:5; Gal. 3:28; Eph. 3:6). *Personally*, it expresses the intimate relationship established between the believer and Christ (Rom. 8:39; Phil. 2:1; 4:7). *Practically*, it expresses the way in which being "in Christ" affects every sphere of life (Rom. 9:1; 1 Cor. 4:17; Phil. 1:13; 4:13; 1 Thess. 4:16). The richness of being "in Christ" stands in sharp contrast to being "in Adam" and makes the necessity of a transfer from the latter to the former all the more significant.

## THE GREAT TRANSFER

In 2 Corinthians, Paul makes it clear that a change takes place at salvation: "[I]f anyone is in Christ, he is a new creature; the old things passed away; behold, new things have come" (5:17). That statement points to something far greater than a minor shift in belief or behavior; it describes nothing less than a total transfer from one sphere of existence to another. Colossians 1:13 makes the idea of transfer explicit: "For He rescued us from the domain of darkness, and *transferred* us to the kingdom of His beloved Son" (emphasis added). For Paul, following Christ involves a radical change in who a person is and how that person lives. He explains this change/transfer in some detail in Romans 5:12–21, and he uses a number of key terms to picture it.[3]

## The Transfer Explained

After demonstrating in Romans 1:18–3:20 that all humankind stands condemned before God, Paul declares that God's righteousness is revealed through faith in Christ (3:21–31). Abraham's experience supports Paul's thesis and proves that a person is justified on the basis of faith apart from human effort, ceremony, or law keeping (4:1–25). Being justified by faith brings certain benefits (5:1–11), but it is equally important to understand that the act of a single individual (Christ) made those benefits possible. Romans 5:12–21 unfolds the typological relationship between Adam and Christ, and explains how Christ's act of obedience counteracts Adam's act of disobedience.

Verses 12–14 make clear Adam's role in redemptive history. By transgressing God's command not to eat of the tree of the knowledge of good and evil, Adam not only brought sin into the world but also spread it to all human beings (5:12). The fact that men and women died between the time of Adam and the giving of the Mosaic Law proves that Adam's offense had far-reaching consequences (5:13–14). It is these far-reaching consequences resulting from the act of a single individual that lead Paul to identify Adam as a "type of Him who was to come"— that is, Christ (5:14).

Before summarizing what Adam and Christ had in common, however, Paul uses verses 15–17 to set out three significant differences between them. First, where Adam's act brought widespread death, Christ's act brings abundant grace (5:15). Second, where Adam's act resulted in condemnation, Christ's act results in acquittal (5:16). Third, where Adam's act caused death to reign, Christ's act causes life to reign (5:17). The other contrast running throughout the verses is the way the acts are characterized: Adam's act was a "transgression" (τὸ παράπτω-μα), while Christ's act is a "gift" (τὸ χάρισμα).

Paul recapitulates and concludes his argument in verses 18–21. In so doing, he sets out the essential differences between the two individuals who are central to redemption history:

---

3. E. P. Sanders uses the helpful phrase "transfer terminology" in his book *Paul, the Law, and the Jewish People* (Philadelphia: Fortress, 1983), 7–8. His suggested list of terms is considerably longer and somewhat more wide-ranging.

| | Adam | Christ |
|---|---|---|
| Nature of the act | Disobedience | Obedience |
| Immediate effect | Condemnation | Acquittal |
| Resulting status | Sinners | Righteous |
| Ultimate effect | Sin reigns in death | Grace reigns in life |

Both Adam's disobedience and Christ's obedience have far-reaching consequences. All human beings are "in Adam" from the day they come into the world. The good news of the gospel is that Christ has made it possible for God to transfer us out of the existence we inherited in Adam and into a brand-new existence in Christ.

## The Transfer Pictured

No single word can adequately communicate the change that takes place when God transfers a person from being in Adam to being in Christ. There are, however, six important terms that help picture the transfer. Each has a different background, and each highlights a different aspect of the change that has taken place. Together, they make clear the total reversal of status that Christ brings.

*Justification* (δικαίωσις) occurs twice in Paul's letters (Rom. 4:25; 5:18).[4] Its background context is the law court, where it denotes the act of declaring someone righteous. It pictures a change in status from being guilty to being righteous. *Redemption* (ἀπολυτρώσις) occurs seven times (Rom. 3:24; 8:23; 1 Cor. 1:30; Eph. 1:7, 14; 4:30; Col. 1:14).[5] Borrowed from the context of the slave market, it speaks of securing freedom by paying a ransom. It pictures a change in status from being slaves to being free men and women (although Romans 6 makes it clear that the change is actually one of a transfer to a new master).

*Propitiation* (ἱλαστήριον) occurs only in Romans 3:25.[6] Borrowed from the context of temple worship, it speaks of turning away wrath by offering a sacrifice. It pictures a change in status from being objects of God's wrath to being objects of his favor. *Sanctification* (ἁγιασμός) occurs eight times (Rom. 6:19, 22; 1 Cor. 1:30; 1 Thess. 4:3–4, 7;

---

4. The cognate verb (δικαιόω) occurs twenty-six times.

5. Paul uses the cognate verb (λυτρόω) only in Titus 2:14.

6. Paul does not use the cognate verb (ἱλάσκομαι) at all.

2 Thess. 2:13; 1 Tim. 2:15).[7] Also taken from a cultic context, it describes the act of setting apart someone or something as holy. It pictures a change in status from being sinners to being saints.

*Reconciliation* (καταλλαγή) occurs four times in Paul's letters (Rom. 5:10; 11:15; 2 Cor. 5:18–19).[8] Its background context is personal relationships, where it denotes the act of bringing opposing parties into agreement. It pictures a change in status from being enemies to being friends. *Adoption* (υἱοθεσία) occurs five times (Rom. 8:15, 23; 9:4; Gal. 4:5; Eph. 1:5). Borrowed from a family context, it denotes the bestowing of the rights and privileges of family membership. With adoption, a person's status changes from that of a stranger to that of a son or daughter.

|  | **Background Context** | **Change in Status** |
|---|---|---|
| Justification | Law court | Guilty to righteous |
| Redemption | Slave market | Slave to free |
| Propitiation | Temple | Wrath to favor |
| Sanctification | Temple | Sinner to saint |
| Reconciliation | Personal relationships | Enemy to friend |
| Adoption | Family | Stranger to son/daughter |

## THE MEANS OF TRANSFER

Paul uses the noun *faith* (πίστις) and the verb *to believe* (πιστεύω) more than 200 times in his letters. The words carry several nuances, but the primary focus is on the means of appropriating the effects of Christ's work. First and foremost, faith is the means of effecting the transfer from being in Adam to being in Christ. It presupposes knowledge on which it rests and from which it derives its strength (2 Tim. 2:25). It relies on God and his provision for salvation, which itself is a gift received by God's favor (Eph. 2:8–9). For that reason, faith alone is the ground of salvation. Although faith results in works (Gal. 5:6; Eph. 2:10), those works are not the basis for salvation (Rom. 2:28).

Two important facets of faith stand out: faith as trust, and faith as obedience. Faith is not mere intellectual assent to facts or propositions;

---

7. The cognate verb (ἁγιάζω) occurs nine times.

8. The cognate verb (καταλλάσσω) occurs six times.

it is a matter of the heart, a matter of trust (Rom. 10:9). Saving faith involves placing trust in Jesus Christ alone for salvation (Rom. 5:1–2; Eph. 2:8–9; Col. 2:12). Occasionally, faith is commitment to the truth of the gospel (Eph. 1:13–14), but predominantly it is a personal commitment to the whole person of Christ (Rom. 3:26; Eph. 1:15; Col. 1:4; 2:5; 2 Tim. 3:15). Faith, however, is broader than the initial reception of the gospel; it is also a matter of obedience. It can carry the sense of following the authoritative apostolic tradition (2 Thess. 2:13–15), but more often it is reliance on God in every aspect of life. Paul makes it clear that we stand by faith (2 Cor. 1:24), walk by faith (2 Cor. 5:7), and live by faith (Gal. 2:20). It should come as no surprise that faith is part of the fruit of the Spirit (Gal. 5:22).

The central role of faith is clearly seen in Ephesians 2, a chapter that includes what is perhaps Paul's best known declaration on the role of faith, "For by grace you have been saved through faith; and that not of yourselves, it is the gift of God; not as a result of works, that no one should boast" (Eph. 2:8–9). That declaration occurs in the context of two extended explanations of what God has accomplished in Christ. Verses 1–10 address the topic on the individual level, while verses 11–22 address the topic on the corporate level. Both explanations highlight the contrast between what we were and what we are.

In verses 1–3 Paul says that apart from Christ we were "dead in [our] trespasses and sins"; we walked "according to the prince of the power of the air"; we lived among "the sons of disobedience"; and we were "children of wrath." Faith, however, results in us being made alive together with Christ, being raised up with Christ, and being "seated . . . in the heavenly places" with Christ (2:4–6). We are also destined for good works (2:10).

In verses 11–22, Paul says that apart from Christ we were "far off" (2:13), as well as "strangers and aliens" (2:19). Faith, however, results in us being "brought near" (2:13) and made "fellow citizens with the saints, and [members] of God's household" (2:19). It is by grace, and through faith, that we are transferred from who we were in Adam to who we are in Christ.

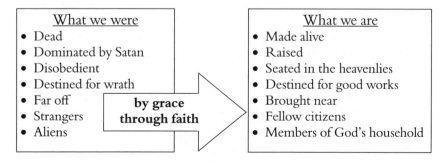

| What we were | What we are |
|---|---|
| • Dead | • Made alive |
| • Dominated by Satan | • Raised |
| • Disobedient | • Seated in the heavenies |
| • Destined for wrath | • Destined for good works |
| • Far off | • Brought near |
| • Strangers | • Fellow citizens |
| • Aliens | • Members of God's household |

by grace through faith

## THE CONGREGATION OF THOSE TRANSFERRED

When God transfers a person from being "in Adam" to being "in Christ," he also incorporates that person into "the church" (ἡ ἐκκλησία). The Greek word ἐκκλησία occurs sixty-two times in Paul's letters (e.g., 1 Cor. 1:2; 2 Cor. 1:2; Eph. 1:22; Col. 1:18). The Septuagint regularly uses ἐκκλησία to translate the Hebrew word that designates Israel as the "assembly" or "congregation" of Yahweh (cf. Deut. 23:2–4, 9; 31:30; Josh. 9:2; 1 Kings 8:14). That congregation is made up of "the saints" (οἱ ἅγιοι). Paul uses the word forty times (e.g., Rom. 1:7; 1 Cor. 1:2; 2 Cor. 1:1; Eph. 1:1; Phil. 1:1) and most likely draws it from the background of Israel as the true people of God who are preserved and delivered from judgment by the Lord (cf. Isa. 4:3; 6:13; Dan. 7:18, 21–22). These saints are both "called" (κλητός, seven times) and "elect" (ἐκλεκτός, six times). It is possible to trace both ideas back to the Old Testament—one to God's historical calling of Israel (Isa. 41:9; 42:6; 43:1; 45:3: 48:12; 51:2), the other to the designation of Israel as God's chosen people (Deut. 7:6–7; 14:2; 1 Kings 3:8; 1 Chron. 16:13; Ps. 105:6).

Paul uses two metaphors to describe this congregation of elect saints: the building and the body. The building metaphor appears in Ephesians where Paul's primary emphasis is the unity of the universal Church (Eph. 2:19–22). The apostles and prophets are the foundation (2:20);[9] Christ is the cornerstone (2:20; cf. Rom 15:20; Col. 2:7); the saints comprise the building that is in the process of construction as the dwelling for God (2:21–22). The Gentiles (2:11) who once were strangers and aliens (2:19) are now being "built together" into God's building. As such, Paul's point is not far from that of Romans 11:17–24, where he uses the imagery of the olive tree to describe the incorporation of the Gentiles into company of God's people.

The body is Paul's more common and distinctive metaphor for the church, appearing in Romans, 1 Corinthians, Ephesians, and Colossians. He uses it in Romans and 1 Corinthians, but with little development. In those letters, the primary emphasis is the body's unity in Christ (Rom 12:5; 1 Cor. 10:17; 11:29), and Paul uses the metaphor to address the issue of believers' relations with one another (1 Cor. 12:12–27). In Ephesians and Colossians, Paul develops the metaphor more fully. It emphasizes the unity of the (universal) Church in the same way as in Romans and 1 Corinthians (Eph. 1:10, 22; 4:4–6, 13),

---

9. Scholars differ over whether the "prophets" are the Old Testament canonical prophets or Spirit-filled prophets who were active in the local congregations of the early church. Given Paul's point that the Gentiles are being incorporated into God's building along with the Jews, it seems most natural to understand the apostles as New Testament spokesmen for God and the prophets as their Old Testament counterparts.

but it also includes the concept of Christ as the head of the body (Eph. 1:22; 4:15; 5:23; Col. 1:18; 2:19). The basic thought is of the Church as one body based on what Christ has accomplished for it (Eph. 2:14–18; 5:23). Christ's headship emphasizes his position of authority as the exalted Lord. As such, God has given him all power (Eph. 1:20–23); he has all spiritual gifts at his disposal (Eph. 4:7–11); and he is the source for the growth of the body (Eph. 4:15–16; 5:25–27; Col. 2:9–10, 14).

To Paul, the church is the context for living the Christian life (Gal. 6:10; 1 Tim. 3:14–16). Judgment by the congregation is appropriate for a believer who has overstepped the boundaries established for it (1 Cor. 5:1–13). When there is a conflict of interest between believers, each person is to seek the things that pertain to "the other" (1 Cor. 10:24; Phil. 2:3–4), and the primary concern should be the health of the congregation (1 Cor. 5:6–8). Two foundational principles govern life in the congregation: the equality of all believers and the distinctiveness of each believer. All believers have equal standing in God's sight (Gal. 3:26–29), and all believers share equally in freedom from sin (Rom. 6:18, 22) because they have been equally set free for that freedom (Gal. 5:11). Yet, each believer is distinct in calling (1 Cor. 7:17–24), in gifting (Rom. 12:3–9; 1 Cor. 12:7–11), in strength of faith (Rom. 12:3, 6; 14:1; 15:1), and in spiritual growth (1 Cor. 3:1–2).

Given these foundational principles of equality and distinctiveness, the believer must exercise discernment in all things (Phil 1:9–11; 1 Thess. 5:21). Comparison among believers is ruled out (Rom. 14:4, 13; 2 Cor. 10:12); proper self-evaluation is essential—neither thinking too highly (Rom. 12:3; 1 Cor. 8:2; 10:12; Gal. 6:3) nor too lowly of oneself (1 Cor. 12:15–17). Believers should pursue certain virtues (Gal. 5:22–23; Eph. 4:23; Col. 3:12–17) and reject certain vices (Gal. 5:19–21; Eph. 4:25–31; Col. 3:5–10). Between these poles of virtue and vice is a comparatively broad area of liberty that requires the exercise of discernment. Actions that are not expressly forbidden are governed by six principles:

1. All actions must be appropriate to the believer's measure of faith (Rom. 12:3; 14:23). Conscience and doubt serve to limit the believer's actions (Rom. 14:14, 23).

2. Certainty and conviction mark out permissible actions (Rom. 14:5, 11).

3. Permissible actions edify other believers (1 Cor. 6:12; 8:1–13; 10:23–33).

4. Permissible actions promote the spread of the gospel (1 Cor. 9:1–27).

5. Permissible actions promote personal sanctification (1 Cor. 10:1–13).

6. Permissible actions promote God's glory (1 Cor. 14–22).

| Virtues Encouraged | Principles of Discernment | Vices Forbidden |
|---|---|---|
| Gal. 5:22–22 Eph. 4:23 Col. 3:12–17 Phil 4:8–9 | Measure of faith Conscience and doubt Certainty and conviction Edification Evangelism Sanctification God's glory | Gal. 5:19–21 Eph. 4:25–31 Col. 3:5–10 |

For Paul, then, the church is the congregation of those God has transferred from one sphere of existence to another. By grace through faith, the members of that congregation have moved from being "in Adam" to being "in Christ," because Christ's life of obedience has counteracted the results of Adam's disobedience. As a result, God has been propitiated and reconciled; believers have been justified, redeemed, sanctified, and adopted. They have been incorporated into a congregation that has its roots in the Old Testament and may be pictured using the metaphors of a building and a body. That congregation is composed of both Jews and Gentiles whom God has brought together into a single people to provide the context for living the Christian life, with prescribed virtues, proscribed vices, and proper principles for exercising discernment.

## MAJOR THEMES IN PAUL'S LETTERS

In addition to the larger contours of Paul's theology, as suggested by the opposing pairs running throughout his letters, it is also possible to trace major themes within related letters. The three groupings of letters identified in Chapter 2 provide a framework for tracing those themes.

## The Missionary Letters

### 1–2 Thessalonians

The Thessalonian letters are among Paul's earliest. They were prompted by Paul's forced separation from Thessalonica after only a short time there. The letters reflect his concern over their responses to the opposition they were facing from their fellow citizens and to

Paul's teaching regarding Christ's return. Significant themes running throughout the letters include the Thessalonians' response to the gospel, the return of Christ, and responsible living in light of that return.

The Thessalonians' response to the gospel is particularly prominent in Paul's first letter to them. They received his preaching as God's Word with joy (1:6) and with full conviction (1:5). In response to that preaching, they turned to God from idols (1:9) and became imitators both of Paul (1:6) and of the churches in Judea (2:14). As a result, faith, love, and hope characterized their lives (1:3), and they became examples to the entire region (1:7; 3:6) by standing firmly in the face of suffering (2:14; 3:8).

A key element in Paul's preaching of the gospel in Thessalonica was the return of Christ. That theme permeates both letters as motivation for multiple aspects of Christian living (1 Thess. 1:10; 2:19; 3:13; 5:23; 2 Thess. 1:7, 10; 2:1). Paul also devotes a major section of each letter to the theme. The first, 1 Thessalonians 4:13–5:11, divides naturally into two parts: the fate of those who have already died in Christ (4:13–18) and the conduct of those who are waiting for his return (5:1–11).

Because the Thessalonians are concerned about the fate of those who have already died in Christ (4:13), Paul seeks to help them understand how Christ's return is a source of comfort. Death is actually a "falling asleep in Jesus" to wait for his return, when he will bring the dead in Christ with him (4:14). His return involves a descent from heaven, accompanied by a shout, the voice of the archangel, and the trumpet of God (4:16). At that time, the dead in Christ will rise first (4:16); then the living will be caught up with the dead to meet Christ in the air (4:17). While they wait, those who are alive in Christ must live in light of his sudden and unexpected return. That return will be like a thief coming in the night (5:2) or like a woman going into labor (5:3)—there is no predicting when it will happen. For that reason, it should motivate Christ's disciples to watchfulness (5:4–6) as well as continued faith, love, and hope (5:8). It should be a source hope and of mutual encouragement (5:9–11).

In 2 Thessalonians 2:1–12, Paul again takes up the topic of Christ's return, this time in response to a letter suggesting that the day of the Lord had already come (2:1–2). To refute that deception, Paul notes that it will not come "unless the apostasy comes first, and the man of lawlessness is revealed" (2:3). The man of lawlessness opposes God and exalts himself above God (2:4), works in accord with Satan's activities (2:9), and deceives with signs and wonders (2:9–10). His activities will delude those who do not receive the truth and will lead them into apostasy (2:11–12). That principle is already at work in the world (2:7), but God restrains its full manifestation until he determines the time is right to remove that restraint (2:6–7).

Responsible living in light of Christ's return involves sanctification, orderliness, and perseverance. Sanctification is God's will (1 Thess. 4:3), his call (1 Thess. 4:7), and his choice (2 Thess. 2:13) for the believer. It is both God's work (1 Thess. 5:23) and the Spirit's work (2 Thess. 2:13). It touches the entire person, including the body (1 Thess. 5:23), and is closely related to sexual purity (1 Thess. 4:3–7). It is cultivated by holding fast to Paul's teaching (2 Thess. 2:15), and it has the believer's glorification as its object (2 Thess. 2:14).

A sanctified life is also an orderly life. Followers of Christ should live quiet, disciplined lives (1 Thess. 4:11; 2 Thess. 3:6–8, 11), attend to their own business (1 Thess. 4:11; 2 Thess. 3:11), and work with their hands (1 Thess. 4:11; 2 Thess. 3:10, 12). They should esteem those who lead them (1 Thess. 5:12–13) and seek the good of others (1 Thess. 5:14–15). If they live in this way, they will behave properly toward outsiders and will not be in any need (1 Thess. 4:12).

Because followers of Christ live in the midst of persecution by those who know them (1 Thess. 2:14–16; 3:3–4; 2 Thess. 1:4), and because that persecution provides an opening for Satan to tempt them (1 Thess. 3:5), they also need perseverance. Persevering in the face of affliction glorifies Christ (2 Thess. 1:12) and makes believers worthy of God's kingdom (2 Thess. 1: 5, 11). God himself provides the resources they need in order to endure (2 Thess. 3:1–5), and they can persevere confidently because they know their persecutors will ultimately be judged while they will ultimately be glorified (2 Thess. 1:6–10).

### 1–2 Corinthians

The canonical letters of 1–2 Corinthians are actually the second and fourth letters Paul wrote to the church, since 1 Corinthians mentions a "previous letter" and 2 Corinthians mentions a "sorrowful letter." It is well known that 1 Corinthians deals with a series of issues within the church: divisions (1:10–4:21), immorality (5:1–13; 6:12–20), lawsuits (6:1–11), marriage (7:1–40), food offered to idols (8:1–11:1), public worship (11:1–34), spiritual gifts (12:1–14:40), and the resurrection (15:1–58). Second Corinthians focuses more on Paul's apostolic ministry and his relations with the Corinthians. Significant themes running throughout the letters include the nature and content of the gospel message, the apostolic (or missionary) ministry, and the Holy Spirit.

Paul's explanation of the gospel in 1–2 Corinthians centers on three aspects: the Cross, the Resurrection, and the new covenant. In each instance, Paul's language is strongly antithetic—as is evident in his teaching on the Cross, where the opposing pairs of wisdom/foolishness and weakness/strength are prominent (1 Cor. 1:18–2:16). While planting the church in Corinth, Paul had determined "to know nothing . . . except Jesus Christ, and Him crucified" (1 Cor. 2:2). From the world's perspective that "word of the Cross" is both a message of foolishness and a demonstration of weakness. Yet God has chosen the foolish things of the world to shame the wise and the weak things of the world to shame the strong (1 Cor. 1:26–31). In fact, God's economy operates in a way that is diametrically opposed to the world's economy. What is foolishness to the wise becomes the wisdom of God, and what is weakness to the strong becomes the power of God (1 Cor. 1:18–25; 3:18–22). In that way, the message of the Cross does not rest on either the wisdom or strength of men; instead, it rests on both the wisdom and power of God (1 Cor. 2:1–5). It is a message that is spiritually discerned because it is God's wisdom, contained in a mystery and revealed through the Spirit (1 Cor. 2:6–15).

| The wise | are shamed | by the foolish things of the world |
| The strong | are shamed | by the weak things of the world |
| The foolishness of the world | becomes | the wisdom of God |
| The weakness of the world | becomes | the power of God |

The link between the Cross and the Resurrection becomes clear when Paul says of Christ: "He was crucified because of weakness, yet He lives because of the power of God" (2 Cor. 13:4). The Resurrection is the supreme demonstration of God's power because it defeats sin, the law, and death (1 Cor. 15:50–58). The Resurrection, therefore, becomes the Christian's source of hope and confidence (1 Cor. 15:12–19), inaugurates Christ's reign (1 Cor. 15:20–28), and brings the promise of heavenly glory (1 Cor. 15:35–48). In this section also, opposing pairs are prominent and reflect the contrast between the "first Adam" and Christ, the "last Adam."

| The "First Adam" | The "Last Adam" |
| --- | --- |
| • Death | • Resurrection |
| • All die | • All made alive |
| • Natural body | • Spiritual body |
| • Perishable | • Imperishable |
| • Dishonor | • Glory |
| • Weakness | • Power |
| • Earthy | • Heavenly |
| • Mortality | • Immortality |
| • Living soul | • Life-giving Spirit |

The other aspect of the gospel Paul addresses is the new covenant Christ inaugurates (2 Cor. 3:1–18). Again, antithetic language permeates the section, highlighting the differences between the old and new covenants in administration, result, and duration. The old covenant's administration was external, "written . . . with ink"; but the new covenant's administration is internal, "written . . . with the Spirit . . . not on tablets of stone but on tablets of human hearts" (2 Cor. 3:3). The old covenant was a covenant of condemnation resulting in death, but the new covenant is a covenant of righteousness resulting in life (2 Cor. 3:6–7, 9). The glory of the old covenant was temporary, but the greater glory of the new covenant is permanent (2 Cor. 3:11).

The proclamation of the gospel is the preeminent task of the apostolic ministry. That ministry takes place in a context of hardship (2 Cor. 4:7–11; 6:4–10; 11:24–27). The hardship encountered includes affliction from outside the church (2 Cor. 1:8–11) as well as opposition from inside the church (2 Cor. 2:4; 7:5). Yet God comforts in the midst of those hardships (2 Cor. 1:3–7; 7:6–7) and provides grace and power to face them (2 Cor. 4:16–18; 12:7-10). The ministry itself involves fulfilling a God-ordained role (1 Cor. 3:1–15) as a trustworthy steward (1 Cor. 4:1–5; 2 Cor. 4:5) while being willing to limit personal liberty for the sake of the gospel (1 Cor. 9:3–23). It also involves serving as an ambassador of reconciliation (2 Cor. 5:18–21) and engaging in spiritual warfare (2 Cor. 10:3–5). Because the ministry is spiritual, God provides the Holy Spirit as an indispensable resource (2 Cor. 1:22; 5:5). Reliance on the Spirit is essential because he reveals the content of the apostolic message (1 Cor. 2:6–16) and enables the proclamation of that message (1 Cor. 2:1–5).

The Holy Spirit is the third major theme in the Corinthian correspondence, although Paul's teaching on the Spirit is scattered throughout the letters rather than concentrated in a single systematic exposition. As noted above, the Spirit reveals the content of the gospel (1 Cor. 2:6–14), administers the new covenant (2 Cor. 3:2–6), and transforms those who participate in that new covenant (2 Cor. 3:17–18). The Spirit baptizes the believer into the body of Christ (1 Cor. 12:13), indwells the believer (1 Cor. 3:16–17; 6:19), and seals the believer as a pledge (2 Cor. 1:22; 5:5). The Spirit also distributes gifts for the common good of the body (1 Cor. 12:4–11), provides the enabling for the use of those gifts in ministry by members of the body (1 Cor. 2:4–5; 12:11; 2 Cor. 6:4–6), and fosters fellowship within the body (2 Cor. 13:14).

### Galatians and Romans

Galatians is Paul's earliest letter, but it has strong affinities to Romans, which he wrote six or seven years later. Those affinities lead some scholars to adopt both a North Galatian destination and a later date. Regardless of a decision on the destination and date of Galatians, the similarities in content are evident; the differences lie in the tone of the argument. The sharp polemical tone of Galatians reflects Paul's defense of the gospel against Judaizing false teachers who were threatening the churches he had planted. In contrast, Romans is a carefully reasoned presentation of Paul's gospel intended to introduce him to a church he had not yet visited. Significant themes running throughout the letters include God's righteousness, the Old Testament law, and living by the Spirit rather than the flesh.

The righteousness in Romans and Galatians is preeminently God's (Rom. 1:17; 3:21-22, 26). Whether the phrase "God's righteousness" (δικαιοσύνη θεοῦ) denotes the righteousness God possesses or the righteousness he bestows has been widely debated, but it seems best to keep both aspects in view. In both letters, Paul bases his understanding of God's righteousness on the life of Abraham (Gen. 15:6; cf. Rom. 4:9; Gal. 3:6) and on the declaration of the prophet Habbakuk (Hab. 2:4; cf. Rom. 1:17; Gal. 3:11). That righteousness is both revealed—from faith to faith (Rom. 1:17) and apart from law (Rom. 3:21; 4:13)—and a gift of God's grace (Rom 3:24; 4:5–6, 16). The gift of righteousness is bestowed apart from works (Rom. 4:1–8), circumcision (Rom. 4:9–12), or law (Rom. 4:13–25). It comes through faith in Christ (Rom. 3:22–30; Gal. 3:5–8) to all who believe (Rom. 3:22) and results in salvation (Rom. 1:16; 10:10). It extends to the Gentiles (Gal. 3:14) and is lived out by faith (Rom. 1:17).

The subject of Paul and the law has generated extensive scholarly debate. That debate generally takes one of three directions: Paul's teaching on the law is a consistent response to Jewish beliefs (e.g., Schoeps and Cranfield); Paul's teaching on the law developed in response to ministry circumstances (e.g., Drane and Hübner); or Paul's teaching on the law was inherently inconsistent (e.g., Sanders and Raisanen). More recently, the so-called "new perspective" on Paul and the law (e.g., Dunn) has suggested that the Jewish attitude toward the law against which Paul argued was one of **covenantal nomism**, in which his opponents viewed circumcision and other "works of the law" as exclusive badges of Jewish pride that they were seeking to force on Gentile opponents.

Paul most commonly uses "law" (νόμος) to describe the divine requirements given to Israel though Moses (e.g., Rom; 2:13–26; 4:15; 7:6–12; 10:5; Gal. 3:12–19; 4:5; 6:13). Its original role was as a standard of obedience for preserving Israel's covenant relationship with God. As such, it is "holy, just, good," and "spiritual" (Rom. 7:12, 14) because it makes sin known (Rom. 3:20; 7:7). In that respect, it codifies what human beings know instinctively through conscience (Rom. 2:14–15). Unfortunately, the law requires perfect obedience (Rom. 2:12–13; 3:23–29; 8:4; Gal 3:10–13) and, so, is weak because of human flesh (Rom. 8:3) in which it arouses sinful passions (Rom. 7:5, 8–11, 14–21). Ultimately, the law increases the number and sinfulness of sins committed (Rom. 5:20–21; 7:7–13; Gal. 3:19) and leads to the slavery of sin and death (Rom. 7:23; 8:2; Gal. 4:25, 31).

In contrast to human sinfulness and the law's weakness stands God's promise, given 430 years before the law and fulfilled in Jesus Christ (Gal. 3:16–17). Understood from the perspective of God's promise, it is clear that the law was never intended to impart life (Gal. 3:21). In fact, it was supplementary (Gal. 3:19), temporary (Gal. 3:25), and served as a pedagogue to lead us to Christ (Gal. 3:24). For those reasons, Christ is the "end of the law . . . to everyone who believes" (Rom. 10:4). Yet followers of Christ are still expected to "fulfill" the law by loving their neighbors as themselves (Rom. 13:8–10; Gal. 5:13–14).

The Holy Spirit is also a major theme in Romans and Galatians. In contrast to 1–2 Corinthians where teaching on the Spirit is scattered throughout the letters, Romans and Galatians each has an extended passage on living by the Spirit rather than by the flesh. The focus in Galatians 5:16–26 is on the difference produced when a person "walk[s] by the Spirit" (5:16, 25) and is "led by the Spirit" (5:18). Because the flesh and the Spirit are in opposition to each other (5:17), Paul sets out that dramatic difference using the contrasting lists of the "deeds of the flesh" (5:19–21) and the "fruit of the Spirit (5:22–23).

Romans 8:1–27 is the longest single passage in Paul's letters on the difference produced when a person lives by the Spirit. That difference is heightened by the contrast between Romans 7 and 8. Romans 7 sets out the futility of trying to live in the flesh (7:5), while Romans 8 sets out the victory of living by the Spirit (cf. 7:6). The Spirit frees the Christian from the law of sin and of death (8:2), focuses on spiritual things (8:5), and leads to life and peace (8:6). Because the Holy Spirit indwells the Christian (8:9, 11; cf. Gal. 4:6), the human spirit is alive now (8:10), and the human body will live again (8:11).

Romans 8:12–27 sets out six practical implications for the walk of those who live "according to the Spirit." First, such individuals reject the demands of the flesh (8:12). Second, they put to death the deeds of the body (8:13). Third, they follow the Spirit's leading (8:14). Fourth, they find assurance of God's acceptance through the Spirit's inner witness (8:15–17). Fifth, they live in hope because the Spirit guarantees the redemption of the body (8:23–25). Sixth, their prayer life is effective because the Spirit intercedes for them (8:26–27). So, whatever the circumstances, Christians can be confident that the Spirit will provide the strength (8:9–14), the assurance (8:15–17), the hope (8:23–25), and the help (8:26–27) they need.

## The Imprisonment Letters

Although Paul wrote Philippians somewhat later than Colossians, Philemon, and Ephesians, the four imprisonment letters may be considered together. Written after his active missionary period, they are somewhat more reflective in tone. Colossians and Ephesians include themes not found in earlier letters (e.g., the universal church) and are written in a more complex style than either Philemon or Philippians. Yet the four letters have much in common. Significant themes running throughout the imprisonment letters include the supremacy of Christ, the nature of the Church, the mystery revealed to Paul, and the believer's future glory with Christ.

Christ's supremacy is particularly prominent in the hymnic passages Paul includes in Colossians and Philippians. In Colossians 1:15–18 he writes:

> He is the image of the invisible God, the firstborn of all creation;
> For by Him all things were created,
>> both in the heavens and on earth, visible and invisible,
>> whether thrones or dominions or rulers or authorities—
> all things have been created through Him and for Him.
> He is before all things, and in Him all things hold together.
> He is also the head of the body, the church;
> and He is the beginning, the firstborn from the dead;
> so that He Himself will come to have first place in everything.

In Philippians 2:9–11, he writes:

> For this reason also, God highly exalted Him,
> and bestowed on Him the name which is above every name,
> so that at the name of Jesus every knee will bow,
>> of those who are in heaven and on earth and under
>> the earth,
> and that every tongue will confess that Jesus Christ is Lord, to the glory of God the Father.

Although Ephesians 1:20–23 is seldom included in the discussion of Christological hymns, it also emphasizes Christ's supremacy using similar language:

> which He brouht about in Christ, when He raised Him from the
> dead and seated Him at His right hand in the heavenly places,
>> far above all rule and authority and power and dominion,
>> and every name that is named, not only in this age but also
>> in the one to come.
> And He put all things in subjection under His feet,
> and gave Him as head over all things to the church,
> which is His body, the fullness of Him who fills all in all.

The ideas found in the preceding passages occur repeatedly in Ephesians and Colossians (e.g., Eph. 3:19; 4:13, 15; Col. 2:9–10, 15). Elsewhere in those letters, Paul states that all deity dwells in Christ (Col. 2:9), that he ascended far above all the heavens (Eph. 4:10), that he sums up all things (Eph. 1:10), that he is the source of all wisdom and knowledge (Col. 2:3; Eph. 1:17), and that he reconciles all things through the blood of his cross (Col. 1:20). For Paul, there is no question that Christ is supreme in all areas, especially in his Church.

Because Christ is the head of the Church, he unifies it. The longest discussion of this theme occurs in Ephesians 2:11–22. In that passage, Paul reminds his readers that prior to Christ's reconciling work, a sharp divide existed between Jews and Gentiles. The Gentiles were separated from Messiah, excluded from God's promises to Israel, without hope, and without God (2:12). Locked behind the barrier of the Old Testament law (2:14–15), they were the "Uncircumcision" (2:11)—strangers and aliens to God's covenant people (2:19). Through his work on the cross, however, Christ brought near those who were far off (2:13), broke down the dividing wall of the Law (2:14–16), established peace (2:17–18), and incorporated the Gentiles into God's household (2:19; cf. 3:6).

The result of Christ's reconciling work is the Church, pictured as a building (Eph. 2:20–22) and as a body (Eph. 4:15–16; Col. 2:19). Seven key elements unite the body (Eph. 4:4–6), and maintaining that unity is a top priority for the members of the body (Eph. 4:1-3; Phil. 2:1–4). Membership in the body transcends socioeconomic levels (Philem. vv. 8–20) and brings with it the expectation that members of the body will practice mutual submission to one another (Eph. 5:21–6:9; Col. 3:18–4:1). As the head of his Church, Christ sets the standard for it (Eph. 2:20–21), provides the resources for its growth (Eph. 2:22; 4:16), and provides the example for the attitude that should characterize it (Phil. 2:5–11).

The Church as a single body that includes both Jews and Gentiles is the embodiment of the mystery God revealed to Paul who, in turn, preached it as central to his gospel. This mystery was previously hidden but now is made known (Eph. 3:4–5, 9; Col. 1:23, 25–26). God, who is the source of all spiritual wisdom and insight (Eph. 1:17; cf. Phil. 1:9; Col. 1:9–10), made it known through his Spirit (Eph. 3:5). The mystery itself consists of God's grace being extended to the Gentiles (Eph. 3:6–8), and results in future glory (Col. 1:27).

The believers' hope of future glory is the inheritance reserved for them as citizens of heaven (Eph. 1:14, 18; Col. 1:5). They are already seated and hidden with Christ at God's right hand (Col. 3:1-3), and they have the Holy Spirit dwelling in them as God's pledge of their inheritance (Eph. 1:13–14). Yet they pursue it as a prize (Phil. 3:12–14) and wait eagerly for its final consummation, knowing when Christ is revealed in glory they will participate in that same glory (Col. 3:4; cf. Eph. 1:14; Phil. 3:20–21).

## The Pastoral Letters

Paul's three letters to Timothy and Titus are different from the other letters ascribed to him. They address individuals in leadership positions— Timothy and Titus are sometimes described as "apostolic representatives"— rather than to local churches. They include instructions on roles, relationships, and attitudes within the church. Titus and 1 Timothy were probably intended to be read aloud to the congregations where those men were ministering. First Timothy is the longest and most comprehensive of the three letters; Titus is the briefest, yet its breadth is comparable to that of 1 Timothy. The second letter to Timothy is more narrowly focused. Because the nature of each letter is different, the content also includes distinct themes. Significant themes running throughout the three letters include false teaching, faithfulness, elders and deacons, and godly conduct.

False teaching is the primary danger confronting both Timothy in Ephesus (1 Tim. 1:3–4) and Titus in Crete (Titus 1:10–11). Individuals propagate false teaching because their minds and consciences are defiled (1 Tim. 4:2; Titus 1:15) and they are ensnared by the devil (2 Tim. 2:25–26). As a result, they are hypocritical (2 Tim. 4:2), deceitful (1 Tim. 4:1), and motivated by profit (1 Tim. 6:9-10; Titus 1:11). They deny God (Titus 1:16), oppose his truth (2 Tim. 2:16–18; 3:8; Titus 1:13–14), misapply his law (1 Tim. 1:7–10), and pervert the good things he has created (1 Tim. 4:3–4). Their teaching promotes controversy, disputes, speculation, and fruitless discussion rather than pure hearts, good consciences, and sincere faith (1 Tim. 1:4–6; cf. 6:4–5). They hold to a form of godliness but deny its power (2 Tim. 3:1–5). By their activities they upset the faith of some (2 Tim. 2:8; Titus 1:11), lead others astray (2 Tim. 3:6–7), and cause still others to shipwreck their faith (1 Tim. 1:19–20).

In response to the false teaching they were facing, Paul challenged Timothy and Titus to remain faithful in teaching sound doctrine. Just as Paul has considered God faithful to guard what Paul entrusted to him (2 Tim. 1:12), so Paul has been faithful to complete the task God entrusted to him (1 Tim. 1:12–14; 2 Tim. 4:1–8). Timothy and Titus can be confident that God will remain faithful even when they are faithless (2 Tim. 2:11–13):

> For if we died with Him, we will also live with Him;
> if we endure, we will also reign with Him;
> if we deny Him, He also will deny us;
> if we are faithless, He remains faithful, for He cannot deny himself. [10]

---

10. 2 Timothy 2:11–13 is one of five "faithful sayings" that occur in the pastoral letters. Each is identified by the phrase πιστὸς ὁ λόγος (cf. 1 Tim. 1:15; 3:1; 4:9; 2 Tim. 2:11; Titus 3:8).

Because faithfulness is a characteristic of God, those who follow him are also expected to demonstrate faithfulness in their conduct (1 Tim. 4:3, 10, 12; 5:16)—whether they are deacons (1 Tim. 3:11), masters (1 Tim. 6:2), or children (Titus 1:6).[11] For this reason, Paul challenges Timothy in particular to remain faithful, both in his conduct and in his ministry (1 Tim. 4:12–16; 6:11–16; 2 Tim. 2:3–10). Further, he is to identify other faithful men to whom he can entrust the sound teaching he has received from Paul (2 Tim. 2:1–2). Some of these faithful men will, no doubt, become elders and deacons in the congregations of which they are a part.

The presence of extended sections devoted to elders and deacons in the pastoral letters is well known, and has led some scholars to suggest that 1–2 Timothy and Titus reflect a period in church history later than when Paul wrote his letters. Since that issue has been addressed in the preceding chapter, the task here is to summarize the content of those sections. Considerably more space is devoted to elders than to deacons; deacons are mentioned only in 1 Timothy 3:8–13, where qualifications for their appointment are listed.

Both 1 Timothy 3:1–7 and Titus 1:5–9 set out the qualifications to apply when appointing elders. The list is extensive and does not need to be itemized, although the qualities fall into four categories: public reputation, personal character, family life, and church life. Titus 1:10–16 sets out the need for elders: They are called to silence false teachers by teaching sound doctrine. 1 Timothy 5:17–22 sets out the proper attitude and conduct to adopt toward elders: They are worthy of double honor, and accusations against them should not be entertained lightly. As leaders of the congregation, they are to be examples of godly conduct to those who follow Christ.

The theme of godly conduct is highlighted by the Greek word εὐσέβεια ("godliness"), which occurs eleven times in the pastoral letters. The purpose of prayer is to insure that followers of Christ may live quiet lives in all godliness (1 Tim. 2:1–8). Women who make a claim to godliness will conduct themselves in a certain way (1 Tim. 2:9–15). Godliness is the profitable goal toward which the good servant of Christ will strive (1 Tim. 4:7–11; cf. 6:11). Godliness is one of the measures of sound doctrine (1 Tim. 6:3–5; 2 Tim. 3:1–5; Titus 1:1) and, in contrast to the love of money, it is a means of great gain when accompanied by contentment (1 Tim. 6:6–10).

In fact, εὐσέβεια has a prominent place in the purpose paragraph of

---

They appear to be one means Paul uses to assure the readers of God's faithfulness.

11.  In all the verses noted, both the translators of the New American Standard Bible and the New International Version use the word "believer" or "believing," but the Greek text uses the adjective "faithful" (πιστός).

1 Timothy (3:14–16), where Paul notes that he is writing, in order that readers "will know how one ought to conduct himself in the household of God, which is the church of the living God, the pillar and support of the truth" (3:15). This statement suggests that the concept of godly living may extend to other sections of the pastoral letters including the conduct of and care for widows (1 Tim. 5:1–16), the conduct of older and younger men and women (Titus 2:1–8), the proper response to God's grace (Titus 2:11–14), and the call to engage in good deeds (Titus 3:1–11).

## TOWARD A THEOLOGY OF PAUL'S LETTERS

The integrating concept in Paul's theology is the transfer from being "in Adam" to being "in Christ." That transfer involves a radical change from one sphere of existence to another and is so significant that Paul must use multiple terms to picture it. The transfer places an individual in the church, which provides the context for living the Christian life. The transfer is effected by faith in the gospel of Christ, which is a mystery previously hidden but now revealed through Paul's apostolic ministry and includes the Gentiles.

Christ's life, death and resurrection are the focus of the gospel. He is the revelation of God's righteousness, the end of the Old Testament law, and the inaugurator of the new covenant. As a result of his virtuous life, his vicarious death, and his victorious resurrection, he is supreme over all things, including the church, which he unifies as its head. At his return, he will be manifested in glory, and the promise of being manifested with him in glory is the believer's hope.

In response to the gospel, the follower of Christ is expected to live a responsible life characterized by orderliness, perseverance, and godliness. The empowerment for godly living is provided by the Holy Spirit, who regenerates, baptizes, indwells, seals, fills, and transforms the believer. The Christian is also expected to remain faithful to sound doctrine, to defend it in the face of false teaching, and to promote it among faithful followers who are able to communicate it to others.

With this overview of Paul's theology added to the authenticity, integrity, and historical background of his canonical letters, it is time to turn to the tasks of establishing what the text is (textual criticism) and what the text says (translation). Those tasks are the focus of Chapter 4.

## The Chapter in Review

Beker's paradigm of "coherence and contingency" is helpful in thinking about the theology of Paul's letters. The coherence lies in Christ's crucifixion and resurrection, because they make possible a transfer from the sphere of "in Adam" to the sphere of "in Christ." In that new sphere, Christ is supreme, believers are righteous, and the Spirit is essential to living. Faith is the means of making the transfer, and the church is the context for living after the transfer.

The contingency may be seen by considering the three groupings of Paul's letters. His missionary letters are more immediate and focus on the challenges facing the local churches he planted. His imprisonment letters are more reflective and focus on the big picture of the universal church. His pastoral letters are more personal and focus on orderliness and godly conduct within "the church of the living God." Yet, it is possible to trace significant themes throughout Paul's letters and so identify the major contours of his thought.

**4**

# PREPARING TO INTERPRET PAUL'S LETTERS

## The Chapter at a Glance

- Textual criticism seeks to establish the text and enable more accurate communication of it.

- A balanced approach to textual criticism attempts to give equal weight to extrinsic, transcriptional, and intrinsic probabilities.

- Translation seeks to arrive at an initial understanding of the text in the target language.

- Although several methods may be used to establish what the text says, preparing a preliminary translation of the entire passage provides the interpreter with the fullest and most direct interaction with the Greek text.

TWO TASKS ARE ESSENTIAL IN PREPARING to interpret Paul's letters. The first is establishing what the text is; the second is establishing what the text says. Establishing the wording of the text is commonly called **textual criticism**, and arriving at an initial understanding of the text in the target language is commonly called translation.

## TEXTUAL CRITICISM: ESTABLISHING WHAT THE TEXT IS

Establishing the most likely original wording of the text is an important preliminary step to interpreting Paul's letters. The issue might be as small as a single letter (e.g., Rom. 5:1), as large as an entire chapter (e.g., Romans 16), or anything in between (e.g., Rom. 6:11; 7:25; 8:28; 11:6). It is, therefore, important to understand the need for textual criticism, to be aware of the resources available, and to be aware of the different approaches used before considering a method for engaging in the task itself.

### The Need for Textual Criticism

Approximately five thousand manuscripts exist that contain all or part of the Greek New Testament. Of the fifteen hundred sets of variant readings in the fourth edition of the United Bible Societies Greek New Testament (UBS4), only fifty are significant. None, however, touches on an article of faith or practice that is not clearly supported elsewhere in the Scriptures. Nevertheless, textual criticism provides a better understanding of the wording of a particular text and enables more accurate communication of that text.

The **textual variant** present in Romans 5:1 provides an example of the need for textual criticism. The text of that verse reads as follows:

Δικαιωθέντες οὖν ἐκ πίστεως εἰρήνην [ἔχομεν / ἔχωμεν]
πρὸς τὸν θεὸν διὰ τοῦ κυρίου ἡμῶν Ἰησοῦ Χριστοῦ

The textual variant is set off in brackets and involves the difference of a single letter. Was the original reading ἔχομεν (present active indicative first plural) or ἔχωμεν (present active subjunctive first plural)?

The first reading is a declarative indicative that makes a statement of fact and highlights our present *status* as the result of God's completed act of justification. It may be translated "Therefore because we are justified by faith, *we are having* peace with God." The second reading is a hortatory subjunctive that issues a call to action and highlights our present *responsibility* in response to God's completed act of justification. It may be translated, "Therefore because we are justified by faith, *let us be having* peace with God." So, is Paul stating a fact or issuing a challenge? Textual criticism seeks to provide an answer to that question. This variant from Romans 5:1 will serve as a test case for applying the method set out below.

## Resources for Textual Criticism

In order to engage in textual criticism, a resource that sets out both the variants and the manuscript support for each reading is essential. *The Novum Testamentum Graecae* (NA27) is the foundational tool for research and study, both in textual criticism and translation. Many, however, find the resource that is easiest to use in this regard is the edition of the Greek New Testament published by the United Bible Societies:

- B. Aland, et al, *The Greek New Testament*, 4th revised edition (New York: United Bible Societies, 1998).

The United Bible Societies also publishes a helpful volume that gives a concise explanation of the readings included in their edition of the Greek New Testament:

- B. M. Metzger, *Textual Commentary on the Greek New Testament*, 2nd edition (New York: United Bible Societies, 1994).

Anyone interested in a more detailed study of the theory and practice of textual criticism, as well as the major approaches to the task, would benefit from one or more of these introductions to the discipline:

- K. Aland and B. Aland, *The Text of the New Testament*, 2nd edition (Grand Rapids, MI: Eerdmans, 1989).

- D. A. Black, *New Testament Textual Criticism. A Concise Guide* (Grand Rapids, MI: Baker, 1994).

- P. W. Comfort, *The Quest for the Original Text of the New Testament* (Grand Rapids, MI: Baker, 1992).

- J. H. Greenlee, *Introduction to New Testament Textual Criticism*, revised edition (Peabody, MA: Hendrickson, 1995).

- B. M. Metzger and B. D. Ehrman, *The Text of the New Testament*, 4th edition (Oxford: University Press, 2005).

- W. N. Pickering, *The Identity of the New Testament Text* (Nashville: Nelson, 1980).

- H. A. Sturz, *The Byzantine Text-type and New Testament Criticism* (Nashville: Nelson, 1984).

## Approaches to Textual Criticism

David Alan Black identifies four modern approaches to textual criticism, although two approaches he mentions may be understood as subsets of a single approach.[1] The Eclectic Approach bases decisions about the preferred original reading solely on intrinsic (i.e., internal) evidence. The Conservative Approach bases decisions about the preferred original reading solely on extrinsic (i.e., manuscript) evidence. The Reasoned Approach bases decisions about the preferred original reading of the text on both intrinsic and extrinsic evidence.

| Eclectic Approach | Reasoned Approach | | Conservative Approach |
|---|---|---|---|
| Bases decisions on internal evidence | Bases decisions on internal and manuscript evidence | | Bases decisions on manuscript evidence |
| | Reasoned Eclecticism | Reasoned Conservatism | |
| | Gives greater weight to Alexandrian manuscripts | Gives greater weight to Byzantine manuscripts | |

Being aware of the of text types into which scholars commonly group New Testament manuscripts helps clarify the two subsets of the Reasoned Approach. These text types relate to the increased manuscript production that took place during the fourth century.[2] The major centers of manuscript production were Egypt (Alexandria) and Asia Minor (Antioch and Constantinople). From these production centers, two test types emerged: the Alexandrian and the Byzantine, each with certain general characteristics.[3] The Alexandrian text tends to retain readings that are "terse or somewhat rough, and . . . superficially

---

1. D. A. Black, *New Testament Textual Criticism: A Concise Guide* (Grand Rapids, MI: Baker, 1994), 36–40.

2. See the discussion in K. Aland and B. Aland, *The Text of the New Testament*, 2nd edition, (Grand Rapids, MI: Eerdmans, 1989), 64–7.

3. Two other text types have been suggested—Western and Caesarean—but they are somewhat less widely embraced.

more difficult."[4] The Byzantine text tends to retain readings that are "smooth, clear, and full."[5]

Within the Reasoned Approach, some scholars give greater weight to Alexandrian manuscripts (Reasoned Eclecticism); other scholars give greater weight to Byzantine manuscripts (Reasoned Conservatism). The text established by giving greater weight to the Byzantine manuscripts is sometimes called the "Majority" text, because Byzantine manuscripts tend to be more numerous than those included in the other families. The criticism often leveled against the Majority text is that the more numerous manuscripts also tend to be later (e.g., eighth or ninth century) and, therefore, might be more likely to reflect additions or changes to the text. In response, advocates of the Majority text argue that these more numerous manuscripts are actually more likely to reflect the widespread distribution of the original reading.

In contrast, proponents of the Alexandrian text give greater weight to a smaller number of earlier manuscripts (e.g., fourth or fifth century) that have been well preserved in the dry climate of Egypt. The criticism often leveled against these Alexandrian manuscripts is that they were less widely circulated and therefore might be more likely to reflect obscure or less well attested readings. In response, advocates of the Alexandrian text argue that these earlier manuscripts are actually more likely to reflect the original reading because less time had elapsed for scribes to incorporate additions or changes.

| Alexandrian Text Theory | Majority Text Theory |
| --- | --- |
| • Variants came into the manuscripts at an early stage. | • The readings in the largest number of manuscripts are most likely original. |
| • Alexandria had a history of preserving the Greek classics against textual corruption. | • Many of the original autographs were written to and preserved by churches in Asia Minor. |
| • The "Byzantine" text is based on an intentionally harmonized edition. | • The major "Alexandrian" manuscripts survived because they were seldom used. |

Both Reasoned Approaches have devoted advocates. Each approach has arguments for and against it. The individual seeking to interpret

---

4.  J. H. Greenlee, *Introduction to New Testament Textual Criticism*, (Grand Rapids, MI: Eerdmans, 1964), 87.

5.  Ibid., 91.

Paul's letters must assess the persuasiveness of those arguments for himself or herself, but a full discussion is beyond the scope of this chapter. The method suggested below seeks to work with both intrinsic and extrinsic probabilities; it also leans toward earlier manuscript support and shorter readings. In those respects it is a reasoned approach and stands somewhat closer to the Alexandrian than to the Majority text theory.

## A Method for Textual Criticism

In doing the work of textual criticism, the interpreter should consider three sets of probabilities: extrinsic, transcriptional, and intrinsic. Extrinsic probabilities focus on manuscript evidence. The guiding principle in evaluating extrinsic probabilities is that the earlier and more widely distributed manuscripts support the more likely original reading. Transcriptional probabilities focus on possible copyist changes (both unintentional and intentional). The guiding principle in evaluating transcriptional probabilities is that the shorter and more difficult reading is the more likely original. Intrinsic probabilities focus on the reading's "fit" with its context. The guiding principle in evaluating intrinsic probabilities is that the original reading is more grammatically harmonious with the context and more congruent with the author's style, vocabulary, and theology.

| Extrinsic Probabilities | Transcriptional Probabilities | Intrinsic Probabilities |
|---|---|---|
| • Earlier<br>• More widely distributed | • Shorter<br>• More difficult | • More harmonious<br>• More congruent |

As noted above, the textual variant present in Romans 5:1 includes two readings: ἔχομεν (present active indicative first plural) and ἔχωμεν (present active subjunctive first plural). What are the results when these guiding principles are applied to each reading?

### Extrinsic Probabilities

Both readings have early manuscript support and include witnesses from both the Alexandrian and Byzantine text types. Reading #1 (ἔχομεν) has somewhat stronger Byzantine support, while Reading #2 (ἔχωμεν) has stronger Alexandrian support (ℵ, B, A, C, 33, 81). The extrinsic probabilities, therefore, are divided, and a decision cannot be based on manuscript evidence alone.

### Transcriptional Probabilities

Since the variant in Romans 5:1 consists of a single letter, neither reading is shorter. It is possible to argue that the subjunctive reading is less likely in the context and, therefore, more difficult, but that discussion belongs more properly to the examination of intrinsic probabilities. The difference most likely reflects an unintentional change as the result of an error of pronunciation or hearing—either o to ω, or vice versa. Variants reflecting a parallel change are present in Romans 14:19 and 1 Corinthians 15:49. In the case of Romans 5:1, however, transcriptional probabilities cannot be decisive.

### Intrinsic Probabilities

Romans 5:1 occurs within the "doctrinal" section of the letter (1:13–11:36) where instruction is more likely than exhortation, although Paul weaves both throughout his letters. The parallel use of ἔχω in the immediate context is in the indicative mode (5:2), and Paul's only other use of the present active subjunctive first plural of ἔχω occurs in Romans 15:4 where it is the verb in a purpose clause introduced by the conjunction ἵνα. Of the twenty-eight occurrences of the present active subjunctive first plural in Paul's letters, ten are hortatory, and all ten are in the "practical" sections of letters.[6] Elsewhere in Paul, "peace" seems more frequently to be something God gives rather than something the believer is responsible to possess or experience (e.g., 2 Cor. 13:11; Phil. 4:7, 9; 2 Thess. 3:16). Based on these pieces of intrinsic evidence, Reading #1 (indicative statement of fact) seems the more probable original reading.

### Conclusion

Neither the extrinsic and nor the transcriptional evidence provides a strong basis for deciding which reading should be preferred. Intrinsic evidence, however, leans in favor of Reading #1 and suggests that the present indicative is the more probable original. Bruce Metzger's *Textual Commentary on the Greek New Testament* reaches the same conclusion: "Although the subjunctive . . . has far better external support . . . internal evidence must take precedence. Since in this passage, it appears that Paul is not exhorting but stating facts . . . only the indicative is consonant with the apostle's argument."[7]

---

6. Rom. 14:13, 19; Gal. 5:25; 6:9, 10; Phil. 3:15; 1 Thess. 5:6 (3x), 8.

7. B. M. Metzger, *Textual Commentary on the Greek New Testament*, 2nd edition (New York: United Bible Societies, 1994), 452.

## TRANSLATION: ESTABLISHING WHAT THE TEXT SAYS

Once the process of textual criticism establishes what the text is, the next step in preparing to interpret Paul's letters is establishing what the text says. There are a variety of approaches the interpreter may use in moving from the Greek text to an English understanding of it. Of those approaches, translating the entire passage provides the fullest and most direct interaction with the text and allows the interpreter to arrive at his or her own independent understanding of what the text says. This portion of the chapter will survey four approaches briefly and, then, will develop a procedure for translation at greater length.

## Approaches to Establishing What the Text Says

There are at least four approaches to establishing what the text says. Each has advantages as well as realities that must be faced when using it. This section seeks to set out briefly both sides of each approach.

### Comparing English Versions

One method of establishing what the text says in the target language (in this case, English) is to compare a selection of vernacular translations. Such a process makes it possible to identify places where translation difficulties might exist and to gain a sense of fine nuances of understanding that might be present. If the interpreter chooses this option, he or she is best served in comparing at least two versions, and it is helpful to understand the basic character of several of the most popular English versions.

- *The New American Standard Bible (NASB)* is a literal translation that is concerned with reflecting the grammar and syntax of the original Hebrew and Greek. It tends to be somewhat "wooden" because it makes fewer interpretive decisions for the reader than some versions.

- *The New International Version (NIV)* uses a dynamic equivalence translation approach and is concerned with literary quality and readability. It tends to make interpretive decisions rather than leaving them to the reader.

- *The New King James Version (NKJV)* seeks to retain the translation principles of the King James Bible while modernizing the language. It attempts to balance a literal translation with literary quality.

- *The English Standard Version (ESV)* uses the Revised Standard Version as its starting point. It is concerned with providing an essentially literal translation in modern language.

The greatest advantage of this method is its time efficiency. The interpreter need not invest time in arriving at his or her own translation of the text. The reality that is sometimes overlooked, however, is that beginning with existing English translations still requires an analysis of the Greek text to resolve any difficulties that might be identified—for if two English versions disagree, how is the interpreter to determine which understanding is closest to the author's intent, apart from comparing it with the original text?

### Working from an Interlinear

The advantage of working from an interlinear is its time efficiency, in that it relates the translation to the Greek text without engaging in the process of developing a full translation. It is important to recognize, though, that an interlinear merely correlates the Greek words of the text with corresponding English words. Because Greek word order differs from that of English, the end product is not really a translation at all, but rather, a series of words that the translator must organize mentally.[8] So, working from an interlinear still requires the interpreter to possess an understanding of and engage in analyzing Greek vocabulary, grammar, and syntax to reach conclusions on the author's most likely intended meaning.

### Translating Part of the Passage

A third approach is to translate central or difficult portions of the passage. This approach has the advantages of working directly with the Greek text while requiring less time commitment than translating the entire passage would. Translating only a portion of the passage, though, can produce a somewhat less contextual result, since all words and grammatical constructions have meaning only in a context beyond the sentence level.[9]

---

8. The example I use when teaching first year Greek is the apparently nonsensical sentence "Order difference word Greek no makes in." (Put in normal English word order the sentence reads: "Word order makes no difference in Greek.")

9. This concern with the broader context is reflected in the growing interest in "discourse analysis." The challenge with discourse analysis is that it is defined and practiced differently by various proponents. For a sample, see D. A. Black, ed. *Linguistics and New Testament Interpretation: Essays on Discourse Analysis* (Nashville: Broadman, 1992).

*Translating the Entire Passage*

Building a preliminary translation of the entire passage affords the fullest and most direct interaction with the Greek text. One reality to be faced when adopting this approach is that it requires a commitment to keeping Greek "fresh." Another is that the process can extend the amount of time required in preparation. Both of these realities, however, can be mitigated by engaging in a regular program of Greek reading and translation. William Larkin sets out a good model for ongoing Greek reading that can also serve as a basis for regular advance translation of passages for future preaching and teaching.[10]

## Elements of Translation

The task of translation involves multiple elements. The two most prominent are the meaning of words (**semantics**) and the relationship between words (**syntax**).

*Semantics*

Only rarely does a word have a single meaning; a range of meaning is far more common. The word "train," for example, has multiple nuances in its range of meaning.[11] As a noun, it can denote (a) a self-propelled connected group of rolling stock, (b) a trailing part that is drawn along, (c) a body of followers or attendants, (d) a series of results proceeding from an event or action, or (e) a succession of connected ideas. As a verb, it can denote (f) the act of forming habits, thoughts, or behaviors, (g) the act of making fit by proper exercise, (h) the act of bringing something to bear on an object, or (i) the act of undergoing discipline or instruction.

Further, some words have both literal and figurative nuances. The noun "light," for example, can denote illumination that makes something visible (literal nuance) or information that makes something clearer (figurative nuance). In both instances, the phrase "to shed light on" communicates accurately only when understood in context. These considerations make it clear that context determines a word's meaning, including its relationship to other words around it. Lexicons and theological dictionaries are important resources for dealing with the semantics of Greek words.

---

10.   W. J. Larkin, *Greek is Great Gain. A Method for Exegesis and Exposition* (Eugene, OR: Wipf & Stock, 2008), 27–38.

11.   In fact, *Webster's Encyclopedic Dictionary of the English Language* (New York: Portland House, 1989) lists twenty-nine different definitions.

## Syntax

Larkin notes that languages communicate through four grammatical phenomena.[12] A **morpheme** is the part of a word that indicates a particular relationship. For example, the difference of a single letter between the nominative form λόγος and the accusative form λόγον can denote the difference between the subject of a sentence and the direct object of that same sentence. A *function word* is a fixed form that makes links between other words; conjunctions and prepositions are the most common function words. *Word order* is the placement of words to indicate boundaries and connections. A simple example is the difference between the attributive construction ὁ πιστὸς λόγος (translated as "the faithful word") and the predicate construction πιστὸς ὁ λόγος (translated as "the word is faithful"). Punctuation is the placement of commas, semicolons, periods, and question marks to indicate connections and/or separations among words, phrases, clauses, and sentences. Intermediate and advanced grammar texts are important resources for dealing with the analysis of Greek syntax.

## Resources for Translation

The starting point for engaging in the task of translation is a version of the Greek text of the New Testament. The fourth edition of the United Bible Societies Greek New Testament (UBS4), which is based on the *Novum Testamentum Graecae* (NT27), is a helpful resource:

- B. Aland, et al., *The Greek New Testament*, 4th revised edition (New York: United Bible Societies, 1998).

An alternate version provides a running Greek–English dictionary that identifies and concisely defines infrequently used words and irregular word forms:

- B. Aland, et al., *The UBS Greek New Testament. A Reader's Edition* (Stuttgart: Deutsche Bibelgesellschaft, 2007).

A third version provides the Greek text on one page with the text of an English translation (New Revised Standard Version) on the facing page:

- B. Aland, et al., *Greek-English New Testament,* eighth revised edition (Stuttgart: Deutsche Bibelgesellschaft, 1994).

---

12. Larkin, *Greek Is Great Gain*, 41–2.

Concordances make it possible to trace all the uses of a Greek word in the New Testament. Some volumes provide the context of the verse in Greek; others provide the context in English:

- J. R. Kohlenberger, E. W. Goodrick, and J. A. Swanson, *The Exhaustive Concordance to the Greek New Testament* (Grand Rapids, MI: Zondervan, 1995).

- G. V. Wigram, *The Englishman's Greek Concordance of the New Testament* (Peabody, MA: Hendrickson, 1996).

Several computer software programs make it possible to perform the same task electronically:

- BibleWorks, BibleWorks LLC, Norfolk, VA, www.bibleworks.com

- Gramcord, Gramcord Institute, Vancouver, WA, www.gramcord.org

- Logos Bible Software, Bellingham, WA, www.logos.com

Lexicons provide important forms for each Greek word used in the New Testament as well as an expanded range of meaning and instances of the various nuances in that range of meaning:

- W. Bauer, W. F. Arndt, F. W. Gingrich, and F. W. Danker, *A Greek-English Lexicon of the New Testament and Other Early Christian Literature*, third edition (Chicago: University of Chicago Press, 2000).

- J. P. Louw and E. A. Nida, *A Greek-English Lexicon of the New Testament based on Semantic Domains*, 2nd edition, 2 volumes (New York: United Bible Societies, 1989).

Multivolume theological dictionaries supply important background for New Testament words and concepts, including background information from Old Testament, Classical, and Koine Greek contexts:

- C. Brown, ed., *The New International Dictionary of New Testament Theology*, 4 volumes (Grand Rapids, MI: Zondervan, 1986).

- G. Kittel and G. Friedrich, eds., *Theological Dictionary of the New Testament*, 10 volumes (Grand Rapids, MI: Eerdmans, 1964–73).

Intermediate grammars set out the fine distinctions of Greek grammar and syntax along with examples of those distinctions:

- D. B. Wallace, *Greek Grammar Beyond the Basics* (Grand Rapids, MI: Zondervan, 1996).

- F. Blass, A. Debrunner, and R. W. Funk, *A Greek Grammar of the New Testament and Other Early Christian Literature* (Chicago: University of Chicago Press, 1961).

## A Procedure for Translation

The premise of the following procedure for translation is that the basic unit of thought is the sentence. The relationship between those units of thought and the author's overall discourse are also important to interpretation. Considering those broader aspects of a passage, however, is more properly the task of exegesis and will be addressed in the next chapter.

### Steps in the Procedure

Since a sentence can extend beyond a single verse, the first step is to use punctuation to determine the length of the sentence. The second step is to use subordinate conjunctions and relative pronouns to identify any segments within the sentence. The third step is to translate the main (independent) clause(s) that constitute the heart of the sentence. This step involves several tasks.

A coordinate conjunction usually introduces each sentence; locate and translate it.[13] Then locate, parse, and translate the main verb; most commonly, that verb will be in the indicative or imperative mood. Next, check for an expressed subject and/or an expressed direct object. If there is an expressed subject, it will usually be a noun or pronoun in the nominative case. Similarly, if there is an expressed direct object, it will usually be a noun or pronoun in the accusative case. Once the subject and direct object are identified, translate them, along with any adjectival modifiers. Then locate and translate any adverbial modifiers. In addition to adverbs, prepositional phrases, participles, infinitives, and nouns in "oblique" cases (dative, genitive, and occasionally accusative) can function as adverbial modifiers. Once the pieces of the clause are identified and translated, build it using normal English word order: subject—verb—direct object—adverbial modifiers.

---

13. Greek writers tend to use coordinate conjunctions to bind sentences together. When a conjunction is not present, the phenomenon is called "asyndeton" (not bound together) and is worth noting because it is less common.

The fourth step in the process is to translate any subordinate (dependent) clauses following the same procedure used to translate the main clause. The fifth step is to build the sentence by arranging the clauses in the order in which they occur in the Greek text. The final step is to check the preliminary translation against an English version and make any necessary adjustments to it.

| Step #1 | Use punctuation to determine the length of the sentence. |
|---------|----------------------------------------------------------|
| Step #2 | Use subordinate conjunctions and relative pronouns to identify any segments within the sentence. |
| Step #3 | Translate the main (independent) clause(s). <br> • Locate the introductory coordinate conjunction. <br> • Locate and parse the main verb(s). <br> • Locate the expressed subject, the direct object, and any adjectival modifiers. <br> • Locate any adverbial modifiers. <br> • Build the clause according to normal English word order. |
| Step #4 | Translate any subordinate (dependent) clauses using the same process. |
| Step #5 | Build the sentence by translating the clauses following the order in which they occur in the Greek text. |
| Step #6 | Check the translation against an English version and make any necessary adjustments. |

## Practicing the Procedure

Since Romans 5:1 provided the example for a case study in textual criticism, Romans 5:1–2 serves as the sample text for practicing the procedure for translation. Although there is a second textual variant in verse 2, this case study will work on the premise that the dative article and noun τῇ πίστει are part of the original text.

> Δικαιωθέντες οὖν ἐκ πίστεως εἰρήνην ἔχομεν πρὸς τὸν θεὸν διὰ τοῦ κυρίου ἡμῶν Ἰησοῦ Χριστοῦ, δι᾽ οὗ καὶ τὴν προσαγωγὴν ἐσχήκαμεν [τῇ πίστει] εἰς τὴν χάριν ταύτην ἐν ᾗ ἑστήκαμεν, καὶ καυχώμεθα ἐπ᾽ ἐλπίδι τῆς δόξης τοῦ θεοῦ.

Step #1: Determine the length of the sentence.

- *The period after* τοῦ θεοῦ *in verse 2 marks the end of the sentence.*

Step #2: Identify any segments within the sentence.

- *Two relative pronouns* δι᾿ οὗ *and* ἐν ᾗ *mark a second and a third clause, both of which are subordinate.*

> δι᾿ οὗ καὶ τὴν προσαγωγὴν ἐσχήκαμεν [τῇ πίστει] εἰς τὴν χάριν ταύτην
>
> ἐν ᾗ ἑστήκαμεν, καὶ καυχώμεθα ἐπ᾿ ἐλπίδι τῆς δό-ξης τοῦ θεοῦ.

Step #3: Translate the main clause.

> Δικαιωθέντες οὖν ἐκ πίστεως εἰρήνην ἔχομεν πρὸς τὸν θεὸν διὰ τοῦ κυρίου ἡμῶν Ἰησοῦ Χριστοῦ

- *The postpositive coordinate conjunction* οὖν *introduces the sentence and may be translated as "therefore."*

- *The main verb* ἔχομεν *is present active indicative first person plural and may be translated as "we are having."*

- *There is no expressed subject, but the accusative noun* εἰρήνην *functions as the direct object and may be translated as "peace."*

- *Adverbial modifiers include the participial phrase* Δικαιωθέντες . . . ἐκ πίστεως *("having been justified out of faith"), the prepositional phrase* πρὸς τὸν θεὸν *("toward God"), and the prepositional phrase* διὰ τοῦ κυρίου ἡμῶν Ἰησοῦ Χριστοῦ *("through our Lord Jesus Christ").*

  "Therefore, having been justified out of faith, we are having peace toward God through our Lord Jesus Christ."

Step #4: Translate any subordinate clauses. For the sake of space, only the composite translation of each clause will be given.

> δι᾿ οὗ καὶ τὴν προσαγωγὴν ἐσχήκαμεν [τῇ πίστει] εἰς τὴν χάριν ταύτην

"through whom we also have had access by faith into this
grace"

ἐν ᾗ ἑστήκαμεν, καὶ καυχώμεθα ἐπ᾽ ἐλπίδι τῆς δόξης τοῦ
θεοῦ.
"in which we are standing and boasting in the hope of the
glory of God."

Step #5: Build the sentence. Following the order of the clauses as they
occur in the Greek text yields the following preliminary translation:
"Therefore, having been justified out of faith, we are having
peace toward God through our Lord Jesus Christ, through
whom also we have had access into this grace in which we
are standing and boasting in the hope of the glory of God."

Step #6: Check the translation against an English version.
Comparing the preliminary translation above with the NASB, for
example, identifies three items to consider:

- *Should the verb ἐσχήκαμεν be translated "we have had" or
  "we have obtained"?*

- *Should the noun προσαγωγὴν be translated "access" or "introduction"?*

- *Should the verb καυχώμεθα be understood as parallel with
  ἑστήκαμεν in the second relative clause, or is it the main verb
  in a separate independent clause?*

Each of these questions would naturally be folded into the process of
exegesis as the interpreter moves forward.

## GETTING TO THE TEXT

Romans 5:1–2 has served as a case study for considering the tasks
of textual criticism and translation. Textual criticism seeks to establish
what the text is, while translation seeks to establish what the text says.
Both tasks are preliminary to interpreting a passage from one of Paul's
letters. In the case of Romans 5:1–2, textual criticism has established
that the passage is a statement of fact rather than an exhortation to action. Building a preliminary translation of the text has identified a number of issues that should be investigated when seeking to interpret the
passage. Comparing that preliminary translation with the NASB raises
the issues of the best understanding of ἐσχήκαμεν, the best understand-

ing of προσαγωγὴν, and the relationship of καυχώμεθα to the rest of the sentence. Further items that could be pursued include the nuance of the adverbial participle Δικαιωθέντες, whether it is significant that Paul chose the preposition πρὸς ("toward") instead of σύν or μετά ("with"), and the nuance of the perfect tenses of ἐσχήκαμεν and ἐστήκαμεν. It is precisely questions such as these that are in view in Chapter 5.

## The Chapter in Review

The large number of extant Greek manuscripts as well as the existence of numerous textual variants in those manuscripts makes the process of textual criticism necessary. When engaging in textual criticism, interpreters may choose to give greater weight to the Alexandrian text type or to the Byzantine text type. In either case, a reasoned approach takes into account extrinsic, transcriptional, and intrinsic probabilities.

Several approaches may be used in moving from the Greek text to an English understanding of it. Of those approaches, preparing a preliminary translation of the entire passage provides the fullest and most direct interaction with the text. Translation necessarily involves the consideration of semantics and syntax. It will also raise questions that can profitably be investigated as the process of interpretation moves forward.

# 5

# INTERPRETING PASSAGES IN PAUL'S LETTERS

## The Chapter at a Glance

- The *"ABCs"* of exegesis include analyzing the historical, literary, and theological aspects of a passage.

- Historical analysis involves an investigation of both the circumstances specific to each letter and any details of first-century history, culture, and/or religion that are not readily understood by the twenty-first-century reader.

- Literary analysis involves an investigation of context, genre, structure, syntax, rhetoric, and word study.

- Theological analysis involves an investigation of both the analogy of Scripture and the analogy of faith.

WITH THE WORDING OF THE TEXT ESTABLISHED, a preliminary translation in place, and interpretive issues identified, the next step in interpreting Paul's letters is a more detailed analysis of the passage. That detailed analysis is commonly called **exegesis** and may be organized under three headings: historical analysis, literary analysis, and theological analysis. This chapter considers each of those areas in turn.

## HISTORICAL ANALYSIS

Paul wrote his letters in historical circumstances specific to each letter. He also wrote in the historical-cultural-religious context of the first century, a context quite different from that of the twenty-first century. It is important, therefore, to investigate both aspects of a passage's historical background. The historical circumstances specific to each letter are usually considered under the heading of introductory matters.

### Introductory Matters

Introductory matters include the author, the date and place of composition, the destination, the characteristics of the audience, and the author's purpose in writing. Since the same introductory information applies to the entire letter, it is unnecessary to re-investigate the details for each passage. It is more helpful to ask, "Which aspects of introductory matters help me better understand the passage I am studying?" For example, the fact that Philippi (destination) was a Roman colony populated by Roman citizens provides important context for both Philippians 1:27 where Paul calls his readers to "conduct yourselves [as citizens] in a manner worthy of the gospel of Christ" (ἀξίως τοῦ εὐαγγελίου τοῦ Χριστοῦ πολιτεύεσθε) and Philippians 3:20 where Paul reminds them that "our citizenship is in heaven" (ἡμῶν τὸ πολίτευμα ἐν οὐρανοῖς ὑπάρχει).

---

**Rights of Roman Citizens**

- To buy and sell property
- To be exempt from direct taxation
- To be exempt from imperial duties (e.g., military service)
- To be exempt from flogging
- To choose a Roman trial when accused
- To appeal following a trial

---

Similarly, the fact that Paul was in prison (place of composition) when he wrote to the Philippians informs those passages where Paul emphasizes his joy in serving Christ (e.g., Phil. 1:12–26).

Helpful resources for investigating introductory matters include:

- D. A. Carson and D. J. Moo, *An Introduction to the New Testament*, 2nd edition (Grand Rapids, MI: Eerdmans, 2006).

- R. H. Gundry, *A Survey of the New Testament*, 4th edition (Grand Rapids, MI: Eerdmans, 2003).

## Historical-Cultural-Religious Details

Any passage in Paul's letters might also include details of first-century history, culture, or religion that are not readily understood by the twenty-first-century reader. Bible dictionaries and encyclopedias will provide background on those details. Again, it is important to relate the background information directly to the passage by asking, "How does this information help me better understand the passage I am studying?" For example, knowing the historical background of the sect of the Pharisees as well as their emphasis on keeping the law, informs Paul's statements in Philippians 3:5–6 that he was "as to the Law, a Pharisee" (κατὰ νόμον Φαρισαῖος) and "as to the righteousness which is in the Law, found blameless" (κατὰ δικαιοσύνην τὴν ἐν νόμῳ γενόμενος ἄμεμπτος). In the same way, without knowing the historical background of Illyricum, Paul's statement in Romans 15:19 that he had preached the gospel "from Jerusalem and round about as far as Illyricum" (ἀπὸ Ἰερουσαλὴμ καὶ κύκλῳ μέχρι τοῦ Ἰλλυρικοῦ) is meaningless.

Helpful resources for investigating historical-cultural-religious details include:

- G. W. Bromiley, ed., *International Standard Bible Encyclopedia*, 4 volumes, revised edition (Grand Rapids, MI: Eerdmans, 1979–88).

- J. D. Douglas and M. C. Tenney, eds., *New International Dictionary of the Bible* (Grand Rapids, MI: Zondervan, 1987).

- C. A. Evans and S. E. Porter, eds., *Dictionary of New Testament Background* (Downers Grove, IL: InterVarsity Press, 2000).

- G. F. Hawthorne and R. P. Martin, eds., *Dictionary of Paul and His Letters* (Downers Grove, IL: InterVarsity Press, 1993).

- M. Silva and M. C. Tenney, eds., *Zondervan Encyclopedia of the Bible*, revised edition, 5 volumes (Grand Rapids, MI: Zondervan, 2008).

## Overview of New Testament History

As the discussion of chronology in Chapter 2 indicated, Paul's ministry covered the years from A.D. 34 through A.D. 68, if a later date for his conversion and a release-and-second-imprisonment scenario for the Pastoral Letters are adopted. For that reason, it will be helpful to sketch the first seventy years of New Testament history as background against which to set his ministry. Those seventy years, in turn, must be understood against the events of the intertestamental period.

When the post-exilic prophet Malachi concluded his ministry (c. 400 B.C.), Persia was the dominant world power. Alexander's conquest of Persia and Egypt in 331 B.C. ended more than a century of conflict between the Persian Empire and the Greek city-states and began nearly one thousand years of Greek cultural dominance in the eastern Mediterranean. Alexander, however, died without an heir in 323 B.C., and his empire was divided among his four leading generals. The Seleucid dynasty with its capital in Syrian Antioch, and the Ptolemaic dynasty with its capital in Alexandria, soon became the dominant powers.

Conflict with each other, the threat of Roman expansion, and internal rivalries eventually weakened the Seleucids and Ptolemies. At the same time in Palestine, the pressures of **hellenization** and religious persecution led first to the Maccabean revolt (167–164 B.C.) and subsequently to Jewish autonomy, first under the Maccabeans (164–135 B.C.), then under the Hasmoneans (135–63 B.C.). The Hasmoneans expanded the area under their control from Judea to Idumea, Samaria, Galilee, and the Transjordan (Perea). In 63 B.C., Judean civil strife enabled the Roman general Pompey to extend Roman influence from western Asia Minor into Syria and Judea. In 27 B.C., Octavius consolidated Roman rule over the entire eastern Mediterranean, including Egypt, and began the era of *Pax Romana*. For bringing peace to the Roman world, Octavius was acclaimed as the chief citizen (*princeps*) of the republic and was given the name Augustus. He ruled Rome under that name until A.D. 14 (cf. Luke 2:1).

*Pax Romana* was the phrase Romans writers used to characterize the two-and-a-half centuries that began with the reign of Octavius. They described it as a time of internal stability, material prosperity, and administrative efficiency.[1] Greek was widely spoken in the eastern empire; a system of permanent roads facilitated freedom of movement; an official postal system facilitated imperial communication; and a legal system provided generally consistent rules that applied to Roman citizens, colonies, and governors' courts.

Octavius (27 B.C.–A.D. 14) rebuilt temples and public buildings, revived religion, and settled the borders of the empire. Tiberius succeeded him (A.D. 14–37) but was more reclusive and chose to rule from Capri rather than Rome during his final ten years. Gaius Caligula (A.D. 37–41) promised reforms. Instead, he centralized power, depleted the imperial wealth, and revived the ruler cult until members of his personal guard assassinated him. Claudius (A.D. 41–54) stabilized imperial

---

1. Residents of the provinces experienced the stability, prosperity, and efficiency differently, depending on the character and/or ability of the individual governors.

control and opposed religious proselytizing. Nero (A.D. 54–68) initially reformed the administration of the empire, but he ignored the provinces and armies. He squandered the imperial wealth on games and theaters. When Nero committed suicide, a period of civil war ensued before Vespasian ascended to power. Vespasian (A.D. 69–79) rebuilt the infrastructure of Rome, secured the borders, restored economic stability, and restored public confidence in the emperor.

By the first century, the four largest cities in the empire were Rome, Alexandria, Antioch, and Ephesus. Alexandria had a population of 500,000 and was the administrative center of the province of Egypt. It was the cultural center of the east and was renowned for its library, which was the largest and best known in the empire. Syrian Antioch had a population of 300,000 and was the administrative center for the eastern empire. Ephesus was the capital of the province of Asia, was famous for its Temple of Artemis, and had a population of 250,000.

The original city-state of Rome remained the administrative center of the empire, while areas it incorporated were organized as provinces. *Legates* were appointed directly by the emperor for indefinite terms and governed imperial provinces where legionary troops were posted for external defense and/or internal security. Syria was one such province, and Roman military control of the Middle East was centered in Syrian Antioch. *Proconsuls* were appointed by the senate for limited terms and governed senatorial provinces where auxiliary troops were posted. Judea was governed as a senatorial province from A.D. 6 through 41. Certain cities throughout the empire were designated colonies and were granted municipal constitutions modeled on that of Rome. Octavius settled many of the veterans from his army in Philippi and granted that city status as a colony in 42 B.C.[2]

Some territories were considered particularly difficult or complicated to govern and were ruled by "client kings" who governed in the interests of Rome. In Palestine, Octavius declared the Idumean, Herod, "King of the Jews" in 40 B.C. and installed him in Jerusalem three years later. Herod ruled the area previously controlled by the Hasmoneans until 4 B.C. Increased hellenization and major building projects characterized his reign.[3] When Herod died, his kingdom was divided among three of his sons. Archelaus ruled as "ethnarch" of Judea, Samaria, and Idumea until Octavius deposed him in A.D. 6. Philip ruled as "tetrarch" of the area north and east of the Sea of Galilee until his death in A.D. 34, and Antipas ruled as "tetrarch" of Galilee and the Transjordan until A.D. 37 when Caligula exiled him to southern Gaul.[4]

---

2. Julius Caesar had conferred the same status on Corinth four years earlier.

3. The building projects included a royal palace in Jerusalem, the Jerusalem Temple, and the port of Caesarea Maritima.

4. Philip's tetrarchy consisted of Gaulanitis, Auranitis, Batanea, Trachonitis, Paneas, and

After Octavius deposed Archelaus, his territory passed to direct Roman rule as a senatorial province under a series of procurators supported by auxiliary troops. The best known procurator was Pilate (A.D. 26–36). When Philip died, his territory was initially annexed to the province of Syria. In A.D. 37, however, Caligula named Herod Agrippa I king, restored Philip's territory to him, and added the Galilean and Transjordan areas formerly ruled by the exiled Antipas. In A.D. 41, Claudius added Judea and Perea to Agrippa's kingdom, and so made the territory he governed virtually the same as that ruled by Herod the Great. When Agrippa I died suddenly in A.D. 44, the entire area reverted to direct Roman rule under another series of procurators, including Felix (A.D. 52–59) and Festus (A.D. 59–62). Although Claudius gave Agrippa II the royal title and the authority to appoint the high priest in A.D. 48, he remained subordinate to the procurators.

Outside Palestine, a number of events are worth noting. Tiberius banished all Jews from Rome in A.D. 19 as the result of a public scandal related to a donation to the temple in Jerusalem. Later, however, they returned in such numbers that in A.D. 41 Claudius restricted the Jews in Rome from assembling together (Dio Cassius, *Roman History* 40.6). Then in A.D. 49, he expelled all Jews (and Jewish Christians) from Rome because they were rioting "at the instigation of Chrestus" (Seutonius, *Claudius* 25.4). The Jews subsequently returned after Claudius's death. When the city of Rome burned in A.D. 64, however, Nero blamed the fire on Christians and instituted what is generally considered the first persecution of the early church. Tradition records that both Peter and Paul were martyred by Nero in A.D. 67–68.[5]

Nero's reign also saw the beginning of the Jewish revolt against Rome after three major incidents occurred in A.D. 66. First, there was a dispute between the Jewish and Gentile citizens of Caesarea Maritima. Then, the proconsul Florus raided the Jerusalem Temple and seized the money in the treasury. In response, the priests in the temple stopped offering the daily sacrifice for the emperor's welfare. This final action led to an open revolt in which Agrippa II fled Jerusalem, the Roman garrison of the city was massacred, and the Zealots occupied the fortress at Masada.

In A.D. 67, Nero commissioned Vespasian to put down the revolt using legionary troops from Syria. By the middle of A.D. 68, he had

---

Iturea; his capital was Caesarea Philippi (completed in A.D. 14). Antipas built the new city of Tiberias in Galilee as his northern capital (completed in A.D. 25).

5.  Eusebius writes, "It is recorded that in [Nero's] time Paul was beheaded in Rome itself, and that Peter likewise was crucified, and the title of "Peter and Paul," which is still given to the cemeteries there, confirms the story, no less than does a writer of the Church named Caius, who lived when Zephyrinus was Bishop of Rome" (*Ecclesiastical History* 2, 25.5).

subdued Galilee, Perea, Western Judea, and Idumea. After Nero committed suicide, the eastern armies proclaimed Vespasian emperor (A.D. 69). When the new emperor left for Rome to assume personal control, he gave the task of ending the revolt to Titus, his oldest son. Titus laid siege to Jerusalem for five months in A.D. 70 and destroyed the temple when the city finally fell. The stronghold of Masada held out until A.D. 73 when the defenders committed suicide rather than surrender to the Romans. Judea became a full imperial province governed by a legate and garrisoned by legionary troops. When the legate gave rabbi Yohanan ben Zakkai permission to set up a school of rabbinical study in Jamnia in western Judea, that city became the new focus of what remained of Jewish national life and the center for codification of the Jewish law.

| Roman Emperors, and Major Events during Their Reigns | |
| --- | --- |
| Octavius (Augustus)<br>27 B.C. – A.D. 14 | • Herod installed as "King of the Jews"(40 B.C.)<br>• Kingdom divided among Archelaus, Philip, and Antipas (4 B.C.)<br>• Archelaus deposed (A.D. 6) |
| Tiberius<br>A.D. 14–37 | • Jews expelled from Rome (A.D. 19)<br>• Philip dies (A.D. 34) |
| Gaius Caligula<br>A.D. 37–41 | • Antipas exiled to Gaul (A.D. 37<br>• Herod Agrippa I named king (A.D. 37) |
| Claudius<br>A.D. 41–54 | • Jews in Rome restricted from assembling (A.D. 41)<br>• Herod Agrippa I dies (A.D. 44)<br>• Herod Agrippa II given royal title but limited authority (A.D. 48)<br>• Jews expelled from Rome (A.D. 49) |
| Nero<br>A. D. 54–68 | • Rome burns (A.D. 64)<br>• Jewish revolt begins (A.D. 66)<br>• Peter and Paul martyred (A.D. 67–68)<br>• Nero commits suicide (A.D. 68) |
| Vespasian<br>A.D. 69–79 | • Jerusalem falls to Titus (A.D. 70)<br>• Masada falls to Titus (A.D. 73) |

## The Locales of the Churches to Which Paul Wrote

Paul's ministry extended from Jerusalem in the east to Rome in the west, and perhaps even farther west to Spain. He planted churches in numerous cities, and his extended ministry in Ephesus resulted in churches being planted throughout the province of Asia. Nevertheless, the destinations of his extant letters are comparatively few. If the cities of South Galatia are considered together and Crete is accepted as the destination for the letter to Titus, it is possible to gather the background of the locales to which Paul wrote under eight headings. It will be helpful to consider each of those locales briefly.

### The Cities of South Galatia

The ethnic Gauls who settled in north-central Asia Minor during the third century B.C. named their new homeland Galatia. In 64 B.C., the Romans designated Galatia a client kingdom and expanded its borders southward. Octavius subsequently reorganized Galatia as a province, and by the time of Paul's ministry its boundaries extended from the Black Sea on the north to the Mediterranean Sea on the south. According to Acts 13–14, Paul and Barnabas visited the South Galatian cities of Psidian Antioch, Iconium, Lystra, and Derbe after traveling to the island of Cyprus.

Of the four South Galatians cities Paul visited, Antioch, Iconium, and Derbe were all located on the major trade route connecting Ephesus with the Euphrates. Lystra lay about ten miles southwest of that trade route, but on a later Roman road running from Iconium to Derbe. Antioch, Iconium, and Lystra were Roman colonies, but Lystra had more in common with Derbe than with the other two cities. Antioch and Iconium were Phrygian, while Lystra and Derbe were Lycaonian.

By the first century, Antioch included Greek, Latin, and Phrygian traditions. It also had a prominent Jewish community that was respected by the other traditions (cf. Acts 13:14). Although it was a Roman colony, Iconium resisted Roman influence. Public documents were in Greek, and an assembly of citizens governed the city after the Greek model. It, too, had a Jewish community large enough to support a synagogue (cf. Acts 14:1).

Lystra became a Roman colony under Octavius. In the middle of the first century its population included a small Roman ruling class who spoke Latin and a number of well-to-do Greek-speaking "Hellenists."[6]

---

6. According to Acts 16:1, Timothy was raised in Lystra by a Jewish mother and a Greek father (cf. 2 Tim 1:5; 3:11, 15).

The majority of the citizens were uneducated Lycaonians who spoke the local language and were not well acquainted with Greek. There was a small Jewish community, but it was not as numerous as in the Phrygian cities.[7] Pagan religions were the norm. Derbe lay about sixty miles southeast of Lystra and had many of the same characteristics, although the Lycaonian element was stronger.

## Thessalonica

After Alexander the Great died, Cassander assumed control of the portion of the empire that is modern Greece. In 315 B.C., the new King of Macedonia founded Thessalonica as a port at the head of the Thermaic Gulf. When the Romans organized Macedonia as a province in 146 B.C., Thessalonica became the capital. By the first century, the city was the most important and populous in the province as well as a military and commercial center. It was also a stop on the Via Egnatia that ran through Macedonia to connect Byzantium in the east with the Adriatic Sea in the west. The city had a large Roman population as well as a Jewish community large enough to support a synagogue (cf. Acts 17:1).

## Corinth

The Romans destroyed the original Greek city-state of Corinth in 146 B.C., but Julius Caesar refounded it as a Roman colony in 44 B.C. When Achaia was organized as a senatorial province in 27 B.C., Corinth became the capital.[8] The city was located on an isthmus connecting southern Achaia with the rest of Greece. Mid-way between the ports of Lechaeum and Cenchrea, Corinth was an international crossroads of travel between Italy and Asia and the leading commercial center in Achaia. Estimates of the first-century population ranged from 150,000 to 300,000, and Strabo described the city as "great and wealthy" (*Geography* 8.6). A melting pot of Roman veterans, freedmen, lower classes, and slaves, Corinth also included a significant Jewish community (cf. Acts 18:4, 12–17). It was known for its vice, sexual corruption, and numerous religious sites, including the Temple of Aphrodite. Corinth was also the site of the Isthmian Games, a biennial athletic competition that was second in fame only to the Olympian Games. An earthquake destroyed the city in A.D. 77.

---

7. In Acts 14:19, Luke notes that Jews from Antioch and Iconium pursued Paul when he fled to Lystra and Derbe.

8. Achaia was designated an imperial province in A.D. 15.

## Rome

By the first century, Rome's population was at least one million and consisted of people of all socioeconomic levels from across the empire. Participation in religious ritual was a way of life and was closely connected to the government. Religion was generally considered a legal matter in which following rituals was a way of maintaining peace with the gods. Foreign religions were assimilated but tended to be viewed with suspicion, at least initially.

As early as 139 B.C. Rome had a Jewish population estimated at 40,000. Both Julius Caesar and Octavius declared Judaism a legal religion, but the Jews in Rome still experienced racial discrimination. Tiberius expelled all Jews in A.D. 19, and Claudius did the same in A.D. 49. Jews from Rome were present at Pentecost (cf. Acts 2:10) and most likely carried the gospel back to Italy with them. Claudius's expulsion of all Jews probably reflects initial Christian presence in the synagogues of Rome. The Jews subsequently returned after Claudius's death, and by A.D. 56–57 Paul expected to encounter an active Christian church when he passed through Rome on his was to Spain (cf. Rom. 1:8–12; 15:22–24; 16:3–16).

## Colossae

In the fifth century B.C., Colossae was the largest city in the Lycus Valley, about one hundred miles east of Ephesus on the main road to the Euphrates. By the first century, however, it had declined in size and importance to the point that Strabo called it a "small town" overshadowed by Laodicea and Hieropolis (*Geography* 12.8). Located in the Roman province of Asia, Colossae was a cosmopolitan city with a largely Gentile population and a variety of cultural and religious influences, including a significant Jewish community in the region. The city was never rebuilt after an earthquake destroyed it (c. A.D. 60–64).

## Ephesus

Ionian colonists founded the original Greek city of Ephesus around 1100 B.C. and constructed the Temple of Artemis in the seventh century B.C. The Persians controlled the city from the sixth century B.C. until Alexander the Great conquered Asia Minor. The temple was rebuilt in the first half of the third century, and Lysimachus redesigned the city to relocate it closer to the harbor. Control of Ephesus passed to Rome in 133 B.C.

By the first century, Ephesus was the fourth largest city in the empire with an estimated population of 250,000 and was the capital of the

Roman province of Asia. Strabo described it as "the greatest commercial center in Asia" west of the Tarsus River (*Geography* 14.1). The city had a theater that seated 24,000, a market that measured 110 meters square, baths and gymnasiums, a medical school, and it was the home of the common games of Asia. The population was predominantly Gentile but also included a Jewish population large enough to support a synagogue (cf. Acts 19:8).[9]

Central to the city was the Temple of Artemis, which was numbered among the seven wonders of the ancient world and measured 220 feet by 425 feet. Much of the city's commerce related to the temple, and two major spring festivals celebrated the Artemis cult. Magic played a major role in the worship of Artemis and made the city a center for occult practices (cf. Acts 19:11–20).

### Philippi

Philip of Macedon founded the city of Philippi in 358 B.C., eight miles from the north end of the Aegean Sea, and named it after himself. The city was subsequently destroyed by wars, but Octavius rebuilt it after he consolidated his control of the empire. He settled the new city with veterans from his army and designated it a colony governed by Roman law.[10] It was a major stop on the Via Egnatia, was served by the port of Neapolis, and was known for its medical school.[11] The population was predominantly Roman with a significant number of Macedonian Greeks. There was a Jewish community, although Luke's comment in Acts 16:13 suggests that it was not large enough to support a synagogue.

### Crete

Located about sixty miles southeast of the Greek mainland, the island of Crete marked the southern limit of the Aegean Sea. Strabo noted

---

9. Luke's account of Paul's ministry in Ephesus suggests some level of tension between the Jewish and Gentile segments of the population (Acts 19:33–34).

10. It was in Philippi that Paul first asserted his Roman citizenship (Acts 16:37). He later stated that he was born a Roman citizen (Acts 22:25–28). Tradition records that Paul's parents were taken to Tarsus as prisoners of war, were enslaved to a Roman, and were later freed and granted Roman citizenship.

11. If Luke was a doctor as tradition records, it is interesting to consider his potential connection to Philippi and its medical school. The fact that the "we" passages begin with Paul's vision of the man from Macedonia (Acts 16:9–11) has led some to suggest that Luke himself is the man in the vision. If Luke came from Philippi, that fact might explain his description of the city as "the leading city of the district of Macedonia" (Acts 16:12) when Thessalonica actually held that distinction.

that it was "mountainous and thickly wooded" (*Geography* 10.4). The main Roman city of Gortyna lay on the southern part of the island, although the best harbors were on the north side. After a golden age from 2000 to 1500 B.C., Crete was best known for its traders and mercenary soldiers. The Romans annexed Crete in 67 B.C. and combined it with Cyrene (Libya) to form the province of Cyrenaica. A significant Jewish community had settled on the island by the middle of the second century B.C. (cf. 1 Macc. 15:23), and Jews from Crete were present in Jerusalem at Pentecost (Acts 2:11).

## LITERARY ANALYSIS

Although they were produced in a largely oral culture, Paul's letters are literary documents and must be studied as such. It is important, therefore, to include literary analysis in the process of exegesis. Literary aspects that should be considered when interpreting Paul's letters are context, genre, structure-syntax-rhetoric, and word study.

## Context

Since "context is king," this aspect of literary analysis is crucial to the process of exegesis. The study of context involves two areas: general context and immediate context. Both areas are important for understanding passages in Paul's letters.

### General Context

Understanding where a passage fits into the outline of the letter in which it occurs can help clarify that passage's role in Paul's argument. Scanning the letter with an eye to the way in which the passage relates to the overall argument serves as a useful check on its general context. Summarizing that relationship in a single sentence brings clarity to the understanding of general context.

As is true with introductory matters, it is not necessary to re-investigate a letter's overall structure and argument before studying each passage. If time permits when beginning the study of a letter, a **synthetic study** is a helpful way to get the "big picture" and establish a framework into which the individual passages within the letter fit.[12] A synthetic study involves reading through a letter three different times, completing each reading at a single sitting. For the first and second readings, read the letter continuously, but take notes only at the end of

---

12. For a fuller description of the process for doing a synthetic study, see Larkin, *Greek Is Great Gain*, 285–91.

each reading. After each reading, record first impressions about the letter's tone, purpose, and key passages. Then, during the third reading, take notes on turning points, movements of thought, and major divisions. Finally, synthesize the results of the three readings by developing a one-page outline or chart that summarizes the theme, content, and progression of thought. A synthetic study of Ephesians, for example, might take a total of three or four hours of work, but the results will help inform the general context of each passage within the letter.

| EPHESIANS | | |
|---|---|---|
| **Theme: Understanding the Church's Wealth and Walk in Christ** | | |
| Salutation (1:1–2) | | |
| Our Wealth in Christ (1:3–3:21) | | |
| Spiritual Blessings (1:3–14) | Enlightened Eyes (1:15–21) | Regeneration (2:1–10) |
| Reconciliation (2:11–22) | God's Mystery (3:1–13) | God's Love (3:14–21) |
| Our Walk in Christ (4:1–6:20) | | |
| Walk Worthily (4:1–16) | Walk Properly (4:17–32) | Walk Purely (5:1–14) |
| Walk Wisely (5:15–21) | Walk Lovingly (5:22–6:9) | Stand Firmly (6:10–20) |
| Closing (6:21–24) | | |

Using the preceding chart of Ephesians, for example, a summary statement of the general context for Ephesians 4:17-24 might be:

> As the paragraph that begins the second "walk" section of the letter, Ephesians 4:17-24 provides the theological basis for Paul's discussion of what it means to walk properly in Christ.

*Immediate Context*

Because any passage relates in some way to what precedes and follows it, it is important to think intentionally about those relationships. The best way to review a paragraph's immediate context is to read continuously, at minimum, (a) the paragraph before the passage under study, (b) the passage itself, and (c) the paragraph following the passage under study. Then, in a single sentence, summarize the way in which the preceding paragraph contributes to understanding the passage under study. Do the same with the following paragraph. Those summaries for Ephesians 4:17-32 might read:

> After explaining how unity and diversity within the body of Christ contributes to believers walking worthily of their calling (4:1-16), Paul moves on to a section challenging them to live out that calling (4:17-32). First, the apostle sets out the standard by which believers are to live (4:17-24). Then, he describes specific ways in which they can respond to his challenge (4:25-32).

## Genre

Since Chapter 1 addressed the topic of the genre of Paul's letters at some length, it is not necessary to review that discussion here. There are, however, two genre-related concerns in exegesis. The first concern is to locate the passage in the proper section of the letter and consider what implications its place in the letter might have for understanding it. For example, Why did Paul choose to place the apostolic parousia of his letter to the Philippians (2:19-30) at the end of first section of the letter body instead of at the end of the letter (as he does in 2 Cor. 13:1–10)? Or, What do the form and elements of the thanksgiving in 1 Thessalonians (1:2–10) suggest about Paul and his relationship with the letter's recipients?

The second concern is to be aware of any subgenres present in the passage and give them proper attention. For example, Why did Paul choose to expand the thanksgiving of his letter to the Colossians by including the Christological hymn of 1:15–20? Or, Is the order of the groups addressed in the household code of Colossians 3:18–4:1 significant?

## Structure, Syntax, and Rhetoric

With the passage's context and genre clearly in focus, the next areas to consider are the structure, syntax, and rhetoric of the passage. This process involves three steps. The first step is to create a graphic representation of the passage's structure. The second step is to examine key elements of grammar and syntax. The final step is to analyze any significant rhetorical features that enhance the meaning of the passage.

*Structure*

Creating a visual representation of the passage is a helpful way to analyze its structure. Various approaches are possible (e.g., grammatical diagram, mechanical layout, discourse analysis), but similar analytical skills are required in all of them. The objective is to understand as precisely as possible the relationships between the clauses and sentences that comprise the passage. The benefit, particularly in Paul's closely argued letters, is that the process requires the interpreter to think one more time about what Paul is seeking to communicate to his readers. The result is a first step along the path to identifying the primary point(s) to communicate in preaching or teaching the passage.

Because English versions sometimes choose to translate dependent clauses in such a way that they appear to be main ideas, the graphic representation of a passage's structure is best done by working directly with the Greek text. The approach can be simple or complex. One approach is to work at the clause level and concentrate on the relationships between those clauses. Romans 5:1–2 will serve as an example.

Δικαιωθέντες οὖν ἐκ πίστεως εἰρήνην ἔχομεν πρὸς τὸν θεὸν διὰ τοῦ κυρίου ἡμῶν Ἰησοῦ Χριστοῦ δι' οὗ καὶ τὴν προσαγωγὴν ἐσχήκαμεν [τῇ πίστει] εἰς τὴν χάριν ταύτην ἐν ᾗ ἑστήκαμεν καὶ καυχώμεθα ἐπ' ἐλπίδι τῆς δόξης τοῦ θεοῦ.

This sentence consists of four main segments: an introductory (adverbial) participial phrase:

Δικαιωθέντες ἐκ πίστεως

one independent clause:

οὖν εἰρήνην ἔχομεν πρὸς τὸν θεὸν διὰ τοῦ κυρίου ἡμῶν Ἰησοῦ Χριστοῦ

and two dependent (relative) clauses:

δι' οὗ καὶ τὴν προσαγωγὴν ἐσχήκαμεν [τῇ πίστει] εἰς τὴν χάριν ταύτην

ἐν ᾗ ἑστήκαμεν καὶ καυχώμεθα ἐπ' ἐλπίδι τῆς δόξης τοῦ θεοῦ.

It is worth noting that the conjunction οὖν ("therefore") occurs within the participial phrase but introduces the independent clause. For that reason, it has been placed with the independent clause.

With the main segments of the sentence identified, it remains to show the relationships between them. Since Greek speakers and authors used word order to show emphasis, it is best to retain the word order of the original text. Place the independent clause at the left-hand margin and, then, indent dependent clauses on the line above or below the word or phrase they modify. In the layout below, the underlined words/phrases indicate items that are modified. Arrows may also be used to make the modification clear.

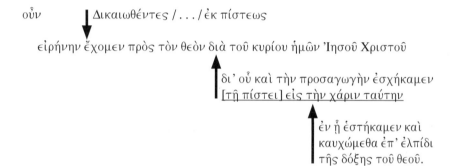

The resulting layout suggests a focus on God's gift of peace to the believer growing out of justification by faith in Christ. The question raised in the preceding chapter as to whether καυχώμεθα in the last segment of the sentence is parallel to ἐστήκαμεν (immediately preceding it) or to ἔχομεν (in the independent clause) still remains. That question, however, is best addressed in the examination of grammar and syntax.

## Grammar and Syntax

It is theoretically possible to engage in an analysis of the grammar and syntax of each word or phrase in a passage, but time constraints seldom permit that much attention to detail. Larkin suggests the helpful categories of "Structure, Verbs, Cases, and the Rest" as a way to organize the step of grammatical/syntactical analysis.[13] That schema reinforces the importance of checking such key elements as:

---

13. Larkin, *Greek Is Great Gain*, 137–41.

- Structure:        The function of coordinate and
                    subordinate conjunctions

- Verbs:            The tense, voice, and mood of verbs as well as
                    the function of participles and infinitives

- Cases:            The special use of noun case forms

- Rest:             The function of prepositional phrases as well as
                    the presence/absence of the definite article

For both the analysis of grammar and syntax as well as the analysis of rhetorical features, a three-step procedure of Collect-Classify-Comment can be useful. Begin by *collecting* those features that appear to warrant study. Then, *classify* the feature as precisely as possible using categories from standard grammar texts. Finally, *comment* on the significance of the classification for understanding the passage. This procedure will structure a brief consideration of each of the items that comprise the introductory participial phrase and the independent clause.

| Collect | Classify | Comment |
|---|---|---|
| οὖν | *Inferential* coordinate conjunction | This discussion of the results of justification grows logically out of the preceding explanation of Abraham's example (Romans 4). |
| Δικαιωθέντες | Adverbial participle of *cause* | The reason peace with God is possible is God's gracious act of justifying those who believe (cf. Rom. 3:22–24). |
| ἐκ πίστεως | Prepositional phrase of *means* | Faith is the means that makes justification possible. |
| εἰρήνην ἔχομεν | *Progressive* present tense | Peace with God is the present and continuing status of the person who has been justified by faith. |
| πρὸς τὸν θεὸν | Prepositional phrase of *direction* | The use of a directional preposition suggests that the aspect of peace highlighted is more objective status than subjective experience. |
| διὰ τοῦ κυρίου ἡμῶν Ἰησοῦ Χριστοῦ | Prepositional phrase of agency | Christ is the personal agent through whom peace is established. |

At the end of the sentence, there are two possible ways of under-standing the relationship of καὶ καυχώμεθα ἐπ᾽ ἐλπίδι τῆς δόξης τοῦ θεοῦ to what precedes it. Either the continuative conjunction καὶ coordi-nates ἑστήκαμεν and καυχώμεθα in the relative clause, or it coordinates καυχώμεθα with ἔχομεν in the earlier independent clause. Most English translations choose the second option and insert a comma or semicolon after "in which we stand" (ἐν ᾗ ἑστήκαμεν).[14] The NIV inserts a period and interprets the remainder of the verse as a separate sentence: "And we boast in the hope of the glory of God." Is that decision the best one? What basis is there for making such a decision?

A handy (but not infallible) rule of thumb is "Closer and simpler are better." That rule of thumb would suggest that καυχώμεθα should be taken as coordinate with ἑστήκαμεν. Are there any reasons to conclude otherwise? The tense change from the perfect (ἑστήκαμεν) to the pres-ent (καυχώμεθα) is not significant, since the perfect tense functions as the present when ἵστημι is intransitive. Since there do not appear to be any other grammatical or syntactical issues to consider, a decision to make καυχώμεθα coordinate with ἔχομεν is most likely rooted in theol-ogy. Is it more theologically appropriate to see "the hope of the glory" rooted in justification or in grace? This brief discussion will not attempt to resolve that question, but the more natural grammatical solution is to leave καυχώμεθα as part of the relative clause rather than to begin a new independent clause.

### Rhetoric

The third area to consider is the presence of any significant rhetori-cal features that enhance the meaning of the passage. Such features may include (but not be limited to) word order, repetition, parallelism, asyn-deton, chiasmus, anaphora, inclusion, and ring-composition.[15] Romans 5:1–2 includes four rhetorical features worth noting.

---

14. Commentaries tend to assume that καυχώμεθα is coordinate with ἔχομεν without providing any rationale for doing so.

15. For a helpful list, see Larkin, *Greek Is Great Gain*, 153–63.

| Collect | Classify | Comment |
|---------|----------|---------|
| Δικαιωθέντες . . . ἔχομεν | Change in word order | Placing the adverbial participle before the main verb makes the connection to the preceding context explicit and highlights the importance of justification by faith to the argument. |
| εἰρήνην ἔχομεν | Change in word order | Placing the direct object before the verb emphasizes "peace" as the benefit of justification that is particularly in view. |
| τὴν προσαγωγὴν ἐσχήκαμεν | Change in word order | Placing the direct object before the verb emphasizes "access" as a second benefit provided through Christ. |
| ἐσχήκαμεν . . . ἐστήκαμεν | Word play (*homoeoteleuton*) | Using two verbs with similar-sounding endings calls attention to the importance of God's grace that the verbs frame. |

Helpful resources for analyzing grammatical and syntactical items as well as rhetorical features include:

- D. B. Wallace, *Greek Grammar Beyond the Basics* (Grand Rapids, MI: Zondervan, 1996).

- F. Blass, A. Debrunner, and R. W. Funk, *A Greek Grammar of the New Testament and Other Early Christian Literature* (Chicago: University of Chicago Press, 1961).

## Word Study

Every passage will include one or more words that are unclear or ambiguous, and yet theologically important. Since every word has a range of meaning, the first step is to focus its meaning in the context of the passage under study. Some words will require further study to illumine their meaning. These two aspects of word study involve slightly different procedures.

### Focus the Meaning

The process of focusing a word's meaning involves four steps. First, use a concordance to collect the uses of the word in Paul's letters. Second, classify the uses into an inductively developed range of

meaning. Third, summarize the word's range of meaning in Paul's letters. Fourth, determine the nuance from the range of meaning that best
fits the context of the passage under study.

Moving away from Romans 5:1–2, the noun κοινωνία in Philippians
3:10 will serve as a useful example. In addition to this verse, κοινωνία occurs twelve times in Paul's letters.[16] Those twelve uses fall naturally into
three categories of meaning: (1) association *with* something or someone
(five times), (2) contribution *to* something or someone (four times), and
(3) participation *in* something or someone (three times). The nuance
of association is slightly more common but not overwhelmingly so. In
Philippians 3:10 the noun is part of the genitive construction κοινωνίαν
παθημάτων αὐτοῦ. Although it is possible to see κοινωνία in this verse as
the fellowship (close association) that believers enjoy because of Christ's
suffering for them (subjective genitive), it seems more likely that Paul is
referring to the participation in Christ's sufferings (objective genitive)
that results from being found "in Him" (3:9).[17]

## Illumine the Meaning

Illumining the meaning of a word involves finding background uses
of the word, either in the Old Testament or in extrabiblical literature.
First, use a lexicon or theological dictionary to identify ancient source
references that use the word. Second, locate one or more ancient source
references and record enough of the immediate context to be helpful in
preaching or teaching the passage. Third, comment on how knowing
the word's background contributes to understanding the passage.

Bringing the study of κοινωνία to this level adds interesting texture to
an understanding of the word. A check of five ancient source references
in which use of the word occurs provides the following results:

| | |
|---|---|
| Wisdom of Solomon 6:16 | in the κοινωνία of her words, a good report |
| 3 Maccabees 4:6 | to enjoy the κοινωνία of marriage |
| Josephus, *Ant.* 2.62 | in accordance with the κοινωνία of similar benefit |
| Appian, *Civil Wars* 1.67 | by reason of their κοινωνία in the present enterprise |
| Appian, *Civil Wars* 5.71 | in order to be admitted to the κοινωνία of the government |

16.   Rom. 15:26; 1 Cor. 1:9; 10:16 (twice); 2 Cor. 6:14; 8:4; 9:13; 13:13; Gal. 2:9; Phil. 1:5; 2:1;
       Philem. 6

17.   The idea, therefore, is parallel to "becoming like him in his death" in 3:10 (cf. Rom. 8:17;
       Gal. 6:17).

These extrabiblical uses demonstrate that κοινωνία carries the idea of active participation in an activity or enterprise, sharing the responsibilities as well as the benefits. When Paul speaks of the "fellowship" of Christ's sufferings, he is speaking not solely of the positive benefits derived from those sufferings (where we tend to focus) but also of his willingness to suffer for the sake of Christ. He is so closely identified with Christ that he is willing to suffer as Jesus did if that is what is required of him (cf. 2 Cor. 1:5; 4:10; Col. 1:24; 1 Pet. 4:13). Just as marriage partners (3 Macc. 4:6) share in the good times and the bad times together, so Paul shares in both the benefits and the sufferings brought about by his relationship to Christ. Just as business partners (Appian 1.67) share in the profit and loss resulting from their enterprise together, so Paul shares in both the blessings and the challenges of his κοινωνία with Christ.

Helpful resources for word study include concordances, lexicons, and theological dictionaries:

## Concordances

- J. R. Kohlenberger, E. W. Goodrick, and J. A. Swanson, *The Exhaustive Concordance to the Greek New Testament* (Grand Rapids, MI: Zondervan, 1995).

- G. V. Wigram, *The Englishman's Greek Concordance of the New Testament* (Peabody, MA: Hendrickson, 1996).

## Lexicons

- W. Bauer, W. F. Arndt, F. W. Gingrich, and F. W. Danker, *A Greek-English Lexicon of the New Testament and Other Early Christian Literature*, third edition (Chicago: University of Chicago Press, 2000).

- J. P. Louw and E. A. Nida, *A Greek-English Lexicon of the New Testament Based on Semantic Domains*, 2nd edition, 2 volumes (New York: United Bible Societies, 1989).

## Theological Dictionaries

- C. Brown, ed., The *New International Dictionary of New Testament Theology*, 4 volumes (Grand Rapids, MI: Zondervan, 1986).

- G. Kittel and G. Friedrich, eds., *Theological Dictionary of the New Testament*, 10 volumes (Grand Rapids, MI: Eerdmans, 1964–73).

## THEOLOGICAL ANALYSIS

Because God has inspired all Scripture, it is both unified and coherent. Every passage will fit into the overall teaching of Scripture, and it is important to place that passage within the theological context of divine revelation. Doing so involves both the analogy of Scripture and the analogy of faith. A related topic is the use of the Old Testament in the New Testament.

## The Analogy of Scripture

"Biblical theology" examines the way in which a given passage relates to parallel, similar, and contrasting passages elsewhere in the Bible. Cross references in a study Bible are the best starting points for identifying passages that might contribute to an understanding of the passage under study. After collecting at least two or three passages that are parallel, similar, or contrasting, write a succinct summary of the way in which each of those passages enhances the interpretation of the main passage.

The UBS4 also has a helpful cross-reference system at the bottom of each page as well as an index of allusions and verbal parallels. The cross references listed for 2 Corinthians 3:7–11, for example, include two Old Testament passages that shed light on Paul's discussion of the contrast between the old and new covenants. Exodus 34:29–35 describes Moses' descent from the mountain with a glowing face. Deuteronomy 27:26 records the final curse that was to be recited by the Israelites on Mount Ebal and Mount Gerizim when the new generation entered Canaan. The former passage provides the background for Paul's allusion to Moses' glowing face (2 Cor. 3:7); the latter passage helps explain how the old covenant was a "ministry of condemnation" (2 Cor. 3:9).

Works on New Testament theology are also helpful resources when considering the analogy of Scripture:

- G. E. Ladd, *A Theology of the New Testament*, 2nd edition (Grand Rapids, MI: Eerdmans, 1993).

- I. H. Marshall, *New Testament Theology: Many Witnesses, One Gospel* (Downers Grove, IL: InterVarsity Press, 2004).

- T. R. Schreiner, *New Testament Theology: Magnifying God in Christ* (Grand Rapids, MI: Baker, 2008).

- R. B. Zuck, ed., *A Biblical Theology of the New Testament* (Chicago: Moody, 1994).

## The Analogy of Faith

"Systematic theology" examines the way in which the passage under study relates to major doctrines of the Bible (e.g., bibliology, Christology, soteriology). The indices of systematic theology texts are helpful starting points to identify the primary doctrine to which a given passage relates. Often, it will be possible to identify several doctrines that apply, but time constraints will determine how many of them can be explored. Writing a concise summary of the way in which the passage under study contributes to the biblical teaching on the primary doctrine provides an opportunity to think theologically about the passage's place in the overall teaching of Scripture.

| Major Categories of Systematic Theology | |
| --- | --- |
| • Prolegomena | • Christology |
| • Bibliology | • Soteriology |
| • Theology Proper | • Pneumatology |
| • Anthropology | • Ecclesiology |
| • Hamartiology | • Eschatology |

Paul's discussion of the new covenant in 2 Corinthians 3:1–11, for example, contributes to the doctrines of pneumatology and ecclesiology. In that passage, Paul highlights the Spirit's role in the internal administration of the new covenant. He also makes clear the new covenant's continuity with—but clear superiority over—the old covenant. Both the ministry of believers under the new covenant and the role of the Spirit in administering that covenant are superior to but not totally discontinuous with the arrangements that were in place under the old covenant.[18]

Works on systematic theology are helpful resources when considering the analogy of faith:

- M. J. Erickson, *Christian Theology* (Grand Rapids, MI: Baker, 1989).

- W. A. Grudem, *Systematic Theology: An Introduction to Biblical Doctrine* (Grand Rapids, MI: Zondervan, 1994).

- R. L. Reymond, *A New Systematic Theology of the Christian Faith* (Nashville: Nelson, 1998).

---

18.  For further discussion of this passage, see J. D. Harvey, *Anointed with the Spirit and Power: The Holy Spirit's Empowering Presence* (Phillipsburg, NJ: P&R Publishing, 2008), 157–61.

## Use of the Old Testament in the New Testament

The use of the Old Testament in the New Testament is a complex topic, and a detailed discussion is beyond the scope of this book.[19] It is possible, though, to sketch the basic outlines of the topic, including different forms of dependence, primary functions of quotations, and common evangelical approaches. The USB4 includes an excellent index of quotations in both Old and New Testament order that serves as a good starting point for identifying passages to examine.

There are four ways in which a New Testament passage can depend on the Old Testament. A *direct quotation* is a verbatim citation from the Old Testament, frequently introduced with an introductory formula. For example, Romans 1:17 includes a verbatim citation of Habakkuk 2:4. *Allusion* involves clauses, phrases, or words that recall a key passage, theme, or incident in the Old Testament. For example, 1 Corinthians 11:8–9 refers to the Genesis account of creation without citing it directly. A *summary* is an abbreviated account of Old Testament history or teaching. For example, 1 Corinthians 10:1–13 provides a brief account of Israel's wilderness wanderings in Exodus and Numbers. *Style* involves the use of phraseology or syntax reflecting that of the Old Testament. For example, Luke's repeated use of ἐγένετο δὲ appears to be a deliberate imitation of Septuagintal narrative style (e.g., Luke 1:8; 2:1).

New Testament authors may use Old Testament quotations in any of four ways. When an author cites an Old Testament passage as predicting an event or situation in the life of Jesus or the early church, the passage has a *fulfillment* function (e.g., Isa. 61:1–2 in Luke 4:17–21). The function is one of *analogy* when an author cites an Old Testament passage as foreshadowing a New Testament aspect of God's redemptive activity (e.g., Gen. 12:3 in Gal. 3:8–9). An Old Testament passage functions to give *proof* if an author cites it to support a New Testament doctrinal teaching (e.g., Ps. 32:1–2 in Rom. 4:5–8). When an author cites an Old Testament passage as teaching a mandate or principle that New Testament believers are to adopt in their lives, the passage has an *application* function (e.g., Ps. 4:4 in Eph. 4:26).

Several approaches to the use of the Old Testament in the New Testament have been identified, but two are most common among evangelical interpreters.[20] The first approach may be described as *full human intent*. It holds that the intent of the human author is *identical* to the divine intent and, therefore, the Old Testament author would have

---

19. A helpful resource for this topic is G. K. Beale and D. A. Carson, eds., *Commentary on the New Testament Use of the Old* (Grand Rapids, MI: Baker, 2007).

20. For a useful, although somewhat older overview, see D. L. Bock, "Evangelicals and the Use of the Old Testament in the New," *Bibliotheca Sacra* (1985): 209–23, 306–19.

understood the New Testament author's use of the passage. The second approach may be described as *divine intent-human words*.[21] It holds that the intent of the human author is *linked* to the divine intent, but the Old Testament author would not necessarily have understood the New Testament author's use of the passage. Both approaches seek to resolve one of the theological challenges raised by the divine-human authorship of Scripture while recognizing both its unity and coherence.

## THE *ABC*s OF EXEGESIS

Exegesis is the most intensive and detailed step in the process of interpreting Paul's letters. It is also an essential step to arriving at an accurate understanding of his message, for three reasons. First, each of Paul's letters had its origins in his personal and ministry circumstances, and was addressed to readers living in a historical-cultural-religious context that was different from those in which twenty-first-century readers live. Historical analysis, therefore, is essential to understanding both the general historical-cultural-religious context and the specific circumstances of both Paul and his readers. Second, each of Paul's letters is a literary document that uses standard conventions of context, genre, structure, grammar, syntax, rhetoric, and word meaning to communicate. Literary analysis, therefore, is essential to establishing an accurate understanding of a passage's message. Third, each of Paul's letters is part of the canon of Scripture that, because it is divinely inspired, has both unity and coherence. Theological analysis, therefore, is essential to setting individual passages within the overall teaching of Scripture.

Together, historical analysis, literary analysis, and theological analysis comprise the *ABC*s of exegesis. Once the detailed work of exegesis is completed, the focus shifts to the tasks of synthesis, appropriation, and homiletical packaging. Those tasks are the topic of Chapter 6.

---

21. This approach is sometimes known as *sensius plenior*, or "fuller meaning."

# The Chapter in Review

Interpreting a passage in Paul's letters requires close attention to its historical, literary, and theological aspects. It is important to consider which aspects of a letter's introductory matters might contribute to a better understanding of the passage, and what historical-cultural-religious research might shed light on details of the passage. It is equally important to consider the passage's context—both its place in the letter's overall argument and its relationship to the paragraphs that immediately precede and follow it—structure, and syntax, as well as key words that occur within the passage. Finally, it is important to consider the ways in which parallel, similar, and contrasting passages contribute to understanding the passage under study and the ways in which the passage contributes to the overall teaching of Scripture.

# COMMUNICATING PASSAGES IN PAUL'S LETTERS

## The Chapter at a Glance

- Formulating the passage's central point and identifying its shared need constitute the task of synthesis.

- Appropriating the message of the passage explores the way it connects to the contemporary audience, the attitudes and actions it corrects, and the attitudes and actions it commends.

- Developing a clear objective and crafting a take-home truth help focus the applied truth of the passage.

- Using a variety of sermon patterns serves listeners who hear and process truth differently.

AFTER COMPLETING THE DETAILED ANALYTICAL work of exegesis, the focus turns to the "big picture" synthetic work of **exposition**. As there were three areas to consider in exegesis, there are three steps to take in exposition. The steps are first-century synthesis, twenty-first-century appropriation, and homiletical packaging. This chapter will consider each step in turn.

# FIRST-CENTURY SYNTHESIS

Exegesis determines the "expository unit," which Bryan Chapell defines as "a large or small portion of Scripture from which the preacher can demonstrate a single spiritual truth, with adequate supporting facts or concepts arising within the scope of the text."[1] In Paul's letters, the expository unit will most commonly be one paragraph, although at times it might extend to two or three paragraphs. Since the objective of exposition is to communicate accurately the message of the expository unit, it is essential to identify that message and to recognize the need Paul sought to address by including that message in his work. The work of synthesis, therefore, addresses two questions: (1) What did Paul say? (2) Why did he say it? The first question seeks to isolate the central point of the passage; the second seeks to establish the shared need of the passage.

## The Central Point of the Passage

Haddon Robinson suggests that every expository unit communicates a single "big idea," consisting of two parts: a **homiletical subject** and a **homiletical complement**.[2] The homiletical subject answers the question, What is the author talking about? The homiletical complement answers the question, What is the author saying about what he is talking about? Together, the subject and complement comprise a single sentence that communicates the central point of the passage. Moving outward from Robinson's big idea, it is also worth noting that the passage's central point develops a narrow aspect of a broader *topic* (e.g., suffering, salvation, service), since no single expository unit can cover every aspect of a topic. Formulating the central point of a passage, therefore, consists of four steps:

1. Identify the general topic addressed.

2. Determine the subject—the narrower aspect of the topic developed in the passage.

3. Clarify the complement—what the passage says about the subject.

4. Summarize the central point—a single sentence consisting of the subject and complement.

---

1. B. Chapell, *Christ-centered Preaching: Redeeming the Expository Sermon* (Grand Rapids: Baker, 1994), 53.

2. H. W. Robinson, *Biblical Preaching: the Development and Delivery of Expository Messages*, second edition (Grand Rapids: Baker, 2001), 31–48.

First Thessalonians 2:17–20 will serve as an example:

> But we, brethren, having been taken away from you for a short
> while—in person, not in spirit—were all the more eager with great
> desire to see your face. For we wanted to come to you—I, Paul, more
> than once—and yet Satan hindered us. For who is our hope or joy or
> crown of exultation? Is it not even you, in the presence of our Lord
> Jesus at His coming? For you are our glory and joy.

What general topic is Paul addressing in this passage? The overall
topic of the first three chapters of the letter is Paul's relationship with
the Thessalonians. In 1:1–10, he remembers their response to the message he, Silas, and Timothy preached in Thessalonica. In 2:1–16, he
reviews his conduct as he labored among them. In 2:17–3:13, he re-
calls both his concern over their well-being and his joy when Timothy
brought good news about their faith and love.

What narrower aspect of the topic (subject) does Paul address in the passage? After being fairly objective in reporting his
own ministry and the Thessalonians' response to that ministry,
the tone of Paul's writing becomes more personal beginning in
2:17. He speaks of being "orphaned" from them (ἀπορφανισθέ-
ντες ἀφ᾽ ὑμῶν) and of being "exceedingly diligent" in trying to see
them (περισσοτέρως ἐσπουδάσαμεν τὸ πρόσωπον ὑμῶν ἰδεῖν). He describes them as his "hope" (ἐλπὶς), his "glory" (δόξα), his "crown
of boasting" (στέφανος καυχήσεως), and twice as his "joy" (χαρά).
This language clearly expresses the depth of Paul's affection for
the Thessalonians.

What does Paul say about that subject in the passage (complement)?
A structural analysis makes it clear that the paragraph divides naturally
in two parts. The first part (2:17–18) describes Paul's desire to see them
and his attempts to see them in the face of Satan's opposition. The second part (2:19–20) expresses his joy in knowing them—they are his
hope, joy, glory, and crown of boasting.

What single sentence communicates the central point of the passage?
Combining the subject and the complement yields the passage's central point. In this instance the central point may be stated this way:
The depth of Paul's affection for the Thessalonians (subject) can be
measured by his desire to be with them and his joy in knowing them
(complement).

| Formulating the Central Point of 1 Thessalonians 2:17–20 | |
| --- | --- |
| Topic: | Paul's relationship with the Thessalonians |
| Subject: | The depth of Paul's affection for the Thessalonians |
| Complement: | It can be measured by two emotions: his desire to be with them (2:17–18) and his joy in knowing them (2:19–20). |
| Central Point: | The depth of Paul's affection for the Thessalonians can be measured by his desire to be with them and his joy in knowing them. |

## The Shared Need of the Passage

Knowing *what* Paul said in a passage is an important starting point, but it is also important to know *why* he said it. What need was he seeking to address by including this particular message in this particular letter? Chapell argues that every expository unit has a purpose that addresses a deep human need.[3] Because Scripture is divinely-inspired, it is also timeless. The twenty-first-century audience shares the same need that the original first-century audience experienced. Identifying the shared need of the passage, therefore, helps build a bridge between Paul's original audience and the twenty-first-century audience. Formulating that shared need consists of two steps:

1. Isolate the need(s) the text addressed in its historical and literary context.

2. Determine the need(s) the contemporary listeners share with the original audience.

First Thessalonians 2:17–20 will again serve as an example. (See the translation above.)

What need was Paul addressing when he wrote this paragraph to the Thessalonians? They were facing persecution at the hands of their countrymen (2:14–15). Paul had only been able to spend a short time with them before Jewish opposition drove him from the city (2:16; cf. Acts 17:1–9). He had been forced to abandon them in their time of need.

---

3. He calls it "the fallen condition focus," (Chapell, *Christ-centered Preaching*, 40–4).

Did his continuing absence reflect indifference toward them? Why had he not returned to visit them? Whatever their precise thoughts and feelings, Paul believed they needed assurance that he loved them and was proud of them. He sought to address that need by telling them of his desire to be with them and his delight in knowing them.

What need does the twenty-first-century audience share with the Thessalonians? Answering that question does not require a lengthy search. Contemporary followers of Christ also face difficulties of varying sorts and severity. Those difficulties might involve persecution such as the Thessalonians faced; they might involve isolation or ostracism; they might involve the loss of a loved one. Whatever the precise difficulties they are facing, members of the twenty-first-century audience also need to be assured that others in the body of Christ care for them and support them. Both audiences share a mutual need for assurance from those who know and love them.

| Identifying the Shared Need of 1 Thessalonians 2:17–20 | |
| --- | --- |
| Original Need: | In the midst of their persecution, the Thessalonians needed assurance that Paul wanted to see them and was proud to know them. |
| Shared Need: | In the midst of our difficulties, we need assurance that others in the body of Christ love us and support us. |

## TWENTY-FIRST-CENTURY APPROPRIATION

Identifying the need the contemporary audience shares with the original audience begins the process of moving the passage's message from "then" to "now." The twenty-first-century appropriation of the message answers three questions: (1) How does the passage *connect* with today's audience? (2) What contemporary attitudes and actions does the passage *correct*? (3) What ways of thinking and/or acting does the passage *commend* to today's audience?[4]

## How Does the Passage Connect?

Every passage contains words, ideas, or images to which people today can readily relate. The task is, first, to note those potential points of contact between the passage and the listeners and, then, to determine how to use them to connect with the listeners. The introduction of a

---

4. See Larkin, *Greek is Great Gain*, 230–4.

sermon or lesson is an obvious place where one or more points of contact can be used profitably. In 1 Thessalonians 2:17–20, two possible points of contact that may be used are the experience of being separated from friends and/or family, and the desire to see a loved one. Either (or both) of these items could be used to introduce a sermon or lesson on the passage. For example:

> Have you ever been separated from someone you love? Perhaps it was a family member. Perhaps it was a boyfriend or a girlfriend. Perhaps it was someone with whom you had shared something special. Have you ever longed to be reunited with that person, but haven't been able to be with him or her? If you have, then you know exactly how Paul felt in 1 Thessalonians 2:17–20.

## What Does the Passage Correct?

Because humankind is fallen and creation has been affected by sin, every passage of Scripture includes ideas, beliefs, values, structures, and/or behavior patterns that run counter to—and therefore judge—contemporary culture.[5] Identifying the ways in which a passage judges contemporary attitudes and actions also makes it possible to articulate how those attitudes and actions can be corrected so they are in line with the teaching of Scripture. These aspects of a passage lead naturally to the task of application. First Thessalonians 2:17–20, for example, corrects western independence and individualism. It judges a "Lone-Ranger Christian" mentality and any tendency to neglect the church as the community of believers. It reminds us that we need one another, and that we have an obligation to encourage and support one another in good times and in bad.

## What Does the Passage Commend?

In addition to correcting contemporary culture, every passage also commends thought forms and behavior patterns that meet human needs in God's way and for his glory.[6] Identifying the ways in which a passage addresses real and felt needs introduces the "good news" for the listeners. It also makes it possible to articulate how those thought forms and behavior patterns can be adopted to live a life that demonstrates increasing growth toward the image of Christ. In the case of 1 Thessalonians 2:17–20, the good news is that God has provided a way to meet the

---

5. See Larkin, *Greek is Great Gain*, 233.

6. Ibid., 234. Chapell speaks of this aspect in terms of the way God's grace reveals itself to meet humankind's need (*Christ-centered Preaching*, 301–2).

human needs to feel part of a community, to feel loved and supported, and to feel missed when separated from loved ones. In light of that good news, we should seek to build deeper relationships with other believers so they know where to turn for support and help in times of need. In thinking about applying both the good news and the bad news of a passage, it is important to be as specific and concrete as possible to help listeners connect the truth of the passage to their own lives.

| Appropriating the Message of a Passage | |
| --- | --- |
| Connect: | To what ideas, words, or images can people today readily relate? |
| Correct: | What ideas, beliefs, values, or behaviors does the passage judge? |
| Commend: | What thought forms and behavior patterns promote God's glory and humankind's good? |

## HOMILETICAL PACKAGING

Expository preaching is often understood as moving verse by verse through a passage while explaining the historical, literary, and theological truths found in it. Donald Hamilton, however, offers a different definition. He suggests that expository preaching is best understood as "allow[ing] the text of Scripture to make its own statement about truth and then apply[ing] that truth to the lives of the hearers."[7] Randy Pope comes at the topic from a slightly different perspective but arrives at the same conclusion. He proposes that the goal of expository preaching is "to aim at a personal life . . . while bringing God's truth to bear upon its need."[8]

Understanding the truth in a passage from one of Paul's letters is the task of exegesis. Considering how that truth applies to the needs of men and women today is the task of synthesis and appropriation. Determining the best way to communicate the applied truth of a passage to a group of listeners is the task of homiletics. Numerous excellent books have been written on the topic of sermon preparation and delivery. The goal in the next few pages is simply to highlight several aspects of homiletical packaging that might be helpful in communicat-

---

7. D. L. Hamilton, *Homiletical Handbook*, (Nashville: Broadman & Holman, 1992), 28.

8. R. P. Pope, *The Prevailing Church: An Alternative Approach to Ministry* (Chicago: Moody, 2002), 197.

ing passages in Paul's letters.

## The "One Thing" Listeners Need to Know (and Do)

Andy Stanley argues passionately that "every message should have one central idea, application, insight, or principle that serves as the glue to hold the other parts together."[9] To identify that central idea, he suggests asking two questions:[10]

1. What is the one thing I want my audience to know?

2. What do I want them to do about it?

Note that Stanley's central idea, therefore, involves both information *and* application. It is more than a statement of truth; it is a call to put the truth into action. It is more than Robinson's "big idea," and it is more than the "central point" discussed earlier in this chapter. This *homiletical* central idea (sometimes called the sermon's "proposition") envisions the action the listeners will take in response to the truth of the passage. Another way of approaching this concept is to formulate a sermon (or lesson) objective:

> I want my listeners to understand _____[truth]_____,
>
> so that they will _____[action]_____.

The steps of first-century synthesis and twenty-first-century appropriation should already have supplied the information needed to develop an objective. Formulating the central point provides the truth the listeners should understand. Identifying the shared need focuses the area of life that should be addressed. Appropriating the message highlights the attitudes and actions that should be corrected and/or adopted. Together, these steps make it possible to develop a sermon objective that grows naturally out of the passage itself.

---

9. A. Stanley and L. Jones, *Communicating for a Change* (Colorado Springs: Multnomah, 2006), 103.

10. Ibid., 104.

| Developing a Sermon Objective for 1 Thessalonians 2:17–20 |
| --- |

| | |
| --- | --- |
| Central Point: | The depth of Paul's affection for the Thessalonians can be measured by his desire to be with them and his joy in knowing them. |
| Shared Need: | In the midst of our difficulties, we need assurance that others in the body of Christ love us and support us. |
| Correct: | Paul's concern for the Thessalonians judges Western attitudes of independence and individualism, as well as any tendency to neglect the community of believers. |
| Commend: | Paul's concern for the Thessalonians challenges us to build deeper relationships with other believers so they know where to turn for support and help in times of need. |
| Objective: | I want my listeners to understand the depth of Paul's affection for the Thessalonians, so that they will commit to building deeper relationships with other believers. |

With a sermon objective in place, the next step is crafting what Donald Sunukjian calls the **take-home truth**.[11] The take-home truth is a succinct memorable statement that summarizes the message the listeners will "take home" with them.[12] Such a statement can take any number of forms, but it is designed to help the listeners remember the central idea of the sermon. Here are three examples.

- From Psalm 90, which enjoins us to "number our days":[13]
  » Count your days to make your days count.

- From Naaman's encounter with Elisha in 2 Kings 5:[14]
  » To understand why: Submit and apply.

- From Paul's enumeration of spiritual blessings in Ephesians 1:3–14:
  » Count your blessings; then praise God.

---

11.  D. R. Sunukjian, *Introduction to Biblical Preaching: Proclaiming Truth with Clarity and Relevance* (Grand Rapids: Kregel, 2007), 136–41.

12.  Stanley addresses the same idea when he challenges his readers to "Make it stick" (*Communicating for a Change*, 110–1).

13.  Sunukjian, *Introduction to Biblical Preaching*, 140.

14.  Stanley, *Communicating for a Change*, 11.

One possible take-home truth for 1 Thessalonians 2:17–20 might be "The deeper your love, the greater your joy."

## Structuring the Sermon

Paul himself wrote, "All Scripture is inspired by God and profitable for teaching, for reproof, for correction, for training in righteousness" (2 Tim. 3:16). For that reason, as Pope notes, the ultimate goal of interpreting Paul's letters (and all Scripture) is to bring the truth of a passage to bear on the lives of men and women. Preaching is one way of pursuing that goal, and focusing each sermon on a central idea makes it more likely that the goal is reached. Ideally, the introduction will lead to the central idea, the illustrations and applications will all relate to the central idea, and the conclusion will bring the central idea to bear on the listener's life in a memorable way.

Focusing a sermon on a central idea, however, does not restrict the strategies that may be used in structuring it. There are two basic approaches to structuring a sermon: deductive and inductive. A **deductive sermon** begins with the central idea and proceeds to "prove" that proposition by presenting evidence in support of it. It moves from

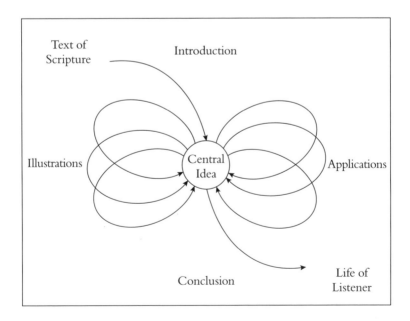

general truth to specific instances. In contrast, an **inductive sermon** moves from specific instances to a general truth. It leads the listeners through the evidence to arrive at the central idea.

| Deductive Approach | Inductive Approach |
| --- | --- |
| Introduction | Introduction |
| Central Idea / Proposition | Point 1 |
| Point 1 | Point 2 |
| Point 2 | Point 3 |
| Point 3 | Central Idea / Proposition |
| Conclusion | Conclusion |

Both approaches have advantages and disadvantages. The deductive approach, for example, has the advantage of alerting the listeners to the central idea at the beginning of the sermon and leading them through the evidence to a clear destination. Some listeners, however, might lose interest in what they see as a dogmatic presentation of a preconceived conclusion. On the other hand, the inductive approach has the advantage of allowing the listeners to interact mentally with the sermon and reach their own tentative conclusion. It also has the disadvantage that some listeners might become frustrated because they do not know the ultimate destination. Since congregations are composed of men and women who hear and process truth differently, the wise communicator will incorporate both deductive and inductive approaches and will utilize a variety of sermon patterns. Fortunately, both basic approaches can be structured using more than one pattern.

*Deductive Patterns*

Hamilton highlights two common deductive patterns: the "keyword" pattern and the "analytical" pattern.[15] The keyword pattern is used with a text that includes two or more parallel constructions or ideas related in the same way to the same subject. For example, the structural analysis of a passage might highlight the fact that it includes four hortatory subjunctives, in which case the logical keyword would be "exhortations."[16] The analytical pattern is used with a text that includes two or more aspects of a subject that are not parallel. For example, a passage might consist of a command, the reason for the command, and

---

15. Hamilton, *Homiletical Handbook*, 39–67.

16. Note that the "keyword" is not the most important word in the passage but, rather, a plural noun that describes each of the parallel main points.

the means by which the command can be obeyed (e.g., the "what," the "why," and the "how").

In either case, the starting point for structuring the sermon is the structure of the passage itself, and the exegetical work done on the passage informs the structure of the sermon. Ephesians 3:14–19 provides an interesting case study:[17]

> Because of this, I am bowing my knees to the Father, from whom every family in heaven and on earth is being named, that (ἵνα) He might give to you, according to the riches of His glory, to be strengthened with power through His Spirit in the inner man, for Christ to dwell in your hearts through faith, having been rooted and grounded in love, that (ἵνα) you might be fully able to comprehend with all the saints what is the breadth and length and height and depth, and to know the love of Christ that is surpassing knowledge, that (ἵνα) you might be filled to all the fulness of God.

One of the prominent grammatical aspects of this passage is the presence of three clauses introduced by the subordinate conjunction ἵνα: "that He might give . . ." (ἵνα δῷ . . .), "that you might be fully able . . ." (ἵνα ἐξισχύσητε . . .), and "that you might be filled . . ." (ἵνα πληρωθῆτε . . .). The question, however, is whether these three clauses are better viewed as parallel or subordinate to one another. In other words, which of the following abbreviated structural layouts is more likely?

Τούτου χάριν κάμπτω τὰ γόνατά μου πρὸς τὸν πατέρα . . .
   ↑ ἵνα δῷ ὑμῖν κατὰ τὸ πλοῦτος τῆς δόξης αὐτοῦ . . .
   ↑ ἵνα ἐξισχύσητε καταλαβέσθαι σὺν πᾶσιν τοῖς ἁγίοις . . .
   ↑ ἵνα πληρωθῆτε εἰς πᾶν τὸ πλήρωμα τοῦ θεοῦ.

Τούτου χάριν κάμπτω τὰ γόνατά μου πρὸς τὸν πατέρα . . .
   ↑ ἵνα δῷ ὑμῖν κατὰ τὸ πλοῦτος τῆς δόξης αὐτοῦ . . .
      ↑ ἵνα ἐξισχύσητε καταλαβέσθαι σὺν πᾶσιν τοῖς ἁγίοις
      . . .
         ↑ ἵνα πληρωθῆτε εἰς πᾶν τὸ πλήρωμα τοῦ θεοῦ.

If the three clauses are parallel, they represent three "requests" that Paul prays for the Ephesians and the sermon would fit the keyword pattern. If, however, the clauses are subordinate, they most likely represent the request, the purpose of the request, and the result anticipated. The second layout points to a sermon that would fit the analytical pattern.

---

17.  Author's translation

Although the specific patterns used would be different, the approach in both instances would be deductive.

| Deductive Approaches to Ephesians 3:14–19 | |
| --- | --- |
| **Keyword Pattern** | **Analytical Pattern** |
| When we pray for the spiritual growth of others, Paul's requests for the Ephesians give us a model.<br>1. He prayed that they would be strengthened by the Spirit's power.<br>2. He prayed that they would comprehend Christ's love.<br>3. He prayed that they would be filled with the Father's fullness. | Analyzing how Paul prayed for the Ephesians will challenge us to follow his example.<br>1. The request: They will experience the Spirit's enabling.<br>2. The purpose: They will comprehend Christ's work in his Church.<br>3. The result: They will appreciate all the Father intends for them. |

## Inductive Patterns

There are also a number of patterns that can be used to structure a sermon inductively. Narrative sermons are inherently inductive, for example, because they tell a story to make a point and that point makes the greatest impact when it comes at the end of the narrative.[18] Galatians 1:11–2:21 is one passage from Paul's letters that lends itself to a narrative approach, since it provides an account of his ministry during the Damascus-Arabia period (A.D. 34–37) and the Syria-Cilicia period (A.D. 37–48). Other inductive patterns include using specific examples from a passage and asking a series of rhetorical questions that are answered either positively (affirmation) or negatively (rebuttal).[19]

An inductive sermon using specific examples from 1 Corinthians 15:12–20 might look like this:

---

18. J. M. Webb argues that preaching any inductive sermon is like telling a story (*Preaching Without Notes* [Nashville: Abindgon, 2001], 28–9).

19. See Hamilton, *Homiletical Handbook*, 99–100.

| Inductive Approach to 1 Corinthians 15:12–20 (Specific Examples) | | |
|---|---|---|
| Thematic Question: | What difference does Christ's resurrection make? | |
| Main Points: | 1. It means our faith has a focus. | (15:14c, 17b) |
| | 2. It means our ministries have meaning. | (15:14b) |
| | 3. It means our witness has worth. | (15:17c) |
| | 4. It means our sins have a solution. | (15:18) |
| | 5. It means our hearts have hope. | (15:19) |
| Proposition: | Christ's resurrection makes all the difference in the world! | |

Romans 4:1–25 could serve as a basis for an inductive sermon using a rebuttal approach.

| Inductive Approach to Romans 4:1–25 (Rebuttal) | | |
|---|---|---|
| Thematic Question: | What does Abraham's experience teach us about why God considers a person righteous? | |
| Main Points: | 1. What role do human works play? None! | (4:1–8) (4:9–12) |
| | 2. What role does religious ritual play? None! | (4:13–25) |
| | 3. What role does law-keeping play? None! | |
| Proposition: | God considers us righteous solely on the basis of faith. | |

Both inductive and deductive approaches can be highly effective. The key is matching the structure of the sermon to the structure of the passage and finding the most persuasive way to bring the overall truth of the passage to bear on the life of the listeners. A mix of inductive and deductive approaches appropriate to the audience will assist in reaching the broadest possible spectrum of listeners.

## BUILDING THE BRIDGE BETWEEN TWO WORLDS

In his book on preaching, John Stott uses the image of the preacher standing "between two worlds."[20] Together, the tasks of exegesis and exposition make it possible to build the bridge between those worlds. Exegesis is the analytical work of understanding what Paul was trying to communicate to the churches and individuals who received his letters while giving proper attention to the historical, literary, and theological contexts of those letters. In particular, exegesis addresses the first-century message. Exposition is the synthetic work of moving the first-century message into the twenty-first-century world.

The work of exposition begins by seeking to formulate the central point of the passage and to isolate the original need the passage addressed. It moves beyond the first-century world, however, to determine the need(s) contemporary listeners share with the original audience. Along with the shared need, it is important to relate the passage's message to the twenty-first-century audience in more specific ways. That task of appropriation considers how the passage connects, what it corrects, and what it commends. Finally, developing a sermon objective and crafting a take-home truth bring focus to the sermon and state it in a memorable way before structuring the sermon to follow either a deductive or an inductive approach.

Exposition completes the process that began with textual criticism. Textual criticism establishes what the text is; translation establishes what the text says. Exegesis uses historical, literary, and theological analysis to understand the message Paul was seeking to communicate. Exposition uses synthesis, appropriation, and homiletical packaging to touch the lives of listeners with that message. Chapter 7 provides detailed examples of moving from text to sermon using two passages from Paul's letters.

---

20. J. R. W. Stott, *Between Two Worlds: The Art of Preaching in the Twentieth Century* (Grand Rapids: Eerdmans, 1982).

## The Chapter in Review

Exposition is the natural sequel to exegesis. Exposition involves the tasks of synthesis, appropriation, and homiletical packing. Each is essential in preparing to communicate a passage from one of Paul's letters.

Synthesis asks the questions, What did Paul say? and Why did he say it? The answers to those questions identify the passage's central point and shared need.

Appropriation moves the message of the passage from the first century to the twenty-first century. It seeks to answer three questions: How does the passage connect? What does the passage correct? What does the passage commend?

Homiletical packaging brings the message of the passage to bear on the lives of listeners by asking, What "one thing" do the listeners need to know and do? and How can I structure the sermon to communicate that 'one thing' most effectively?

# 7

# FROM TEXT TO SERMON: TWO EXAMPLES

## The Chapter at a Glance

- Paul had never visited the church and Colossae, but he had received a report that it was being influenced by false teachers who leaned heavily on human tradition and philosophy. How does he address that situation in Colossians 3:1–4, and how does what he writes relate to our lives today?

- The Philippians knew Paul well and had followed his ministry closely. From prison, he shared with them valuable insight on living the Christian life. How does he motivate both them and us to pursue Christ by what he wrote about his own experience in Philippians 3:12–16?

CHAPTERS 4–6 SET OUT A PROCESS FOR INTERPRETING and communicating passages in Paul's letters. First, textual criticism and translation establish the text. Then, exegesis analyzes the message the first-century author communicated to his original audience. Exposition then builds a bridge to twenty-first-century listeners and packages the message in a way that makes it both memorable and practical. This chapter applies the entire process to Colossians 3:1–4 and Philippians 3:12–16 as case studies.

## COLOSSIANS 3:1–4

Εἰ οὖν συνηγέρθητε τῷ Χριστῷ, τὰ ἄνω ζητεῖτε, οὗ ὁ Χριστός
ἐστιν ἐν δεξιᾷ τοῦ θεοῦ καθήμενος· τὰ ἄνω φρονεῖτε, μὴ τὰ
ἐπὶ τῆς γῆς· ἀπεθάνετε γάρ, καὶ ἡ ζωὴ ὑμῶν κέκρυπται σὺν τῷ
Χριστῷ ἐν τῷ θεῷ. ὅταν ὁ Χριστὸς φανερωθῇ, ἡ ζωὴ ὑμῶν, τότε
καὶ ὑμεῖς σὺν αὐτῷ φανερωθήσεσθε ἐν δόξῃ.

## Textual Criticism

The UBS4 includes a textual variant in verse 4. Was the more likely
original reading ἡ ζωὴ ὑμῶν ("your life") or ἡ ζωὴ ἡμῶν ("our life")?
Interestingly, the NIV chooses the former, while the NASB chooses the latter. The NKJV, which prefers the Byzantine text type, also
chooses ἡ ζωὴ ἡμῶν. Which reading does the process of textual criticism
suggest should be preferred?

### Extrinsic Probabilities

Geographical distribution is not decisive, since Alexandrian-Western
and Byzantine manuscripts support both variants. Nor is age decisive,
since early uncial manuscripts support both variants as well.[1] The second person plural variant (ὑμῶν) has the stronger Alexandrian-Western
manuscript support,[2] while the first person plural variant (ἡμῶν) has
the stronger Byzantine manuscript support.[3] Ultimately, the support
of P46 (about A.D. 200) tips the scale of extrinsic probabilities in favor
of ὑμῶν.[4]

### Transcriptional Probabilities

Neither variant is shorter or more difficult. There does not appear
to be any reason to suspect that a change from ὑμῶν to ἡμῶν (or vice
versa) might be the result of an unintentional error of sight or hearing.
It is possible to argue that a change from ἡμῶν to ὑμῶν might be an intentional assimilation to the second person plural pronouns in verse 3
(ὑμῶν) and verse 4 (ὑμεῖς). Murray Harris, however, suggests that "The
change from ὑμῶν to ἡμῶν may have been occasioned by the universal-

---

1. Fourth and fifth century manuscripts support both ὑμῶν (ℵ, C, D*) and ἡμῶν (B, D1).

2. ℵ, C, D*, F, G, P, Ψ, 33, 81, 104, 1912

3. 365, 436, 1241, 1573, 1852, 1962, 2200, 2464

4. Metzger reflects the committee's preference for Alexandrian-Western manuscripts when
   he notes that the committee gave ὑμῶν a {B} rating because of its "considerably stronger
   manuscript evidence" (*Textual Commentary*, 557).

izing instinct of a scribe who did not want it to appear that Christ was 'the life' solely of the Colossian Christians."[5] The transcriptional probabilities might lean slightly toward ἡμῶν.

## Intrinsic Probabilities

The guiding principle in considering intrinsic probabilities is that the preferred original reading is more grammatically harmonious with the context and more congruent with the author's style, vocabulary, and theology. The second person plural (ὑμῶν) is clearly more grammatically harmonious with the context since it agrees with the pronouns in verses 3 and 4. It also appears to be more congruent with Paul's style, both in the third chapter (six occurrences) and throughout the letter (a total of twenty-four occurrences).[6] Since Colossians 3:1–4:1 is the section in the letter where Paul moves from the indicative to the imperative, the second person plural variant is more harmonious with the context and congruent with Paul's style.[7]

## Conclusion

Extrinsic probabilities support the second person plural reading, primarily because of the early papyrus manuscript P[46]. On the other hand, transcriptional probabilities support the first person plural reading. Intrinsic probabilities, however, lean strongly toward the second person plural reading and provide the decisive evidence in concluding the most likely original reading was ἡ ζωὴ ὑμῶν.

## Translation

The passage consists of four parts, with the end of each marked by a semi-colon or period:

Εἰ οὖν συνηγέρθητε τῷ Χριστῷ, τὰ ἄνω ζητεῖτε, οὗ ὁ Χριστός ἐστιν ἐν δεξιᾷ τοῦ θεοῦ καθήμενος·

τὰ ἄνω φρονεῖτε, μὴ τὰ ἐπὶ τῆς γῆς·

ἀπεθάνετε γάρ, καὶ ἡ ζωὴ ὑμῶν κέκρυπται σὺν τῷ Χριστῷ ἐν τῷ θεῷ.

---

5. M. J. Harris, *Colossians & Philemon*, (Nashville: B&H Publishing, 2010), 122.

6. In comparison, the first person plural occurs only five times elsewhere in the letter and nowhere else in the third chapter.

7. There are nine second person plural verbs in 2:6–23, compared to twenty-seven in 3:1–4:1.

ὅταν ὁ Χριστὸς φανερωθῇ, ἡ ζωὴ ὑμῶν, τότε καὶ ὑμεῖς σὺν αὐτῷ φανερωθήσεσθε ἐν δόξῃ.

Without showing all the steps in the process, the resulting preliminary translation is:

> Therefore, if you were co-raised with Christ, keep on seeking the things above, where Christ is being seated at the right {hand} of God;

> keep on setting your mind on the things above, not the things upon the earth;

> for you died, and your life has been hidden with Christ in God.

> Whenever Christ—your life—might be made manifest, then you also will be made manifest with him in glory.

Checking this preliminary translation against the NASB and NIV highlights four items to consider as part of literary analysis: (1) the class of the conditional clause (εἰ) in the first sentence, (2) the weight of the periphrastic participle (ἐστιν . . . καθήμενος) in the first sentence, (3) the nuances of the aorist tense (ἀπεθάνετε) and the prefect tense (κέκρυπται) in the third sentence, and (4) the best translation of the verb φανερόω in the fourth sentence.

## Historical Analysis

What historical information helps in understanding Colossians 3:1–4? That question may be addressed by considering introductory matters related to the letter as a whole and historical-religious-cultural details related to the passage in particular. Chapter 2 set out the basic historical background of Paul's letters. The following sections develop that background in more detail as it relates to Colossians.

### Introductory Matters

Paul wrote to the church in Colossae (1:2) while he was in prison (4:3, 10, 18), most likely from Rome, around A.D. 61–62. Paul had never visited Colossae personally (2:1), but apparently Epaphras (4:12–13) and/or other Christians Paul discipled during his ministry in Ephesus planted the church (cf. Acts 19:8–10). While Paul was in prison Epaphras arrived in Rome with news from Colossae (1:7–8). Paul wrote with a dual purpose: to express his personal interest in the young church and to refute false teachers who have infiltrated it. None of these aspects of introductory matters sheds significant light on Colossians 3:1–4, but the nature of the false teaching that threatened the young congregation contributes to an understanding of the passage.

### Historical-Cultural-Religious Details

It is impossible to consider any passage in Colossians without taking into account what has come to be labeled "the Colossian heresy." E. T. Mayerhoff (1838) first connected the false teaching Paul was addressing in the letter to second century Gnosticism. F. C. Baur (1873) adopted a similar understanding of the false teaching and made the late date of Gnosticism one of the major reasons for rejecting Pauline authorship of Colossians. Since Mayerhoff and Baur, other scholars have suggested numerous explanations for the teaching Paul sought to address.[8] James Dunn notes that the pendulum of scholarly opinion has tended to swing between the poles of Hellenistic Gnosticism and Jewish Mysticism.[9]

This plethora of scholarly opinions most likely results from several elements that appear in the letter. The false teaching appears to have been a "philosophy" based on "tradition" (2:8) that emphasized food regulations and holy days (2:16–17), worship of angels (2:18–19), and severe treatment of the body (2:20–23). These elements could reflect the influence of Jewish legalism, Oriental mysticism, and/or Greek asceticism, depending on which aspect a commentator chooses to emphasize.

| Elements of "the Colossian Heresy" | | |
|---|---|---|
| Legalism (2:16–17) | Mysticism (2:18–19) | Asceticism (2:20–23) |
| • Dietary laws<br>• Holy days | • Worship of angels<br>• Heavenly visions | • Do not handle, taste, touch<br>• Severe treatment of body |

Since Colossae was a cosmopolitan city with a largely Gentile population and a variety of cultural and religious influences, including a

---

8. P. T. O'Brien notes one source that identifies forty-four different suggestions. He also provides a good summary of five major contributions to the discussion (*Colossians, Philemon* [Waco, TX: Word, 1982], xxx–xxxviii).

9. J. D. G. Dunn, *The Epistles to the Colossians and to Philemon*, (Grand Rapids: Eerdmans, 1996), 27–35.

significant Jewish community, perhaps the best understanding of the
false teaching about which Paul was concerned is that it was an amal-
gam of several influences. Regardless, Paul saw the teaching as standing in direct contrast to the gospel of Christ. That contrast is clear
in 2:8 where the apostle notes that the "philosophy" and "tradition"
were κατὰ τὰ στοιχεῖα τοῦ κόσμου καὶ οὐ κατὰ Χριστόν. In 2:20 he also
writes that the Colossians had died with Christ ἀπὸ τῶν στοιχείων τοῦ
κόσμου.

Whether τὰ στοιχεῖα τοῦ κόσμου are understood as somehow related to the elements of the physical world (e.g., earth, air, fire, water) or
to the heavenly bodies that influence human destiny,[10] the Colossians
should not focus on them. Instead, the proper focus is Christ. He is
pre-eminent in creation and in redemption (1:15–20); all the trea-
sures of wisdom and knowledge reside in him (2:2–3); and all the
fulness of deity dwells in him (2:9). Further, he sits at God's right
hand waiting to be revealed in glory (3:1–4). So, Paul's injunctions in
Colossians 3:1–4 relate directly to the false philosophy that concerned
him. Christ and "the things above" should be their focus, not "the
things below." He alone controls their destiny, not the observance
of holy days, the worship of angels, or the severe treatment of their
bodies.

## Literary Analysis

A genre-informed synthetic study of Colossians readily identifies the salutation (1:1–2). A thanksgiving (1:3–8) and prayer report
(1:9–14) flow seamlessly into the well-known Christological hymn of
1:15–20, which leads Paul to reflect on Christ's reconciling work on
behalf of the Colossians (1:21–23). The body of the letter begins with
a joy formula in 1:24 that introduces a description of Paul's ministry
(1:24–29) and his concern for the Colossians (2:1–5). Both descrip-
tions are particularly important because Paul had neither planted the
church nor met the Colossians. The heart of the letter is Colossians
2:6–4:1, where Paul focuses on the completeness the Colossians possess in Christ (2:6–23) and the way in which they are to live out that
completeness (3:1–4:1). A brief section of summary advice (4:2–6) and
the apostolic parousia (4:7–9) round out the letter body. A somewhat
longer than usual list of greetings (4:10–18a) and a brief benediction
(4:18b) close the letter. The following summary chart reflects the results of that synthetic study.

---

10. See Dunn, *Colossians and Philemon*, 148–51.

| COLOSSIANS<br>Proclaiming Completeness in Christ | | | |
|---|---|---|---|
| Salutation<br>(1:1–2) | | | |
| Extended Thanksgiving<br>(1:3–23) | | | |
| Paul's Ministry<br>(1:24–2:5) | Complete in Christ<br>(2:6–23) | Life in Christ<br>(3:1–4:1) | Summary Advice<br>(4:2–9) |
| 1:24–29<br>His<br>commission<br>2:1–5<br>His concern | 2:6–15<br>God's provision<br><br>2:16–23<br>False obligations | 3:1–4<br>Seek the<br>heavenly<br>3:5–11<br>Put off the old<br>3:12–17<br>Put on the new<br>3:18–4:1<br>Serve one<br>another | 4:2–6<br>Prayer &<br>wisdom<br>4:7–9<br>Paul's<br>messengers |
| Closing<br>(4:10–18) | | | |

## General Context

The summary chart makes it clear that Colossians 3:1–4 stands at the turning point of the letter body. Having set out the truth of God's complete provision in Christ (2:6–15) and having warned the Colossians of the heretical obligations his opponents are seeking to lay on them (2:16–23), Paul turns to instruction on how they can live out their new status in a Christ-honoring way (3:1–4:1). The first four verses of this new sub-section call them to lift their eyes from the earthly focus of the syncretistic false teachers who were seeking to lead them astray and, instead, fix their eyes firmly on their true heavenly position in Christ. Some people might characterize followers of Christ as "too heavenly minded to be any earthly good." Paul, however, turns that assessment upside down and says, in effect, "Only as you are truly heavenly-minded will you ever be *any* earthly good!"

## Immediate Context

Together, the opening words of 2:20 and 3:1 highlight what constitute for Paul the key elements of the transfer from one sphere of existence to the other:

> Col. 2:20    "If you died with Christ . . ."
>
> Col. 3:1     "If you were raised with Christ . . ."

So, Paul links Colossians 3:1–4 not only logically (οὖν) but also theologically to the paragraph that precedes it (2:20–23). The theological
reality of dying with Christ carries with it the practical reality that we
are no longer tied to the "elementary principles" of the world. The
theological reality of being raised with Christ carries with it the practical reality that we are forever tied to the "things above" where we
are now seated with him. In the paragraphs that follow, Paul develops
that practical reality by setting out specific steps to take: putting off old
earthly vices (3:5–11) and putting on new heavenly virtues (3:12–17).
Colossians 3:1–4, therefore, sets forth the key theological truth that informs the way in which we are to live the Christian life: Our true existence is a heavenly existence.

## Structure

As noted in the translation, the passage divides naturally into four
sentences. The first two sentences (one complex, one simple) are built
around parallel present tense imperatives.

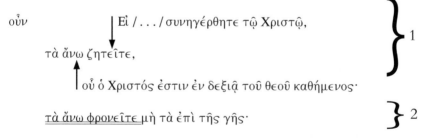

οὖν          Εἰ / . . . / συνηγέρθητε τῷ Χριστῷ,

        τὰ ἄνω ζητεῖτε,

             οὗ ὁ Χριστός ἐστιν ἐν δεξιᾷ τοῦ θεοῦ καθήμενος·      } 1

τὰ ἄνω φρονεῖτε μὴ τὰ ἐπὶ τῆς γῆς·      } 2

The third (compound) sentence consists of two independent clauses
introduced by the conjunction γάρ and joined by the conjunction καὶ.

γάρ     ἀπεθάνετε / . . . /

καὶ     ἡ ζωὴ ὑμῶν κέκρυπται σὺν τῷ Χριστῷ ἐν τῷ θεῷ.      } 3

The fourth (complex) sentence is not introduced by a coordinate conjunction and is built around an independent clause with its verb in the future tense.

$$\left. \begin{array}{l} \text{ὅταν ὁ Χριστὸς φανερωθῇ ἡ ζωὴ ὑμῶν,} \\[6pt] \text{τότε καὶ ὑμεῖς σὺν αὐτῷ φανερωθήσεσθε ἐν δόξῃ.} \end{array} \right\} 4$$

*Grammar, Syntax, and Rhetoric*

A number of significant grammatical/syntactical/rhetorical elements in the passage merit comment. As noted above, the inferential conjunction οὖν connects Colossians 3:1–4 to the preceding context and draws a logical conclusion from Paul's argument in 2:20–23. The commands to focus on τὰ ἄνω grow naturally out of the truth that believers have died to τὰ στοιχεῖα τοῦ κόσμου. The first class conditional clause (Εἰ συνηγέρθητε τῷ Χριστῷ) that introduces the first sentence affirms the reality of the believers' position—they have, indeed, been raised with Christ—and effectively functions as one of the reasons for the commands that follow.[11] Placing the object (τὰ ἄνω) before the verb in each of the first two sentences emphasizes the heavenly focus Paul is seeking to cultivate. The two imperatives (ζητεῖτε . . . φρονεῖτε) are most likely customary or habitual presents that should be understood as carrying the idea of "make it your fixed and regular habit to . . ." The adversative phrase in the second sentence (μὴ τὰ ἐπὶ τῆς γῆς) again emphasizes the contrast between the heavenly and the earthly. If the combination ἐστιν . . . καθήμενος is a periphrastic participle, it highlights the present continuing reality of Christ's session at the Father's right hand. Even if it is not, the double use of the present tense reminds the believer of the present reality of Christ's position and activity: he is at God's right hand (the place of honor and authority), and he is seated (the posture of one who has completed his work).[12]

The causal conjunction (γάρ) that introduces the third sentence provides the reason to focus on the heavenly realm: not only is Christ there, so is the believer. First, she died (ἀπεθάνετε); second, her life has been hidden (κέκρυπται) with Christ in God. Although the first verb is aorist and the second is perfect, they most likely both emphasize the present state resulting from a completed action.[13] The prepositional

---

11. See J. P. Louw, "Reading a Text as Discourse," *Linguistics and New Testament Interpretation: Essays on Discourse Analysis*, ed., D. A. Black (Nashville: Broadman, 1992): 26.

12. Both Harris and O'Brien reject the construction as periphrastic (Harris, *Colossians*, 120; O'Brien, *Colossians*, 161).

13. If so, both tenses should be understood as "consummative." This understanding is reflected

phrase σὺν τῷ Χριστῷ repeats an idea that Paul introduced in the first sentence (συνηγέρθητε τῷ Χριστῷ) and that he will repeat again in the fourth sentence (σὺν αὐτῷ φανερωθήσεσθε). This threefold repetition of σὺν emphasizes the believer's complete identification with Christ in his resurrection, his heavenly life, and his future glory.[14] Futhermore, it is also appropriate to infer that the death in this sentence (ἀπεθάνετε) also refers to the death with Christ Paul mentions in 2:20 (Εἰ ἀπεθάνετε σὺν Χριστῷ). What Christ has experienced (and will experience), the believer has experienced (and will experience) also; where Christ is, the believer is also. Not only is Christ seated at the Father's right hand in heaven, so is the one who is identified with Christ through his death and resurrection.

The omission of a coordinate conjunction at the beginning of the fourth sentence (asyndeton) sets the idea apart from the first three sentences. O'Brien writes, "The very abruptness of the expression helps to underline the assurance of the hope more vividly."[15] The verb φανερωθῇ is an indefinite subjunctive that states the circumstances under which the main verb will occur. The use of ὅταν . . . τότε makes clear the sequence of the events Paul is describing ("when . . . then"). The adjunctive use of καὶ ("also") and the intensive use of ὑμεῖς both reinforce the action of the main verb φανερωθήσεσθε. The future tense of that verb is predictive, and the passive voice without an expressed agent lays special emphasis on the expressed subject of the verb (ὑμεῖς). The significance of the prepositional phrase (σὺν αὐτῷ) has been noted previously.

Bringing together the results of structural analysis and grammatical/ syntactical/ rhetorical analysis results in an exegetical outline that consists of two commands supported by four reasons.

| Colossians 3:1-4 | |
| --- | --- |
| Command #1: Keep seeking the heavenly | 3:1b |
| Command #2: Keep pondering the heavenly | 3:2 |
| Reason #1: Raised with Christ | 3:1a |

---

in the NASB translation of ἀπεθάνετε as "you have died," although the translators then render κέκρυπται as "your life is hidden." More consistent would be "you have died and your life has been hidden."

14. For a fuller study of this idea in Paul's letters see J. D. Harvey, "The 'With Christ' Motif in Paul's Thought," *Journal of the Evangelical Theological Society* 35 (1992): 329–40.

15. O'Brien, *Colossians*, 166.

| Colossians 3:1-4 | |
| --- | --- |
| Reason #2: Died with Christ | 3:3a |
| Reason #3: Hidden with Christ | 3:3b |
| Reason #4: Future glory with Christ | 3:4 |

## Word Study

The verb in the first command (ζητεῖτε) occurs nineteen other times in Paul's letters, with three nuances in its range of meaning: (1) to try to find something (e.g., Rom. 10:20; 2 Tim. 1:17); (2) to ask for, request, or demand (e.g., 1 Cor. 1:22; 2 Cor. 13:3); (3) to devote serious attention to realizing a desire (e.g., Rom. 2:7; Gal. 1:10). The third nuance is by far the most common (fifteen times) and best fits Colossians 3:1. The closest uses elsewhere in Paul are 1 Corinthians 10:24 (μηδεὶς τὸ ἑαυτοῦ ζητείτω ἀλλὰ τὸ τοῦ ἑτέρου), 1 Corinthians 13:5 (οὐ ζητεῖ τὰ ἑαυτῆς), 2 Corinthians 12:14 (οὐ γὰρ ζητῶ τὰ ὑμῶν ἀλλὰ ὑμᾶς), and Philippians 2:21 (οἱ πάντες γὰρ τὰ ἑαυτῶν ζητοῦσιν, οὐ τὰ Ἰησοῦ Χριστοῦ). Jesus uses the same word in Matthew 6:33 when he commands his disciples to "seek first the kingdom of God and his righteousness" (ζητεῖτε πρῶτον τὴν βασιλείαν τοῦ θεοῦ καὶ τὴν δικαιοσύνην αὐτοῦ). In the Old Testament, it is used most frequently of seeking wisdom (e.g., Prov. 14:6), of seeking love (e.g., Jer. 2:33), and of seeking God (e.g., 1 Chron. 16:11; 22:19; 2 Chron. 11:16; 15:12; Ps. 105:3–4). So, the command to "keep seeking the heavenly" is not a casual suggestion to give intermittent attention to something. Instead, it is a call to give the same attention and priority to seeking heavenly things as we give to seeking God, his kingdom, and his character.

The verb in the second command (φρονεῖτε) occurs twenty-two other times in Paul's letters, with three nuances in its range of meaning: (1) to have an opinion with regard to something (e.g., Rom. 15:5; Phil. 1:7); (2) to develop an attitude based on careful thought (e.g., Phil. 2:5); (3) to give careful consideration to something (e.g., Rom. 14:6; Phil. 3:19). Although the first nuance is the most common (fourteen times), the third fits Colossians 3:2 the best.[16] The closest uses elsewhere in Paul are Romans 8:5 (οἱ γὰρ κατὰ σάρκα ὄντες τὰ τῆς σαρκὸς φρονοῦσιν, οἱ δὲ κατὰ πνεῦμα τὰ τοῦ πνεύματος) and Philippians 3:19 (οἱ τὰ

---

16. The second nuance occurs in the well-known Christological hymn of Philippians 2:5–11. It is one of ten occurrences in Philippians, the highest concentration of the word in Paul's letters.

ἐπίγεια φρονοῦντες). Jesus uses the same word in Matthew 16:23 when he rebukes Peter for "not setting [his] mind on the things of God, but the things of men" (οὐ φρονεῖς τὰ τοῦ θεοῦ ἀλλὰ τὰ τῶν ἀνθρώπων). The word only occurs eight times in the Old Testament, primarily with the idea of "to think, understand" (e.g., Ps. 94:8; Isa. 44:18).[17] O'Brien describes it as "a rather neutral term [that] acquires its proper meaning from its immediate context."[18] It appears that, for Paul, the verb has more weight than it does in the Old Testament and carries overtones of "sober consideration and firm purpose."[19]

## Theological Analysis

Because God has inspired all Scripture, it is both unified and coherent. Colossians 3:1–4, therefore, fits into the overall teaching of Scripture and the theological context of divine revelation. The analogy of Scripture considers the way in which a given passage relates to parallel, similar, and contrasting passages elsewhere in the Bible. The analogy of faith considers the way in which the passage under study relates to major doctrines of the Bible.

### Analogy of Scripture

The critical apparatus of the UBS4 points to multiple passages that parallel Paul's message in Colossians 3:1–4. As noted above, the idea of being raised with Christ in Colossian 3:1 is closely connected with the idea of dying with him in Colossians 2:12. Although those twin ideas receive only brief mention in these verses, they receive fuller treatment in Ephesians 2:4–6 and Romans 6:1–11. After describing his readers as dead, dominated, disobedient, and doomed in Ephesians 2:1–3, Paul describes the transfer that God's mercy and love make possible (2:4–6): we are made alive (συνεζωοποίησεν) with Christ; we are raised (συνήγειρεν) with Christ; and we are seated (συνεκάθισεν) with Christ in the heavenlies.[20] For this reason, Paul calls us not only to recognize the by-grace-alone nature of salvation (2:8–9) but also to demonstrate the surpassing riches of God's grace by walking in the good works that God has prepared for us (2:7, 10).

If Ephesians 2:4–6 highlights the raised-with-Christ side of the transfer, Romans 6:1–11 highlights the died-with-Christ side.[21] We

---

17.  More frequent is the noun φρόνησις with the idea of "prudence, wisdom" (e.g., Prov. 3:19).

18.  O'Brien, *Colossians*, 163.

19.  Ibid., 164.

20.  The Greek words Paul uses might be translated as "co-quickened, co-raised, and co-seated."

21.  The same idea also appears in 2 Corinthians 5:14 where Paul writes ". . . judging this: that one on behalf of all died; therefore all died."

were crucified (συνεσταυρώθη) with Christ (6:6); we were buried (συ-νετάφημεν) with Christ through baptism into his death (6:4); and we are united (σύμφυτοι) with Christ in the likeness of his death (6:5). If we died with Christ (εἰ ἀπεθάνομεν σὺν Χριστῷ)—and the first class condition assumes that we have—we believe that we will also live (συ-ζήσομεν) with him (6:8). Again, Paul calls us to action as a result of these truths: we should consider ourselves dead to sin and alive to God (6:11). Appropriating those truths will lead us to walk in newness of life (6:4; cf. 6:12–14).

Both Ephesians 2 and Romans 6, therefore, reinforce the truth of Colossians 3: our identification with Christ has significant implications for the way we live our lives. A comprehensive understanding of that truth involves three aspects. The past aspect of being crucified, buried, raised, and seated with Christ makes possible our transfer to the new sphere of existence in him. The future aspect of being manifested with Christ in glory gives us hope to endure until he returns. The present aspect of suffering with Christ challenges us to rely on the experiential power of his resurrection to live in conformity with him.

The truth that Christ is seated at God's right hand (his "session") appears in multiple New Testament passages, especially in the formally anonymous letter to the Hebrews (Heb. 1:3; 8:1; 10:12; 12:2). In Ephesians 1:20–21, Paul expands the description considerably when he writes, "[The Father] seated Him at His right hand in the heavenly places, far above all rule and authority and power and dominion, and every name that is named, not only in this age but also in the one to come." The Old Testament root of this idea is Psalm 110 where David declared, "The Lord says to my Lord, 'Sit at my right hand until I make your enemies a footstool for your feet'" (110:1). The rest of the psalm goes on to describe the universal rule the one who sits at the Lord's right hand will exercise (110:2–7). Other New Testament verses explicitly apply this verse to Christ (e.g., Acts 2:34–35; Heb. 1:13), as did Christ himself (Matt. 22:44 and parallels). The reminder for Colossians 3:1–4 is that we, too, are seated with Christ above all rule and authority and power and dominion while we wait with him for the time when he will assume his rightful rule over the nations.

The idea of "Christ your life" in Colossians 3:4 echoes the same sentiment in Philippians 1:21 ("For me to live is Christ . . .") and reminds us that "the life [we] now live" is the result of the work of "the Son of God, who loved [us], and gave Himself up for [us]" (Gal. 2:20). The idea of future glory with Christ also occurs elsewhere in Paul (e.g., Phil. 3:21), but it is not unique to his letters (e.g., 1 John 3:2; 1 Pet. 5:1). The promise that we will ultimately share in Christ's glory regularly serves as a source of hope and as a motivation for the way we are to live in the present (e.g., Rom. 8:23–25). Again, these truths about our identification with Christ serve as reasons for us to "keep on seeking heavenly things" and "keep on setting [our] mind on heavenly things" (Col. 3:1–2).

### Analogy of Faith

Colossians 3:1–4 touches on three major Bible doctrines: Christology, eschatology, and soteriology. The first two doctrines overlap and may be considered together. Christ's exaltation is clearly in view, since the passage mentions both his session (3:1) and his return (3:4). Christ's return is also included in the doctrine of eschatology, although the discussion within that doctrine often focuses on the *timing* of his return in relation to other events of the end times. Since Paul simply asserts that Christ will return— without reference to timing (ὅταν ὁ Χριστὸς φανερωθῇ . . .)—it is probably better to view the passage in light of Christology than eschatology.

Salvation, however, is the primary doctrine to which the passage contributes—in particular, salvation applied (often termed "subjective soteriology"). Within the doctrine of salvation applied, Colossians 3:1–4 touches on two areas: union with Christ and sanctification. In fact, the first of these areas is a basis for the second. The prominence of the believer's union "with Christ" has been highlighted above.[22] That union provides motivation for the commands of verses 1 and 2.

Sanctification may be understood as having three aspects: initial, progressive, and final. Initial sanctification is the past/positional declaration of God by which believers are set apart as holy (e.g., 1 Cor. 6:11; 2 Thess. 2:13). Progressive sanctification is the present/experiential growth and development of holiness within believers' lives (e.g., Rom. 1:19–22; 1 Thess. 4:3). Final sanctification is the future/complete confirmation of the believer in holiness (e.g., 1 Thess. 5:23–24; Eph. 5:25–27). Colossians 3:1–4 relates to both progressive and final sanctification. The commands to keep on seeking and keep on pursuing heavenly things clearly call the readers (and us) to grow in holiness. Based on our union with Christ, Paul is able to command us to become every day more nearly who we already are in Christ. Verse 4 points forward to final sanctification, but it does so as a further motivation for progressive sanctification.

## Synthesis

The task of synthesis is the first step in exposition. It addresses two questions: (1) What did Paul say? (2) Why did he say it? The first question seeks to isolate the central point of the passage; the second seeks to establish the need twenty-first-century readers share with the first-century audience.

---

22. Specifically, the believer is described as raised with Christ (3:1), hidden with Christ (3:3), and revealed with Christ in glory (3:4). Paul also alludes to dying with Christ (3:3; cf. 2:20).

## Central Point

As noted in the discussion of General Context, Colossians 3:1–4 stands at the point in the letter body where Paul turns to practical instruction on how his readers can live out their new status in a Christ-honoring way. It is, therefore, most natural to understand the overall topic of the passage (the homiletical subject) as Sanctification. Given the two commands in the passage, the narrower aspect of that topic might be stated as the Call to Sanctification. What does Paul say about that topic in the passage (the homiletical complement)? He reminds his readers that those commands rest on their union with Christ in his death, resurrection, session, and return. The central point of the passage may be stated in a single sentence: **The call to sanctification rests on the believer's union with Christ in his death, resurrection, session, and return.** This "big idea" reflects a common pattern in Paul's letters: he bases our obligation on God's provision.

## Shared Need

What need in the Colossians' lives did this passage address? They were being influenced by individuals who taught a brand of human philosophy that would lead them to follow earthly traditions and observe earthly commandments. In the face of these earthly distractions, the Colossians needed to focus on the heavenly reality of who they were in Christ. Is there a comparable need in the lives of the twenty-first-century audience? Indeed, it is all too easy for contemporary followers of Christ to become distracted by earthly philosophies, traditions, and practices. In the face of those earthly distractions, they, too, need to focus on the heavenly reality of who they are in Christ.

# Appropriation

Identifying the need the contemporary audience shares with the original audience begins the process of moving the passage's message from "then" to "now." The twenty-first-century appropriation of the message answers three questions: (1) How does the passage *connect* with today's audience? (2) What contemporary attitudes and actions does the passage *correct*? (3) What ways of thinking and/or acting does the passage *commend* to today's audience?[23]

Contemporary listeners can *connect* with the idea of "seeking" something. When something important is lost, we seek (search) diligently for it. When we want to possess something we view as important, we seek

---

23. See Larkin, *Greek is Great Gain*, 230–4.

(pursue) it with single-minded commitment. Paul calls us to exercise the same diligence and commitment in seeking the heavenly things that are truly important.

Paul's emphasis on heavenly things *corrects* the contemporary attitude that only what we see is real. It also corrects the idea that only our present life is important. Instead, Paul reminds us that what we cannot see is truly important and that we can anticipate a future that is drastically different from the present we currently experience.

Paul explicitly *commends* the truth of our union with Christ and the importance of focusing on what is eternally important (φρονεῖτε). He also commends the active pursuit of those same eternally important realities (ζητεῖτε). The good news is that it is possible for us look beyond this world and let that heavenly perspective inform the way we live on a daily basis.

## Homiletical Packaging

Understanding the truth in a passage is the task of exegesis. Considering how that truth applies to the needs of men and women today is the task of synthesis and appropriation. Determining the best way to communicate the applied truth of a passage to a group of listeners is the task of homiletics. Before developing a sermon outline it is crucial to formulate an objective and craft a take-home truth.

### Sermon Objective and Take-Home Truth

Chapter six suggested this template for formulating a sermon objective:

> I want my listeners to understand_____[truth]_____,
>             so that they will_____[action]_____.

Applying that template to Colossians 3:1–4 leads to this objective: **I want my listeners to understand the full extent of their union with Christ, so that they will make living with a heavenly focus a top priority.** The take-home truth seeks to capture the central idea of the passage in a succinct statement listeners will "take home" with them. For Colossians 3:1–4, such a statement might be: **Our priorities should reflect our position.**

### Sermon Outline

As discussed in Chapter 6, sermons may be structured deductively or inductively. The difference was set out this way:

| Deductive Approach | Inductive Approach |
|---|---|
| Introduction | Introduction |
| Central Idea / Proposition | Point 1 |
| Point 1 | Point 2 |
| Point 2 | Point 3 |
| Point 3 | Central Idea / Proposition |
| Conclusion | Conclusion |

It is somewhat more common to adopt a deductive approach with a passage such as Colossians 3:1–4. Since this particular passage includes two commands and four reasons supporting those commands, it seems a likely candidate for the keyword pattern. Either the commands or the reasons could serve as the main points. Since, however, the two commands address the same basic concept (focusing on heavenly things), and since the sermon objective set out above emphasizes the believer's union with Christ, using "reasons" as the keyword seems more logical.

The take-home truth both captures well the central point of the passage and fits well in a proposition of obligation for the keyword pattern.[24] The four reasons that support the commands answer the "why" question that naturally follows such a proposition. The basic elements of a sermon outline for Colossians 3:1–4 might look like this.

| | |
|---|---|
| Proposition: | Our priorities should reflect our position. |
| Interrogative: | Why? |
| Transitional Sentence: | Our priorities should reflect our position because of the four *reasons* we see in Colossians 3:1–4. |

Main Points (in logical order):
1. We died with Christ (3:3a).
2. We were raised with Christ (3:1a).
3. We are hidden with Christ (3:3b).
4. We will be revealed with Christ in glory (3:4).

Although including a full manuscript for the sermon is not within the scope of this book, Sunukjian provides a helpful approach to sermon introductions.[25] He suggests this sequence: (1) engage the lis-

---

24. See Hamilton, *Homiletical Handbook*, 42–3.
25. Sunukjian, *Biblical* Preaching, 192.

teners' interest, (2) focus the message on the topic, (3) set the stage biblically, including (as appropriate) context, background, setting, and (4) announce the passage. Adapting that pattern to a sermon on Colossians 3:1–4 might result in the following introduction, which extends through the proposition to the first main point.

---

### Is Your Head in the Clouds?

Have you ever heard someone described this way: "He has his head in the clouds."? Or how about this comment: "She's so heavenly minded she's no earthly good."? What conclusion do you draw from those statements? That the person is impractical and lacks common sense, right? But it might surprise you to know that Paul has a radically different perspective.

The church in Colossae was being influenced by individuals who taught a brand of human philosophy that would lead them to follow earthly traditions and observe earthly commandments. In the face of these earthly distractions, the Colossians needed to focus on the heavenly realities of who they were in Christ. That's the reason Paul writes what he does in Colossians 3:1–4. Let's take a look at that passage.

### [Announce and read Colossians 3:1–4.]

Did you notice the two commands in verses 1–2? Essentially, Paul says the same thing twice: "Keep on seeking the things above" and "Keep on setting your mind on the things above." Both commands carry the idea of "make it your fixed and regular habit" to do something. And both verbs are strong words that suggest devoting serious attention and effort to securing something. In fact, the verb "seek" is the same one Jesus uses when he tells us to "seek first God's kingdom and his righteousness" in Matthew 6:33.

So, what's Paul's point? You can summarize it in six words: **Our priorities should reflect our position.** Of course, the logical question to ask Paul is "Why?" *Why* should our priorities reflect our position? The answer lies in a proper understanding of our union with Christ. In our passage, Paul explains that union and gives us **four reasons our priorities should reflect our position.** Let's take them in logical order. **First, our priorities should reflect our position because we died with Christ (3:3a) . . .**

## PHILIPPIANS 3:12–16

Οὐχ ὅτι ἤδη ἔλαβον ἢ ἤδη τετελείωμαι, διώκω δὲ εἰ καὶ καταλάβω, ἐφ' ᾧ καὶ κατελήμφθην ὑπὸ Χριστοῦ ['Ιησοῦ]. ἀδελφοί, ἐγὼ ἐμαυτὸν οὐ λογίζομαι κατειληφέναι· ἓν δέ, τὰ μὲν ὀπίσω ἐπιλανθανόμενος τοῖς δὲ ἔμπροσθεν ἐπεκτεινόμενος, κατὰ σκοπὸν διώκω εἰς τὸ βραβεῖον τῆς ἄνω κλήσεως τοῦ θεοῦ ἐν Χριστῷ 'Ιησοῦ. Ὅσοι οὖν τέλειοι, τοῦτο φρονῶμεν· καὶ εἴ τι ἑτέρως φρονεῖτε, καὶ τοῦτο ὁ θεὸς ὑμῖν ἀποκαλύψει· πλὴν εἰς ὃ ἐφθάσαμεν, τῷ αὐτῷ στοιχεῖν.

## Textual Criticism

The UBS4 notes textual variants in verses 12, 13, 15, and 16. Since space does not permit a full analysis of all four variants, this section will summarize the issues related to each of them.

Four different names for Christ appear in manuscripts of verse 12: (a) Χριστοῦ 'Ιησοῦ, (b) τοῦ Χριστοῦ 'Ιησοῦ, (c) 'Ιησοῦ Χριστοῦ, and (d) Χριστοῦ. The first and fourth readings have the strongest manuscript support.[26] The second reading might well be an addition to formalize the messianic title Χριστός. Although the third reading ('Ιησοῦ Χριστοῦ) occurs elsewhere in Philippians (1:11, 19; 3:20; 4:23), the manuscript support for it is far weaker.[27] Gordon Fee concludes that the decision between Χριστοῦ 'Ιησοῦ and Χριστοῦ "is nearly impossible to call." He continues, "On the one hand, omission could easily have occurred by homoeoteleuton . . . on the other hand, an 'addition' like this does not require intentionality on the part of scribes, since they would often write the name in full without even thinking about it. Very likely the shorter reading is original, but one has no guarantee here."[28] The uncertainty is reflected both by the {C} rating in Metzger's *Textual Commentary* and by the UBS4's inclusion of ['Ιησοῦ].

The issue in verse 13 is whether the original reading was οὐ ("not") or οὔπω ("not yet"). Both readings have strong early manuscript support, although the latter is somewhat more widely distributed geographically. Peter O'Brien notes, however, "the context implies 'not yet', and this suggests that scribes replaced an original οὐ with οὔπω."[29] Metzger's *Textual Commentary* assigns οὐ a {B} rating.

---

26. P46, ℵ, and A support Χριστοῦ 'Ιησοῦ; B, D, and 33 support Χριστοῦ.

27. Four Alexandrian manuscripts and three Majority manuscripts; the earliest are from the fifth century. Overall, Paul uses Χριστοῦ 'Ιησοῦ (83 times) far more frequently than 'Ιησοῦ Χριστοῦ (26 times).

28. G. D. Fee, *Paul's Letter to the Philippians* (Grand Rapids: Eerdmans, 1995), 338.

29. P. T. O'Brien, *Commentary on Philippians* (Grand Rapids: Eerdmans, 1991), 418. Fee adds, ". . . had Paul originally written οὔπω, there is no conceivable reason for 'yet' to be omitted" (Fee, *Philippians*, 338).

The variant readings in verse 15 raise the same question as that addressed in the discussion of Romans 5:1 (Chapter 4): Was the original reading more likely subjunctive (φρονῶμεν) or indicative (φρονοῦμεν)? The subjunctive reading has the support of the vast majority of manuscripts, including all the major uncials except ℵ (fourth century) and L (eighth century). It has wide geographical distribution, and it fits well with the hortatory context of 3:12–16. Metzger's *Textual Commentary* gives φρονῶμεν an {A} rating.

At first glance, verse 16 presents a bewildering array of five readings with three basic elements: (1) τῷ αὐτῷ στοιχεῖν, (2) τὸ αὐτὸ φρονεῖν, and (3) κανόνι.[30]

| Textual Variants in Philippians 3:16 |
| --- |
| (a)   τῷ αὐτῷ στοιχεῖν |
| (b)   τὸ αὐτὸ φρονεῖν |
| (c)   τῷ αὐτῷ στοιχεῖν, τὸ αὐτὸ φρονεῖν |
| (d)   τὸ αὐτὸ φρονεῖν, τῷ αὐτῷ κανόνι στοιχεῖν |
| (e)   τῷ αὐτῷ στοιχεῖν κανόνι, τὸ αὐτὸ φρονεῖν |

The manuscript evidence is divided, with Alexandrian texts strongly favoring (a) and Majority texts supporting (e). Only one comparatively late manuscript (1881) supports (b), and the reading itself appears to be an assimilation to 2:2 and 4:2. Nevertheless (a) and (b) together explain (c), and (c) appears to lie behind (d) and (e). If the shorter reading is to be preferred, (a) and (b) are the best options. Of those two readings, τῷ αὐτῷ στοιχεῖν has the stronger manuscript support, which explains the {A} rating in Metzger's *Textual Commentary*.

## Translation

The passage consists of six segments, with the end of each marked by a period or a semicolon:

Οὐχ ὅτι ἤδη ἔλαβον ἢ ἤδη τετελείωμαι, διώκω δὲ εἰ καὶ καταλάβω, ἐφ᾽ ᾧ καὶ κατελήμφθην ὑπὸ Χριστοῦ [Ἰησοῦ].

---

30. Note Galatians 6:16 where ὅσοι τῷ κανόνι τούτῳ στοιχήσουσιν brings together κανόνι and στοικέω and might well have influenced readings (d) and (e).

ἀδελφοί, ἐγὼ ἐμαυτὸν οὐ λογίζομαι κατειληφέναι·

ἓν δέ, τὰ μὲν ὀπίσω ἐπιλανθανόμενος τοῖς δὲ ἔμπροσθεν ἐπεκτεινόμενος, κατὰ σκοπὸν διώκω εἰς τὸ βραβεῖον τῆς ἄνω κλήσεως τοῦ θεοῦ ἐν Χριστῷ Ἰησοῦ.

Ὅσοι οὖν τέλειοι, τοῦτο φρονῶμεν·

καὶ εἴ τι ἑτέρως φρονεῖτε, καὶ τοῦτο ὁ θεὸς ὑμῖν ἀποκαλύψει·

πλὴν εἰς ὃ ἐφθάσαμεν, τῷ αὐτῷ στοιχεῖν.

Without showing all the steps in the process, the resulting preliminary
translation is as follows:

> {I am} not {saying} that I already attained or have already become
> mature, but I am pursuing if indeed I might lay hold, because indeed
> I was laid hold of by Christ Jesus.

> Brothers, I am not considering myself to have laid hold;

> but one thing: on the one hand forgetting the things behind, on the
> other hand stretching out to the things ahead, I am pursuing toward
> the mark for the prize of the upward call of God in Christ Jesus.

> Therefore as many as {are} mature, let us be thinking this way;

> and if you are thinking anything in another way, God will also reveal
> this to you;

> nevertheless, to what we attained, by the same {standard} be walking.

Checking this preliminary translation against the NASB and NIV
highlights three items to explore in literary analysis: (1) the proper interpretation of εἰ καὶ in verse 12, (2) the best understanding of ἐφ' ᾧ in
verse 12, (3) the meaning of κατὰ σκοπὸν in verse 14.

## Historical Analysis

The historical analysis of Philippians 3:12–16 includes both a consideration of how introductory matters inform the interpretation of the
passage and an investigation of any historical-cultural-religious details
that might be unclear to the twenty-first-century audience.

## Introductory Matters

Paul wrote to the church in Philippi (1:1) while he was in prison (1:7, 13, 16), most likely from Rome (cf. 1:13; 4:22) around A.D. 62–63. Paul and Silas had planted the church on their first visit to Macedonia (cf. Acts 16:11–40) and apparently had maintained a close connection with the believers there (cf. Phil. 4:15–16). In fact, it was Epaphroditus's arrival with a gift from the church that prompted Paul to write (2:18). None of this background information sheds significant light on Philippians 3:12–16, but Paul's past informs the entire discussion beginning at 3:4.

In verses 4–6, Paul set out seven advantages in which he could have placed confidence if he so chose. The first four were inherited privileges: circumcised on the eighth day, of the nation of Israel, of the tribe of Benjamin, and a Hebrew of Hebrews. Circumcision was the mark of God's covenant with Abraham, and the Old Testament law mandated that it be performed when a male child was eight days old (Lev. 12:3). Direct Israelite descent set Paul apart from both Gentiles and proselytes. Israel's first king came from the tribe of Benjamin (1 Sam. 9:1–2); Jerusalem and its Temple were located within the territory allotted to Benjamin (Judg. 1:21); Benjamin was one of the two tribes that remained loyal to David's descendents when the kingdom divided (1 Kings 12:21); and Benjaminites were prominent among the Israelites who returned to Palestine after the exile (Ezra 4:1). Even in Jerusalem, Hebrew-speaking Jews tended to keep themselves separate from Greek-speaking Jews (cf. Acts 6:1–8). Although he had lived among Hellenistic Diaspora Jews in Tarsus, Paul's parents had raised him in strict accordance with an Hebraic-Jewish way of life.

The last three advantages were personal achievements: a Pharisee, a persecutor of the Church, and blameless with regard to the law and righteousness. The Pharisees were one of the prominent religious groups within Second Temple Judaism. They observed a strict exclusivism, held themselves subject to both the written law and the oral law, and were viewed as models of piety by the Jewish people. As a persecutor of the Church, Paul had demonstrated his zeal for his Jewish heritage (cf. Acts 22:3–5; Gal. 1:13–14). As a follower of both the written and oral laws, Paul had lived in strict conformity to both, which was a significant achievement. It was these privileges and achievements that Paul chose to forget as "the things behind" (Phil. 3:13) as he pursued the prize of "the upward call of God in Christ Jesus" (3:14).

## Historical-Cultural-Religious Details

Although Paul uses the verb διώκω (to pursue) rather than τρέχω (to run) to describe his approach to following Christ, the imagery of the Olympian races appears to lie behind his language (cf. 1 Cor. 9:24–25). Those races included a goal that marked the end of the race, a herald who announced both the competitors and the winner, a prize awarded to the winner, and judges who bestowed the prize.[31] The first and third elements appear to have the strongest connections to Philippians 3:13–14. The noun σκοπός was commonly used to designate a target or goal toward which one shot (Job 16:12; Lam. 3:12), steered (EpArist. 251), or studied (2 Cl. 19:1). In a race, the σκοπός was the "mark" that provided direction and incentive for the runners.

Paul uses the noun βραβεῖον in 1 Corinthians 9:24 to denote the "prize" for which the runners ran. That prize was most commonly a wreath made out of amaranth leaves that supposedly did not fade. Both Paul and Peter allude to that perishable prize and contrast it with the "imperishable" and "unfading" reward awaiting the runner who wins the Christian race (1 Cor. 9:25; 1 Pet. 5:4). It might also be that the κλῆσις Paul mentions reflects the herald's "calling" the winner forward to receive the prize.[32] The Greek games were highly competitive, and the winners were highly honored. By invoking the imagery of those games, Paul challenges his readers to invest the same single-minded energy and focus in following Christ that the runners invested in winning the races that were part of the Olympian games.

## Literary Analysis

A genre-informed synthetic study of Philippians notes the characteristic Pauline salutation (1:1–2) and thanksgiving (1:3–11). A disclosure formula at 1:12 introduces the letter body that extends through 4:20. The letter body, however, differs from what some consider "standard" Pauline letter structure. A report on Paul's ministry situation at the beginning of the letter (1:12–26) balances an extended "thank-you note" for the Philippians' support of his ministry at the end of the letter (4:10–20). The apostolic parousia (2:19–30) is somewhat longer than usual and divides the remainder of the body into two major sections (1:27–2:18 and 3:1–4:9) rather than coming at the end of it. The following summary chart reflects the results of that synthetic study.

---

31.   J. F. Gates, "Race" in *Zondervan Pictorial Bible Dictionary* (Grand Rapids: Zondervan, 1972), 702.

32.   See Hawthorne, *Philippians*, 154–5.

| PHILIPPIANS<br>Responding Joyfully to Difficult Circumstances | | |
|---|---|---|
| Salutation and Thanksgiving<br>(1:1–11) | | |
| Missionary Report<br>(1:12–26) | | |
| Proper Attitude<br>(1:27–2:18)<br><br>1:27–30 Live worthily of the gospel.<br>2:1–4 Think the same thing.<br>2:5–11 Follow Christ's example.<br>2:12–18 Work out your salvation. | Prime Examples<br>(2:19–30)<br><br>2:19–24 Timothy<br>2:25–30 Epaphroditus | Proper Perspective<br>(3:1–4:9)<br><br>3:1–11 Consider former things loss.<br>3:12–16 Press on to the prize.<br>3:17–4:1 Follow Paul's example.<br>4:2–9 Live in harmony and peace. |
| Note of Thanks<br>(4:10–20) | | |
| Greetings and Benediction<br>(4:21–23) | | |

## General Context

The summary chart shows that Philippians 3:12–16 is part of the second major section of the letter body (3:1–4:9). Interestingly, the two sections of the letter body follow similar patterns of challenge (1:27–2:4; 3:1–16), example (2:5–11; 3:17–4:1), and exhortation (2:12–18; 4:2–9). In the first section, Christ provides the example; in the second section, Paul provides the example. Having called his readers (and us) to adopt the attitude of selfless humility that Christ demonstrated (1:27–2:18) and having held up Timothy and Epaphroditus as prime examples of selfless service (2:19–30), Paul uses his own experience to demonstrate the proper perspective that should characterize followers of Christ (3:1–4:9). Within that section, 3:1–11 calls us to forget our past heritage and achievement, while 3:12–16 calls us to focus on pursuing what is now ours in Christ.

## Immediate Context

As noted, Philippians 3:1–4:9 follows the basic pattern of challenge (3:1–16), example (3:17–4:1), and exhortation (4:2–9). After a brief warning against false teachers (3:1–3), Paul uses his own experience to challenge his readers. Philippians 3:4–16 is, essentially, his personal testimony. He begins with the inherited privileges and personal achievements of his past (3:4–6). Those items have been addressed under Historical Analysis above.

The adversative conjunction ἀλλὰ that begins verse 7 marks a major shift in Paul's discussion; he moves from the way he *used* to think to the way he *now* thinks. Verses 7–11 describe the new perspective he has on life. Three times in verses 7–8 he says that all the privileges and achievements he had just itemized he now considers to be worthless. The reason Paul's perspective changed was that he met Jesus (διὰ τὸν Χριστὸν). Rather than focusing on his own heritage or achievements, Paul now focuses all of his energies on knowing Christ and being found in him (3:8b–9). Verse 10 is a powerful statement of Paul's new perspective: he wants to know the person of Christ (τοῦ γνῶναι αὐτὸν), the power of Christ (τὴν δύναμιν τῆς ἀναστάσεως αὐτοῦ), and the passion of Christ (τὴν κοινωνίαν παθημάτων αὐτοῦ). His ultimate purpose is to enjoy future fellowship with Christ in glory (3:11).

The absence of an introductory conjunction marks a new section of his argument and receives added emphasis by the **elliptical** οὐχ ὅτι that begins it. In 3:7–11 Paul has explained *what* he pursues and *why*; in 3:12–16, he explains *how* he pursues it. Verse 12 echoes the focus on Christ from the preceding paragraph (ἐφ᾽ ᾧ καὶ κατελήμφθην ὑπὸ Χριστοῦ Ἰησοῦ). Verses 13–14 bring the focus back to Paul's personal example. Verses 15–16 move from the indicative to the imperative and set the stage for his challenge to join in following his example in 3:17 (συμμιμηταί μου γίνεσθε). So, Philippians 3:12–16 forms the hinge in Paul's argument, where he continues to use himself as an example but redirects his readers to consider their own attitudes and actions in light of that example.

## Structure

The six segments of the paragraph form three sentences. The first sentence draws a contrast, with the positive aspect captured by the verb διώκω.

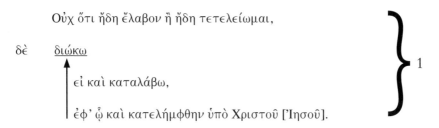

The second sentence also draws a contrast, with the positive aspect again captured by the verb διώκω.

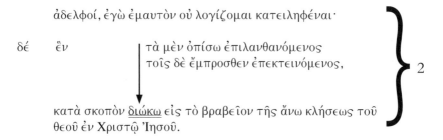

The third sentence consists of three independent clauses and two dependent clauses.

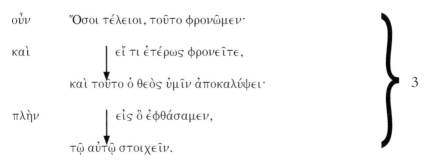

## Grammar, Syntax, and Rhetoric

A number of grammatical, syntactical, and rhetorical elements in the passage merit comment. Paul marks the shift in his argument both by omitting the expected coordinate conjunction (asyndeton) and by using the elliptical οὐχ ὅτι. The latter construction occurs six other times in the New Testament, including two uses elsewhere in Philippians (4:11, 17).[33] It serves to introduce a clarifying explanation and is most

---

33. Of the other four uses, two are in Paul letters (2 Cor. 1:24; 2 Thess. 3:9), and two are in John's Gospel (6:45; 7:22)

likely a shortened form of οὐ λέγω ὅτι.[34] It also establishes the first of two οὐ . . . δὲ contrasts in verses 12–14, both of which incorporate the progressive present tense verb διώκω to highlight Paul's persistent pursuit of Christ.[35]

The verb ἔλαβον is best understood as a constative aorist that summarizes Paul's statements in verses 8–11. More significant rhetorically, it begins a word play that extends into verse 13 (ἔλαβον . . . καταλάβω . . . κατελήμφθην . . . κατειληφέναι) and calls attention to Paul's determination to "lay hold" of Christ. The construction εἰ καὶ καταλάβω is not concessive (as would be the case if the verb were in the indicative). It is a first class condition similar to εἴ πως καταντήσω in 3:11 and expresses expectation rather than doubt.[36] The reason Paul expects to lay hold is that he was "laid hold of by Christ" (κατελήμφθην ὑπὸ Χριστοῦ). The prepositional phrase ἐφ' ᾧ carries causal force three other times in Paul's letters (Rom. 5:12; 2 Cor. 5:4; Phil. 4:10) and is most likely a substitute for the longer ἐπὶ τούτο ὅτι ("for this reason that").[37]

The vocative ἀδελφοί at the beginning of the second sentence catches the listeners' attention as do the absence of a coordinating conjunction, the subject focus provided by including ἐγὼ, and the use of the reflexive pronoun ἐμαυτὸν. The elliptical ἓν δέ that introduces the second half of the sentence similarly catches the attention and anticipates the fuller explanation that follows. Again, the present tense verb διώκω (in verse 14) is Paul's focus in that explanation, but two present tense adverbial participles precede it. The antithetic parallelism between those participial phrases is highlighted by the correlative conjunctions μὲν . . . δὲ

| τὰ | μὲν | ὀπίσω | ἐπιλανθανόμενος |
|-----|-----|-------|-----------------|
| τοῖς | δὲ | ἔμπροσθεν | ἐπεκτεινόμενος |

Although classifying the exact nuance of the adverbial participles is a challenge, manner seems most likely. That is, Paul's pursuit is characterized by an attitude that is totally forward looking. The prepositional phrase κατὰ σκοπὸν denotes the direction of Paul's pursuit ("toward the mark"), and εἰς τὸ βραβεῖον denotes the purpose of his pursuit ("for the sake of the prize"). Both of the genitives in the compound construction

---

34. See *BAGD*, 732 and *BDF* §480(5).

35. In fact, Paul uses the present tense eight times in the passage as compared to four uses of the aorist, two uses of the perfect, and one use of the future. This repeated use of the progressive present makes it clear that the actions Paul describes characterize the way he lives his life on a continuing basis.

36. See O'Brien, *Philippians*, 411, 424.

37. *BAGD*, 365.

τῆς ἄνω κλήσεως τοῦ θεοῦ are probably best understood as subjective genitives, so that the entire phrase concluding the sentence would read something like "for the sake of the prize that comes from God's upward call in Christ Jesus."

The inferential conjunction οὖν applies the first two sentences and introduces the present tense hortatory subjunctive φρονῶμεν. Placing the object τοῦτο before the verb reinforces the connection to what precedes and adds emphasis. The subordinate conjunction εἴ introduces a first class condition that assumes (at least of the sake of argument) the condition is true. The second person plural of the verb φρονεῖτε makes more pointed the possibility that some of the readers have adopted a different attitude. Both the adjunctive use of καὶ ("also") and placing τοῦτο at the beginning of the apodosis reinforce God's gracious action among them. Paul uses the adverb πλὴν as a conjunction both to contrast and to call attention to what he considers most important.[38] The verb ἐφθάσαμεν is best understood as a constative aorist summarizing their progress to date, and the present tense infinitive στοιχεῖν is imperatival, giving a command the readers are to "keep on" obeying.[39]

Bringing together the results of structural analysis and grammatical/ syntactical/ rhetorical analysis results in an exegetical outline that divides into two parts and reflects the repetition within the passage.

| Philippians 3:12-16 | |
|---|---|
| Paul's Approach: Pursuing the prize | 3:12b, 14a |
| • Disclaimer: Has not yet laid hold | 3:12a, 13a |
| • Cause #1: Christ has laid hold | 3:12c |
| • Manner: Focuses on what lies ahead | 3:13b |
| • Cause #2: God has called in Christ | 3:14b |
| Paul's Appeal: Think and live maturely | 3:15a, 16 |
| • Promise: God will reveal wrong thinking | 3:15b |

---

38. *BAGD*, 826. See similar uses in Phil. 4:14; 1 Cor. 11:11; Eph. 5:33.

39. Compare Rom. 12:15.

## Word Study

The verb διώκω occurs twice in Philippians 3:12–16 and in many ways captures the primary thrust of Paul's message in the passage. In addition to those two uses (Phil. 3:12, 14), διώκω occurs nineteen times in Paul's letters.[40] Those nineteen uses fall naturally into two categories of meaning: (1) to follow with harmful intent (eleven times), and (2) to seek after with the aim to secure (eight times). Those categories may be summarized using the common definitions of "to persecute" and "to pursue." The immediate context of verse 14 identifies the objective as "the prize of the upward call of God in Christ Jesus" (τὸ βραβεῖον τῆς ἄνω κλήσεως τοῦ θεοῦ ἐν Χριστῷ 'Ιησοῦ) and leads to the conclusion that in these verses διώκω carries the second nuance of to seek after with the aim to secure (i.e., to pursue).

A check of five ancient source references in which use of the word occurs provides the following results:

| Sirach 27:8 | If you <u>follow after</u> (διώκω) righteousness, you will attain it and put it on as a robe of glory. |
|---|---|
| 1 Maccabees 5:22 | And he <u>pursued</u> (διώκω) them . . . and many fell . . . about 300 men . . . |
| Philo, *Virt.* 30 | Just as hungry or thirsty people, when some food or drink presents itself <u>race in pursuit</u> (διώκω) of it without a backward glance in their eagerness to partake of it . . . |
| Josephus, *Ant.* 6.263 | They are kindly and moderate and <u>pursue</u> (διώκω) only what is right and turn thereto their every thought and endeavor. |
| Josephus, *Ant.* 12.272 | Many soldiers <u>pursued</u> (διώκω) the Jews into the wilderness. |

The same two categories of meaning are evident: to follow with harmful intent (1 Macc. 5:22; Jos. *Ant.* 12.272), and to seek after with the aim to secure (Sir. 27:8; Philo, *Virt.* 30; Jos. *Ant.* 6:263). What is interesting, however, is the color these ancient source references add to the word. This "seeking" or "following after" has several special characteristics:

---

40. Rom. 9:30, 31; 12:13, 14; 14:19; 1 Cor. 4:12; 14:1; 15:9; 2 Cor. 4:9; Gal. 1:13, 23; 4:29; 5:11; 6:12; Phil. 3:6; 1 Thess. 5:15; 1 Tim. 6:11; 2 Tim. 2:22; 3:12.

- It turns every thought and action to what is pursued.

- It is done eagerly, without looking back.

- It has a positive, beneficial objective.

- It is done expectantly, with the intent of attaining its objective.

So, when Paul writes, "I press on toward the goal for the prize of the upward call of God in Christ Jesus" (Phil. 3:14), he is doing more than simply plodding along. He engages in his pursuit eagerly and expectantly, without looking back (cf. Phil. 3:13), and focusing his every thought and action on attaining the reward that lies before him. Similarly, the prophet Hosea exhorts his audience "Let us press on (διώκω) to know the LORD" (Hos. 6:1). This "pursuit" is serious business, and using himself as an example, Paul challenges the Philippians (and us) to "have this attitude" (Phil. 3:15).

Other significant words in the passage include καταλαμβάνω (three times in verses 12–13), τέλειος/τελειόω (verses 12 and 15), φρονέω (twice in verse 15), and στοικέω (verse 16). The verb καταλαμβάνω occurs fifteen times in the New Testament, including four occurrences elsewhere in Paul's letters (Rom. 9:30; 1 Cor. 9:24; Eph. 3:18; 1 Thess. 5:4). The uses in Philippians 3 most naturally carry the nuance "to make one's own." Interestingly, in 1 Corinthians 9:24 Paul uses the same verb in the context of running a race in order to win (καταλαμβάνω) a prize (βραβεῖον). In Sirach 11:10 καταλαμβάνω is linked with διώκω, although in a negative context (ἐὰν διώκῃς, οὐ μὴ καταλάβῃς).

Since Paul uses the verb τελειόω only in Philippians 3:12, it has generated considerable scholarly discussion.[41] On the other hand, he uses the adjective τέλειος seven times elsewhere in his letters. When it refers to abstract concepts (e.g., God's will, love), it carries the nuance of "perfect" (Rom. 12:2; Col. 3:14). When it refers to people, however, it carries the nuance of "mature" (1 Cor. 2:6; 14:20; Eph. 4:13; Col. 4:12). It is most natural, therefore, to let the clearer sense of the adjective in verse 15 ("mature") inform the less clear sense of the verb in verse 12 and translate τετελείωμαι as "I have become mature."

The verb φρονέω occurs twenty-two other times in Paul's letters in-

---

41. O'Brien argues that it reflects the language of Paul's opponents and is related to the mystery religions (*Philippians*, 423). Fee disagrees and concludes that "there is nothing elsewhere in this letter, not anywhere else in the Pauline churches . . . that smacks of 'perfectionism'" (*Philippians*, 344).

cluding nine other times in Philippians. In 3:15 it echoes the four previous uses in the letter, including Philippians 2:5, where the word carries the idea of "to develop an attitude based on careful thought" and describes the attitude that characterized Christ himself.[42] The double use of this verb calls the Philippians to adopt the attitude Paul has articulated in 3:13–14.

The verb στοικέω occurs five other times in the New Testament. Four of the uses are in Paul's letters (Rom. 4:12; Gal. 3:25; 5:25; 6:16); the fifth is in Acts (21:24). Its basic meaning is "to stand in a row," or "to agree with." In Romans 4:12 it describes walking in another's footsteps; in Galatians 5:25 it is synonymous with "to walk" (cf. 5:16). The closest parallel is Galatians 6:16 where the NASB translates ὅσοι τῷ κανόνι τούτῳ στοιχήσουσιν as "those who will walk according to this standard." When he chooses this word, Paul not only calls his readers to align themselves with his own perspective but also "stresses the importance of harmony and mutual cooperation in spite of whatever divergence of opinion may exist."[43]

## Theological Analysis

The analogy of Scripture considers the way in which Philippians 3:12–16 relates to parallel, similar, and contrasting passages elsewhere in the Bible. The analogy of faith considers the way in which the passage relates to major doctrines of the Bible.

### Analogy of Scripture

The UBS4 critical apparatus provides fewer cross references for Philippians 3:12–16 than it did for Colossians 3:1–4. Nevertheless, there are three that are worth noting. The most obvious parallel is to the race imagery of 1 Corinthians 9:24–27. The Historical Analysis section above discussed the connections to Philippians 3:14, including the common race elements of a goal (σκοπός), a prize (βραβεῖον), and perhaps, the calling (κλῆσις) issued to the winner.

Paul's statement in 3:12 that he was "laid hold of by Christ" (κατελήμφθην ὑπὸ Χριστοῦ) most likely is an allusion to his conversion experience on the road to Damascus recorded in Acts 9:1–16. That account not only documents the radical change of direction Paul experienced, it also includes two uses of the verb διώκω, both with the negative connotation of "to persecute" (Acts 9:5–6). The contrast highlights the way in which Christ redirected Paul's zeal from *persecuting* the Church (3:6) to *pursuing* Christ (3:12, 14).

---

42. See the longer discussion in connection with Colossians 3:2 above.
43. G. F. Hawthorne, *Philippians* (Grand Rapids: Eerdmans, 1983), 157.

The object of Paul's pursuit in Philippians 3:12–16 has been the source of considerable discussion, since the verb καταλαμβάνω ("lay hold of") has no object in either 3:12 or 3:13. It might be that the uses of the **cognate** verb ἐπιλαμβάνομαι ("take hold of") in 1 Timothy 6:12 and 19 clarify the object of Paul's pursuit. In 6:12 Paul exhorts Timothy to "take hold of the eternal life to which you were called," and in 6:19 he states that those who are generous and ready to share will "take hold of that which is life indeed." These cross references are not definitive, but they are at least suggestive.

### Analogy of Faith

Philippians 3:12–16 most naturally relates to the doctrine of sanctification (salvation applied), specifically progressive sanctification. The passage sets out the basis, the attitude, and the motivation for pursuing growth in holiness. Christ's initiative in claiming men and women for himself is the basis for sanctification. Paul's single-minded, forward-looking pursuit of the prize is the attitude every believer should adopt toward his or her sanctification. God's call to go "farther up and farther in" provides the motivation for sanctification. Finally, the realization that we will never "arrive" in this lifetime provides the proper perspective for the ongoing pursuit of holiness.

## Synthesis

Synthesis addresses two questions: (1) What did Paul say? (2) Why did he say it? The first question seeks to isolate the central point of the passage; the second seeks to establish the need twenty-first-century readers share with the first-century audience.

### Central Point

As noted under Theological Analysis above, Philippians 3:12–16 most naturally relates to the doctrine of sanctification. The Immediate Context section noted that the passage forms the hinge in Paul's argument, where he continues to use himself as an example but redirects his readers to consider their own approach in light of that example. The overall topic of the passage (the homiletical subject) is most naturally understood to be Sanctification. Since Paul calls his readers to adopt his approach to the Christian life as their own, the narrower aspect of the topic might be stated as The Proper Approach to Sanctification. What does Paul say about that topic in the passage (the homiletical complement)? He remembers Christ's work in his life; he recognizes that he has not yet "arrived"; he races after the prize of God's call; and he remains open to God's instruction. The central point of the passage may be stated in a single sentence as **The proper approach to sanctification remembers Christ's work in our lives, recognizes our imperfect progress, races after the prize of God's call, and remains open to God's instruction.**

### Shared Need

What need in the Philippians' lives did this passage address? Paul's exhortation in verses 15–16 addresses that question. Regardless of the level of maturity they might have achieved, they have not yet "arrived." There is still room for growth in godliness. If the apostle Paul recognized his need to continue pursuing his relationship with Christ, so should they. He wrote to help them recognize their need for continued growth and to challenge them to act accordingly. Is there a comparable need in the lives of the twenty-first-century audience? Every follower of Christ in every age has the same need. We cannot stand still; we must continue growing in our walk with Christ. Verse 16 says it well: "Let us keep living by that standard to which we have attained."

## Appropriation

The twenty-first-century appropriation of Paul's message in Philippians 3:12–16 seeks to answer three questions: (1) How does the passage *connect* with today's audience? (2) What contemporary attitudes and actions does the passage *correct*? (3) What ways of thinking and/or acting does the passage *commend* to today's audience?

Contemporary listeners can *connect* with the idea of "pursuing" something. One of the fundamental rights in the United States is "the pursuit of happiness." Action movies and Internet games include the element of pursuit. Every four years the Olympic Games feature the same sort of activities to which Paul alludes as men and women pursue the prize of gold, silver, and bronze medals. As Paul notes in the parallel passage of 1 Corinthians 9:24–27, those athletes run to win and focus all their energies on their pursuit of the prize. He calls his readers (and us) to exercise the same focus and energy in pursuing God's call in Christ.

Paul's teaching in this paragraph corrects two wrong approaches to the Christian life. On the one hand, no follower of Jesus Christ should ever think that he or she has reached such a level of maturity that growing in grace can become a secondary priority. If the apostle Paul understood that he needed to keep moving forward, how much more do we need to do the same? On the other hand, Paul's approach to sanctification undercuts any suggestion that the Christian life is one solely of passive reliance on God. Paul's active pursuit of holiness is diametrically opposed to a "let-go-and-let-God" attitude.

The fact that Paul *commends* the active pursuit of Christ speaks to the innate human impulse to seek God. Assiduously following religious tradition or seeking special religious status will never adequately satisfy that impulse. Adopting Paul's attitude of continuously moving forward toward a standard set by God and being open to God's instruction along the way, however, makes it possible both to grow in our relationship with Christ and to find fulfillment in the process.

## Homiletical Packaging

The discipline of homiletics seeks to determine the best way to communicate the truth of a passage to a group of listeners. Before developing a sermon outline for Philippians 3:12–16, however, it is crucial to formulate a sermon objective and craft a take-home truth.

Chapter 6 suggested this template for formulating a sermon objective:

> I want my listeners to understand_____[truth]_____,
> so that they will_____[action]_____.

Applying that template to Philippians 3:12–16 leads to this objective: **I want my listeners to understand Paul's approach to living the Christian life, so that they will commit to a lifelong pursuit of holiness.** The take-home truth seeks to capture the central idea of the passage in a succinct statement listeners will "take home" with them. For Philippians 3:12–16, such a statement might be: **You can't win the prize you don't pursue.**

### Outline

The overall structure of Philippians 3:12–16 is at least semi-inductive in that Paul's appeal comes at the end of the paragraph rather than at the beginning. Since Philippians 2:5–8 uses the verb φρονέω to make a similar appeal, a comparison of the basic structures of the two passages makes the difference clear.

| Philippians 3:12–16 | Philippians 2:5–8 |
|---|---|
| Details of Paul's attitude (3:12–14) | Call to adopt Christ's attitude (2:5) |
| διώκω εἰ καὶ καταλάβω . . . <br><br> διώκω εἰς τὸ βραβεῖον . . . | τοῦτο φρονεῖτε ἐν ὑμῖν ὃ καὶ ἐν Χριστῷ Ἰησοῦ . . . |
| Call to adopt Paul's attitude (3:15–16) | Details of Christ's attitude (2:6–8) |
| Ὅσοι οὖν τέλειοι, τοῦτο φρονῶμεν . . . | οὐχ ἁρπαγμὸν ἡγήσατο τὸ εἶναι ἴσα θεῷ . . . <br><br> ἀλλὰ ἑαυτὸν ἐκένωσεν . . . <br><br> ἐταπείνωσεν ἑαυτὸν . . . |

Since the structure of the passage is inductive, it might be worthwhile considering an inductive approach for a sermon based on that passage. As a reminder, the following table sets out the difference between the inductive and deductive approaches.

| Inductive Approach | Deductive Approach |
|---|---|
| Introduction | Introduction |
| Point 1 | Central Idea / Proposition |
| Point 2 | Point 1 |
| Point 3 | Point 2 |
| Central Idea / Proposition | Point 3 |
| Conclusion | Conclusion |

A thematic question introduces the main points of an inductive sermon. In the case of Philippians 3:12–16, the main points will most naturally be specific examples from Paul's own experience. The take-home truth can serve as the proposition that follows the main points. The central elements of an inductive sermon based on this passage, therefore, might look like this:

Thematic Question:      What does Paul's experience teach us about the
                        proper approach to living the Christian life?

Main Points:
1. He remembers Christ's work in his life (3:12c).
2. He recognizes his imperfect progress (3:12a, 13a).
3. He races after the prize of God's call (3:13b–14a).
4. He remains open to God's instruction (3:15b).

Take-home Truth:        Paul's experience teaches us that you can't win the
                        prize you don't pursue.

A deductive approach to the passage might follow an analytical pattern and state the main points as aspects of a single theme such as "living the Christian life." Verses 15–16 would serve as a natural challenge at the end of the sermon.

Proposition:        Analyzing Paul's approach to living the Christian life in
                    Philippians 3:12–16 will challenge us to commit to a life-
                    long pursuit of holiness.

Main Points:
1. We see Paul's perspective on living the Christian life in 3:12a.
2. We see Paul's foundation for living the Christian life in 3:12b.
3. We see Paul's approach to living the Christian life in 3:13–14a.
4. We see Paul's motivation for living the Christian life in 3:14b

## FROM TEXT TO SERMON

Careful attention to textual criticism and translation, as well as to the historical, literary, and theological aspects of a passage, makes it possible to understand a passage's message accurately. Identifying the central point of the passage and the need the original and contemporary audiences share provides focus for a sermon based on the passage. Exploring how the passage connects with the contemporary audience, corrects contemporary attitudes and/or behaviors, and commends God-honoring attitudes and actions makes the sermon relevant to the listeners. Thoughtful homiletical packaging matches the structure of the sermon to the structure of the passage and brings the message of the passage to bear on the listeners in a persuasive way. Applying this process to passages in Paul's letters leads to sermons that are true to the text, appropriate to the audience, and powerful in their impact.

## The Chapter in Review

In Colossians 3:1–4 Paul calls us to live with a heavenly perspective. Since we are united with Christ in his death, resurrection, session, and return, our priorities should reflect our position. In contrast to philosophies that focus on the "here and now," it is only as we are heavenly minded that we are any earthly good.

In Philippians 3:12–16 Paul sets out his approach to following Christ. Forgetting what lies behind and focusing on what lies ahead, he pursues the prize God has promised. If we are truly mature, we will commit to a lifelong pursuit of holiness and will be open to God's correction in areas where we are not living according to his standard.

# 8

# SELECTED RESOURCES

- A variety of resources facilitate the process of interpreting passages from Paul's letters.

- Understanding the character and intent of major commentary series helps build a balanced library for interpreting Paul's letters.

- Helpful commentaries on Paul's letters include those based on the Greek text, those based on the English Bible, and those focused primarily on the expository task.

THE PRECEDING CHAPTERS INCLUDED resources related to the various tasks involved in interpreting and communicating passages from Paul's letters. This chapter brings those resources together into a composite list. It then provides an overview of important commentary series and lists three different types of commentaries for each of Paul's letters.

## RESOURCES FOR INTERPRETING PAUL'S LETTERS

The following list compiles those resources noted in the first seven chapters.

### Editions of the Greek New Testament

- B. Aland, et al., The Greek New Testament, 4th revised edition (New York: United Bible Societies, 1998).

- B. Aland, et al., The UBS Greek New Testament. A Reader's Edition (Stuttgart: Deutsche Bibelgesellschaft, 2007).

- B. Aland, et al., Greek-English New Testament, eighth revised edition (Stuttgart: Deutsche Bibelgesellschaft, 1994).

- E. Nestle, et al., Novum Testamentum Graecae, 27th revised edition (Stuttgart: Deutsche Bibelgesellschaft, 1999).

### Resources for Textual Criticism

- K. Aland and B. Aland, *The Text of the New Testament*, 2nd edition (Grand Rapids, MI: Eerdmans, 1989).

- D. A. Black, *New Testament Textual Criticism: A Concise Guide* (Grand Rapids, MI: Baker, 1994).

- P. W. Comfort, *The Quest for the Original Text of the New Testament* (Grand Rapids, MI: Baker, 1992).

- J. H. Greenlee, *Introduction to New Testament Textual Criticism*, revised edition (Peabody, MA: Hendrickson, 1995).

- B. M. Metzger, *Textual Commentary on the Greek New Testament*, 2nd edition (New York: United Bible Societies, 1994).

- B. M. Metzger and B. D. Ehrman, *The Text of the New Testament*, 4th edition (Oxford: University Press, 2005).

- W. N. Pickering, *The Identity of the New Testament Text* (Nashville: Nelson, 1980).

- H. A. Sturz, *The Byzantine Text-type and New Testament Criticism* (Nashville: Nelson, 1984).

## Greek-Based Concordances

- J. R. Kohlenberger, E. W. Goodrick, and J. A. Swanson, *The Exhaustive Concordance to the Greek New Testament* (Grand Rapids, MI: Zondervan, 1995).

- G. V. Wigram, *The Englishman's Greek Concordance of the New Testament* (Peabody, MA: Hendrickson, 1996).

## Lexicons and Theological Dictionaries

- W. Bauer, W. F. Arndt, F. W. Gingrich, and F. W. Danker, *A Greek-English Lexicon of the New Testament and Other Early Christian Literature*, third edition (Chicago: University of Chicago Press, 2000).

- C. Brown, ed., *The New International Dictionary of New Testament Theology*, 4 volumes (Grand Rapids, MI: Zondervan, 1986).

- G. Kittel and G. Friedrich, eds., *Theological Dictionary of the New Testament*, 10 volumes (Grand Rapids, MI: Eerdmans, 1964–73).

- J. P. Louw and E. A. Nida, *A Greek-English Lexicon of the New Testament Based on Semantic Domains*, 2nd edition, 2 volumes (New York: United Bible Societies, 1989).

## Intermediate Greek Grammars

- D. B. Wallace, *Greek Grammar Beyond the Basics* (Grand Rapids, MI: Zondervan, 1996).

- F. Blass, A. Debrunner, and R. W. Funk, *A Greek Grammar of the New Testament and Other Early Christian Literature* (Chicago: University of Chicago Press, 1961).

## New Testament Introductions

- D. A. Carson and D. J. Moo, *An Introduction to the New Testament*, 2nd edition (Grand Rapids, MI: Eerdmans, 2006).

- R. H. Gundry, *A Survey of the New Testament*, 4th edition (Grand Rapids, MI: Eerdmans, 2003).

## Bible Dictionaries and Encyclopedias

- G. W. Bromiley, ed., *International Standard Bible Encyclopedia*, 4 volumes, revised edition (Grand Rapids, MI: Eerdmans, 1979–88).

- J. D. Douglas and M. C. Tenney, eds., *New International Bible Dictionary* (Grand Rapids, MI: Zondervan, 1999).

- C. A. Evans and S. E. Porter, eds., *Dictionary of New Testament Background* (Downers Grove, IL: InterVarsity Press, 2000).

- G. F. Hawthorne and R. P. Martin, eds., *Dictionary of Paul and His Letters* (Downers Grove, IL: InterVarsity Press, 1993).

- M. Silva and M. C. Tenney, eds., *Zondervan Encyclopedia of the Bible*, revised edition, 5 volumes (Grand Rapids, MI: Zondervan, 2008).

## New Testament Theologies

- G. E. Ladd, *A Theology of the New Testament*, 2nd edition (Grand Rapids, MI: Eerdmans, 1993).

- I. H. Marshall, *New Testament Theology: Many Witnesses, One Gospel* (Downers Grove, IL: InterVarsity Press, 2004).

- T. R. Schreiner, *New Testament Theology: Magnifying God in Christ* (Grand Rapids, MI: Baker, 2008).

- R. B. Zuck, ed., *A Biblical Theology of the New Testament* (Chicago: Moody, 1994).

## Systematic Theologies

- M. J. Erickson, *Christian Theology* (Grand Rapids, MI: Baker, 1989).

- W. A. Grudem, *Systematic Theology: An Introduction to Biblical Doctrine* (Grand Rapids, MI: Zondervan, 1994).

- R. L. Reymond, *A New Systematic Theology of the Christian Faith* (Nashville: Nelson, 1998).

## Resources for Preaching

- J. D. Arthurs, *Preaching with Variety: How to Re-create the Dynamics of Biblical Genres* (Grand Rapids, MI: Kregel, 2007).

- B. Chapell, *Christ-centered Preaching: Redeeming the Expository Sermon* (Grand Rapids, MI: Baker, 1994).

- D. L. Hamilton, *Homiletical Handbook* (Nashville: Broadman, 1992).

- H. W. Robinson, *Biblical Preaching: The Development and Delivery of Expository Messages*, second edition (Grand Rapids, MI: Baker, 2001).

- A. Stanley, *Communicating for a Change* (Colorado Springs: Multnomah, 2006).

- D. R. Sunukjian, *Invitation to Biblical Preaching: Proclaiming the Truth with Clarity and Relevance* (Grand Rapids, MI: Kregel, 2007).

## Use of the Old Testament in the New Testament

- G. K. Beale and D. A. Carson, eds., *Commentary on the New Testament Use of the Old* (Grand Rapids, MI: Baker, 2007).

## Greek Language Computer Software

- BibleWorks, BibleWorks LLC, Norfolk, VA, www.bibleworks.com

- Gramcord, Gramcord Institute, Vancouver, WA, www.gramcord.org

- Logos Bible Software, Bellingham, WA, www.logos.com

## NEW TESTAMENT COMMENTARY SERIES

The usual recommendation is to obtain one good set of commentaries on the entire New Testament (e.g., Expositor's Bible Commentary, Tyndale New Testament Commentaries). Then, it is usually most helpful to obtain separate volumes on individual books, adding them evenly across the New Testament (i.e., one major commentary on each book, then a second major commentary on each book, and so on). The following listing seeks to capture the basic character of several important commentary series.

### Baker Exegetical Commentary on the New Testament (BECNT) Baker.

This Greek-based series seeks to combine scholarship for pastors with readability for inquiring lay readers. Each volume includes the original Greek text, a transliteration, and the author's own English translation.

### Bible Speaks Today (BST). InterVarsity Press.

The stated threefold ideal of this popular-level series is "to expound the biblical text with accuracy, to relate it to contemporary life and to be readable."

### Expositor's Bible Commentary (EBC), Volumes 1–12. Zondervan.

EBC is an advanced-level series of generally good quality. Several works are in the excellent category. Technical issues are addressed in notes following the discussion of each section of Scripture.

### International Critical Commentaries (ICC). T & T Clark, Ltd.

This technical, Greek-based series is intended for the user with some formal training. It provides exhaustive discussion of virtually every issue in a given passage.

IVP New Testament Commentary (IVPNTC). InterVarsity Press.

With exposition and application in the text and exegesis in the footnotes, this series moves by preaching portions. It aims to combine middle-level exegesis with readability.

New American Commentary (NAC). Broadman.

This Southern Baptist series provides middle-level volumes designed to help in the practical work of preaching and teaching. According to the dust jacket, it "assumes inerrancy, focuses on the intrinsic theological and exegetical concerns of each biblical book, and engages the range of issues raised in contemporary biblical scholarship."

New International Commentaries on the New Testament (NICNT). Eerdmans.

NICNT is an advanced-level series and is good for in-depth study. Technical issues are handled in footnotes.

New International Greek Testament Commentaries (NIGTC). Eerdmans.

This technical, Greek-based series is intended for the user with some formal training. A limited number of volumes are presently available.

NIV Application Commentary (NIVAC). Zondervan.

This middle-level series seeks to "bridge the gap between the gap between the world of the Bible and the world of today." It focuses on the contemporary application of the text's original meaning.

Pillar New Testament Commentary (PNTC). Eerdmans.

PNTC is designed to give serious readers of the Bible access to important contemporary issues without becoming overwhelmed by technical details. It seeks to combine serious exegesis with scholarship and pastoral sensitivity.

Tyndale New Testament Commentaries (TNTC). Eerdmans.

This reasonably-priced, popular-level series is a good option for starting to build a library.

Word Biblical Commentaries (WBC). Word.

This advanced-level series uses Greek extensively but is still accessible to the general user. It provides excellent bibliographical information.

Zondervan Exegetical Commentary on the New Testament (ZECNT). Zondervan.

This new series is designed "especially for pastors and students who want some help with the Greek text." The discussion of each passage includes seven components: literary context, main idea, translation and graphical layout, structure, exegetical outline, explanation of the text, and theology in application.

## COMMENTARIES ON PAUL'S LETTERS

For each of Paul's letters, three commentaries are listed. The first is an exegetical commentary based on the Greek text; the second is an exegetical commentary based on the English Bible; the third is an expositional commentary.

Romans

- C. E. B. Cranfield, *A Critical and Exegetical Commentary on the Epistle to the Romans*, 2 volumes, ICC (Edinburgh: T & T Clark, 1980).

- D. J. Moo, *The Epistle to the Romans*, NICNT (Grand Rapids, MI: Eerdmans, 1996).

- J. R. W. Stott, *Romans: God's Good News for the World* (Downers Grove, IL: InterVarsity Press, 1994).

## 1 Corinthians

- A. C. Thistelton, *The First Epistle to the Corinthians: A Commentary on the Greek Text*, NIGTC (Grand Rapids, MI: Eerdmans, 2000).

- G. D. Fee, *The First Epistle to the Corinthians*, NICNT (Grand Rapids, MI: Eerdmans, 1997).

- C. L. Blomberg, *1 Corinthians*, NIVAC (Grand Rapids, MI: Zondervan, 1994).

## 2 Corinthians

- M. E. Thrall, *A Critical and Exegetical Commentary on the Second Epistle to the Corinthians*, 2 volumes, ICC (Edinburgh: T & T Clark, 2000).

- P. Barnett, *The Second Epistle to the Corinthians*, NICNT (Grand Rapids, MI: Eerdmans, 1997).

- L. L. Belleville, *2 Corinthians*, IVPNTC (Downers Grove, IL: InterVarsity Press, 1995).

## Galatians

- R. N. Longenecker, *Galatians*, WBC (Dallas: Word, 1990).

- T. George, *Galatians*, NAC (Nashville: Broadman, 1994).

- G. W. Hansen, *Galatians*, IVPNTC (Downers Grove, IL: InterVarsity Press, 1994).

## Ephesians

- H. W. Hoehner, *Ephesians: An Exegetical Commentary* (Grand Rapids, MI: Baker, 2002).

- P. T. O'Brien, *The Letter to the Ephesians*, PNTC (Grand Rapids, MI: Eerdmans, 1999).

- W. L. Liefeld, *Ephesians*, IVPNTC (Downers Grove, IL: InterVarsity Press, 1997).

## Philippians

- P. T. O'Brien, *The Epistle to the Philippians: A Commentary on the Greek Text*, NIGTC (Grand Rapids, MI: Eerdmans, 1991).

- G. D. Fee, *Paul's Letter to the Philippians*, NICNT (Grand Rapids, MI: Eerdmans, 1995).

- F. Thielman, *Philippians*, NIVAC (Grand Rapids, MI: Zondervan, 1995).

## Colossians and Philemon

- J. D. G. Dunn, *The Epistles to the Colossians and to Philemon: A Commentary on the Greek Text*, NIGTC (Grand Rapids, MI: Eerdmans, 1996).

- D. J. Moo, *The Letters to the Colossians and to Philemon*, PNTC (Grand Rapids, MI: Eerdmans, 2008).

- J. MacArthur, *Colossians & Philemon* (Chicago: Moody, 1992).

## 1–2 Thessalonians

- F. F. Bruce, *1–2 Thessalonians*, WBC (Waco, TX: Word, 1982).

- G. D. Fee, *The First and Second Letters to the Thessalonians*, NICNT (Grand Rapids, MI: Eerdmans, 2009).

- J. R. W. Stott, *The Message of Thessalonians: The Gospel and the End of Time*, BST (Downers Grove, IL: InterVarsity Press, 1994).

## 1–2 Timothy and Titus

- G. W. Knight, *The Pastoral Epistles: A Commentary on the Greek Text*, NIGTC (Grand Rapids, MI: Eerdmans, 1992).

- T. D. Lea and H. P. Griffin, *1, 2, Timothy, Titus*, NAC (Nashville: Broadman, 1992).

- J. R. W. Stott, *The Message of 1–2 Timothy & Titus*, 2 volumes, BST (Downers Grove, IL: InterVarsity Press, 2001).

# GLOSSARY

**apostolic apologia.** The sections of Paul's letters in which he discusses his ministry as an apostle.

**apostolic parousia.** The sections of Paul's letters in which he makes his "presence" as an apostle felt.

**asceticism.** A system of thought holding that the body is evil and should be treated severely.

**asyndeton.** The omission of a conjunction where one would normally be expected.

**authenticity.** The question of whether a biblical book was written by the author mentioned in it.

**cognate.** Related to the same root word.

**compliance formula.** A group of words that calls the readers to implement previously communicated instructions.

**composite letter.** The suggestion that a canonical letter consists of two or more shorter letters or letter fragments.

**confidence formula.** A group of words that uses praise to create a sense of obligation.

**covenantal nomism.** The understanding that the Jewish people viewed the observance of the Mosaic law as a means of maintaining their status as God's people rather as a means of gaining acceptance before God.

**critical apparatus.** Information provided in an edition of the Greek New Testament that supplements the text (e.g., textual variants, alternative punctuation, cross-references).

**deductive sermon.** Sermon structure that begins with a passage's central idea and presents specific evidence in support of that idea.

**diatribe.** A stylized form of argumentation using dialogical objection and response to correct wrong thinking or behavior.

**disclosure formula.** A group of words that introduces new information or reminds the readers of previously communicated information.

**elliptical.** Omitting from a sentence one or more words that would complete or clarify the construction.

**epistolary convention.** A formulaic element used in first-century letters (e.g., salutation, thanksgiving, disclosure formula).

**exegesis.** The analytical work of interpreting the first-century message of a passage.

**exposition.** The synthetic work of moving the first-century message of a passage into the world of the contemporary listeners.

**genre.** A class or type of literature.

**Gnosticism.** A system of thought holding that special knowledge is the key to salvation.

**Hauptbriefe.** The four "main letters" ascribed to Paul: Romans, 1–2 Corinthians, and Galatians.

**hellenization.** The adoption of Greek language, culture, customs, and ideas.

**homiletical complement.** What a passage says about the homiletical subject.

**homiletical subject.** The narrow aspect of a topic that a passages addresses.

**household code.** A list of instructions on proper behavior for members of a family.

**inductive sermon.** Structure that moves from specific evidence to the statement of a passage's central idea.

**integrity.** The question of whether a biblical book was originally a single document.

**joy formula.** A group of words that expresses joy as the basis for a request or commendation.

**lacuna.** A missing portion of a manuscript, argument, or sequence.

**legalism.** A system of thought holding to strict obedience of a set of laws.

**literacy.** A culture's widespread use of written communication.

**literary dependence.** The suggestion that one document is based on another.

**morpheme.** A minimal grammatical unit constituting a meaningful part of a word.

**mysticism.** A system of thought holding that it is possible to transcend the ordinary means of understanding.

**orality.** A culture's widespread reliance on spoken communication.

**oral pattern.** A devise used in oral composition that enables listeners to follow the train of thought in an extended discourse.

**ostraca.** Small fragments of pottery used for writing brief items such as notes, letters, or receipts.

**papyrus.** A document written on material made from the papyrus plant.

**paraenetic.** Characterized by a series of ethical admonitions or exhortations.

**postpositive conjunction.** A coordinate conjunction that cannot stand first in the phrase or clause it introduces.

**preformed traditions.** Confessions, creeds, hymns, or sayings created by the early church and used by the authors of the biblical documents.

**previous letter.** The lost letter mentioned in 1 Corinthians 5:9 that Paul had sent to the church prior to writing canonical 1 Corinthians.

**proem.** An introductory section.

**request formula.** A group of words that asks the readers to respond positively to a stated course of action.

**rhetoric.** The science of communicating persuasively in order to influence the way others think and act.

**semantics.** The meaning of words.

**sorrowful letter.** The lost letter mentioned in 2 Corinthians 2:2–3 and 7:8 that Paul had sent to the church prior to writing canonical 2 Corinthians.

**syncretism.** The merging of elements from two or more systems of thought.

**syntax.** The relationship between words.

**synthetic study.** The process of reading a biblical book multiple times in order to develop a one-page overview of the book's theme, structure, and content.

**take–home truth.** The memorable statement of a passage's message that a sermon seeks to impress on the listeners.

**textual criticism.** The process of reconstructing the original wording of a text.

**textual variants.** Differences in wording found in ancient manuscripts.

**topos.** A self-contained unit that advocates a topic of proper thought or action.

**Tübingen School.** A group of nineteenth century German scholars connected with University of Tübingen.

**vice list.** A list of attitudes and behaviors that readers should reject.

**virtue list.** A list of attitudes and behaviors that readers should adopt.